R A C E   A N D   P O L I T I C A L   T H E O L O G Y

RACE AND POLITICAL THEOLOGY

Edited by Vincent W. Lloyd

STANFORD UNIVERSITY PRESS
STANFORD, CALIFORNIA

Stanford University Press
Stanford, California

This book has been published with the assistance of the Edgar M. Kahn Memorial Fund
and Syracuse University's Department of Religion.

Printed in the United States of America on acid-free, archival-quality paper

Library of Congress Cataloging-in-Publication Data

Race and political theology / edited by Vincent W. Lloyd.
pages cm
Includes bibliographical references and index.
ISBN 978-0-8047-7314-0 (cloth : alk. paper) -- ISBN 978-0-8047-7315-7 (pbk. : alk. paper)
1. Political theology and race. I. Lloyd, Vincent W., 1982– editor of compilation.
BT83.59.R33 2012
201'.72089--dc23

2011040053

Typeset by Bruce Lundquist in 11/15 Bembo

Contents

List of Contributors   vii

Introduction   1
VINCENT W. LLOYD

1. Political Theology and the Case of Otto Brunner   22
VINCENT P. PECORA

2. "The Politicization of Heaven":
Wilhelm Stapel's Political Theology of Nationalist Sovereignty   54
CHRISTOPH SCHMIDT

3. Between W. E. B. Du Bois and Karl Barth:
The Problem of Modern Political Theology   83
J. KAMERON CARTER

4. There Are No Clean Souls:
The Promise and Perils of Political Theology
in *The Souls of Black Folk*   112
JONATHON S. KAHN

5. The Race for Theology:
Toward a Critical Political Theology of Freedom   134
COREY D. B. WALKER

6. The Enemy's Two Bodies (Political Theology Too)   156
GIL ANIDJAR

7. The Double Mark of the Male Muslim:
Eracing Othello   174
DANIEL BOYARIN

8. Between Sacred and Secular?
Michael Walzer's Exodus Story   188
BONNIE HONIG

9. The State between Race and Religion:
A Conversation   213
MARTIN LAND AND JONATHAN BOYARIN

10. From Political Theology to Vernacular
Prophecy: Rethinking Redemption   234
GEORGE SHULMAN

Index   249

Contributors

GIL ANIDJAR teaches in the Department of Religion and the Department of Middle Eastern, South Asian, and African Studies at Columbia University. His books include *The Jew, the Arab: A History of the Enemy* (2003) and *Semites: Race, Religion, Literature* (2008).

DANIEL BOYARIN is Hermann P. and Sophia Taubman Professor of Talmudic Culture in the Departments of Near Eastern Studies and Rhetoric at the University of California, Berkeley. He is the author, most recently, of *The Jewish Gospels: The Story of the Jewish Christ* (2012).

JONATHAN BOYARIN is Leonard and Tobee Kaplan Distinguished Professor of Religious Studies at the University of North Carolina. His publications include *The Unconverted Self: Jews, Indians, and the Identity of Christian Europe* (2009) and, with Martin Land, *Time and Human Language Now* (2009).

J. KAMERON CARTER is Associate Professor of Theology and Black Church Studies at Duke Divinity School. He is the author of *Race: A Theological Account* (2008) and *The Secular Jesus: Political Theology from Columbus to the Age of Obama* (forthcoming).

BONNIE HONIG is Sarah Rebecca Roland Professor of Political Science at Northwestern University and Research Professor at the American Bar Foundation. Her publications include *Democracy and the Foreigner* (2001), *Emergency Politics: Paradox, Law, Democracy* (2009), and *Antigone, Interrupted* (forthcoming).

JONATHON S. KAHN is Assistant Professor of Religion at Vassar College. He is the author of *Divine Discontent: The Religious Imagination of W. E. B. Du Bois* (2009). His research focuses on race, religion, and democratic theory.

MARTIN LAND is Senior Lecturer in Computer Science at Hadassah College in Jerusalem and president of the International Association for Relativistic Dynamics. He is the author, with Jonathan Boyarin, of *Time and Human Language Now* (2009).

VINCENT W. LLOYD is Assistant Professor of Religion at Syracuse University. He is the author of *Law and Transcendence: On the Unfinished Project of Gillian Rose* (2009) and *The Problem with Grace: Reconfiguring Political Theology* (2011).

VINCENT P. PECORA is Gordon B. Hinckley Professor of British Literature and Culture at the University of Utah. His publications include *Households of the Soul* (1997) and *Secularization and Cultural Criticism: Religion, Nation, and Modernity* (2006).

CHRISTOPH SCHMIDT teaches in the Department of German Literature at Hebrew University and is a Fellow at The Van Leer Jerusalem Institute. His most recent books are *The Theopolitical Moment: Twelve Perspectives on the Eschatological Problem of Modernity* (in German, 2009) and *The Return of the Dead Souls* (forthcoming).

GEORGE SHULMAN teaches political theory and American studies at New York University's Gallatin School of Individualized Study. He is the author, most recently, of *American Prophecy: Race and Redemption in American Political Culture* (2008).

COREY D. B. WALKER is Associate Professor and Chair of Africana Studies at Brown University. He is the author of *A Noble Fight: African American Freemasonry and the Struggle for Democracy in America* (2008) and editor of "Theology and Democratic Futures," a special issue of *Political Theology*.

RACE AND POLITICAL THEOLOGY

INTRODUCTION

VINCENT W. LLOYD

The French prime minister looked "like a communion wafer dipped in shit."[1] It is hard to understand Aimé Césaire's description of Georges Bidault as anything but a metaphor that troubles the core of political theology, the homology between political sovereign and God. In light of the colonial massacres of nonwhite populations—Bidault led the Fourth Republic at the start of the Indochina War and was foreign minister during the Malagasy Uprising—the French sovereign is profaned, grotesque. In Césaire's characteristic reversal, he inverts the civilized and the savage, locating "howling savagery" at the heart of Europe. But the image is equivocal; savagery mimes civilization, and paganism mimes Christianity. The image suggests the possibility of cleansing, purifying, and returning to the sovereign who properly looks like a communion wafer, like the Body of Christ.

Césaire's is a political theology from the perspective of the nonwhite, from the perspective of negritude—often euphemistically left untranslated instead of exhibited in its intended ugliness: niggerness. Race as color, as ideology, as institutional logic, as resource, as imagination is joined with religion as symbol, as practice, as ethos, as resource, as imagination, joined by Césaire in political critique. *Discourse on Colonialism*, Césaire's 1950 prose-poem, opens by declaring Europe to be "spiritually indefensible."

The opposition of Europe, civilization, and Christianity to non-Europe, savagery, and paganism is unsustainable. Césaire's target is more than false consciousness; for him, Christianity is more than symbol or belief held superficially. Christianity is also an ethos, a set of virtues and values. To be a good Christian—to be among the "virtuous young men educated by the Jesuit Fathers"—is to be a good bourgeois, and this is to have the habits that make for a successful colonial administrator. Missionaries are among the most virulent racists, Césaire suggests.[2]

After studying in France, Césaire returned to his home in Martinique and wrote his autobiographical poem, *Notebook of a Return to the Native Land*. It was an impossible return. In the poem Césaire describes himself, seeing his land again, as "a lone man imprisoned in whiteness," finding his home a place of fear and hunger and exhaustion, the morning "slowly vomiting out its human fatigue," a place where "neither the teacher in his classroom, nor the priest at catechism will / be able to get a word out of this sleepy little nigger." Yet childhood memories of "foolish and crazy stunts" along with "the bread, / and the wine of complicity" remind of youthful communion, since lost, perhaps educated away. And there was Christmas, with joys and dreams and tastes and smells and laughter and gossip and song: Alleluia, Christ is risen. It is ecstatic song that moves from voices to bodies to spirits, "the hands, the feet, the buttocks, the genitals, and your entire being liquefies into sounds, voices, and rhythm"; it "starts pulling the nearest devil by the tail," muting laments and fears.[3]

After Christmas, fear and exhaustion return: the town "crawls on its hands without the slightest desire to drill the sky with / a stature of protest," the risen Christ an opiate and no more. The whiteness that imprisons is not only the outsider's perspective; it is the whiteness of religion, of Christianity, as well. But there is a response, a transformation of values, realigned from the perspective of niggerness. Whiteness and niggerness are asymmetrical; niggerness congeals the inchoate identities of the nonwhite, starting with the Jew and proceeding to the Kaffir, the Hindu, the Harlem man, and proceeding to the "famine-man," "insult-man," and "torture-man." Reason is displaced by the madness of memory, lament, visions, dreams. "An apostate," the narrator proclaims himself, "I too / have assassinated God," "Worshipped the Zambeze." The poetry turns to incantation, punctuated by a sorcerer's calls, "voum rooh oh," that wake the dead and control the skies. Christian impotence is displaced by pagan conjuring, with human capacity to control the world—"Leaving Europe utterly twisted with screams."[4]

Yet in his "virile prayer" to be granted "the savage faith of the sorcerer," it is possible to read a thickening, rather than a rejection, of Christianity. The ecstatic moment of Christmas and the ecstatic cries of the African sorcerer are moments of fantasy to be traversed. What remains is not the secular but a religiosity complicated. Having passed through the language of virility, the poem praises those who have not explored or conquered, those who "yield, captivated, to the essence of things / ignorant of surfaces but captivated by the motion of all things / indifferent to conquering, but playing the game of the world." The weak and the simple are saved, not the strong and knowledgeable. Grief and joy and love are extolled in the ordinary, not relegated to ecstasy. The greatest of these, all that is left once the world is accepted as it is and the poet finds himself "only a man," is love. Rejecting his identity as a father, a brother, a son, or a husband, the poet wishes to be a lover, not of a woman but of a people. After the poet accepts laughter and fear and agony, it becomes possible to set them aside, "my eyes fixed on this town which I prophesy, beautiful." The new town, the heavenly city, is the vision of the lover, born not of hatred but of "universal hunger" and "universal thirst." It is a vision that was made possible by, and required, acceptance—undistorted accounting, and feeling, of the world as it is. And it is a vision that motivates action: protest, prophecy, and revolution (the place to begin, Césaire writes, is at the end of the world).[5]

For Césaire, we might say, there is a political theology of Christmas as holiday and a political theology of the sorcerer, both entranced by the exceptional moment of religious ecstasy that ultimately reaffirms European sovereignty, white privilege. There is an alternative political theology, visible from the perspective of niggerness, that transforms the sovereign exception into the everyday, that sees each individual—every famine-man, insult-man, and torture-man, everyone who recognizes in themselves a universal hunger and thirst—into a creator, capable of dancing and conjuring, of seeing the miraculous in the ordinary, of protesting injustice, of loving.[6] To cleanse the communion wafer of excrement requires seeing communion everywhere, not just in the face of the (racist and genocidal) prime minister. But this is a difficult communion, a communion of the future, of an imagined town, prophesied by means of the careful analysis of the problems of the day.

WHAT CÉSAIRE'S WORK ILLUSTRATES is how conversations about political theology might be complicated and thickened when race is taken into account. Similarly, discussions of race that avoid political theology limit theoretical imagination. The burgeoning interest in political theology across the humanities has curiously ignored discussions such as these.

This burgeoning interest results, in part, from changing background assumptions about religion. Scholars have realized that treating religion as most essentially a private belief is a very specific, very Protestant approach.[7] Many Christianities, and many other non-Christian traditions, see religion just as much about community as about the individual or do not make this distinction at all. Closely related to this descriptive claim about the essence of religion is the normative claim that religion ought to be a private matter. The reasoning goes that religion has the potential, perhaps the unique potential, to cause discord and violence when it is permitted to show its face in public.[8] Clearly, the imperative to restrict religion to the private sphere complements the Protestant notion that religion is primarily a private matter. As the descriptive claims about what religion is and how violent it is are called into question, the foundations of the normative claim are weakened; the normative claim appears increasingly like a passive-aggressive assertion of Protestant hegemony. Political theology presents itself as an alternative approach to both descriptive and normative questions, an approach that leaves behind implicit assumptions and adds complexity to these conversations.

Recent years have also displayed the limitations of the secularization thesis, the claim that religions will wither away in the modern world.[9] The contemporary religious landscape is, as all can see, robust and dynamic. One might hypothesize that the forms of religiosity in decline are those that ostensibly reject political theology, seeing religious commitment as a personal matter distinct from political ideas and beliefs; those that are on the rise, and increasingly visible, embrace a deep connection between religious and political ideas. Charles Taylor's recent revision of the secularization thesis could be read as an attempt to push those religious communities traditionally allergic to political theology to accept that secularization itself should be understood as a theological transformation, necessitating a theological response.[10]

The phrase "political theology" is sometimes used in a very narrow sense, sometimes in a very broad sense, and sometimes in a sectarian sense. Most narrowly, political theology refers to claims by the German jurist Carl Schmitt concerning the role of religious concepts in political theory. According to Schmitt, in a given place and time in European history there is a homology between particularly significant Christian concepts and particularly significant political concepts.[11] Crudely put, the king is like God; theorizing the powers of the king, or the state, parallels the work of theology. Intellectual historians have investigated the context in which Schmitt's ideas arose, political theorists have investigated the relevance of Schmitt's claims for understanding contemporary democracies, and philosophers have parsed the political theological concepts Schmitt identified.

In the broadest sense, political theology is used almost interchangeably with the phrase "religion and politics." Political theology in this sense refers to the many ways that religion (religious ideas, but religious ideas are hardly separable from religious practices and institutions) shapes politics (political ideas, but, again, political ideas are hardly separable from political practices and institutions). If Catholics and Evangelicals support different political parties, the explanation may have to do with political theology. Or it may not; the explanation may be reductionist, turning to nontheological factors such as demographic or cultural differences to explain the difference in political affiliation. The investigation of political and religious concepts that arise, and conjoin, takes place throughout the humanities, from literary studies to anthropology to political theory and religious studies. If social scientists approach religion and politics by reducing religion away, political theology just names the approach that scholars of the humanities take to these same questions, allowing religion a robust, multifaceted meaning.

It would be tempting, but misleading, to associate "religion and politics" with the empirical and "political theology" with the theoretical. Indeed, understood in the broad sense, political theology is often empirical, beginning with careful examination of specific religious communities and their religious ideas. No claims need to be made about the relationship of religious and political ideas in general (or "in theory"); the scholar of political theology may be content with one particular location or one particular text. As a result, political theology need not have any particular affiliation with Christianity. There is a flourishing literature on Jewish political theology, and an increasing literature on Islamic political theology, with other religions sure to follow suit.

Yet the broad sense of political theology can become frustrating in its expansiveness. What is frustrating is not necessarily the variety of contexts, and texts, to which the term is brought to bear but the distance that the term moves away from the rich and subtle understanding of religion and politics that characterizes Schmitt's work at its best. Religion and politics are both concepts with complicated genealogies. The best work in political theology has an impulse to use the conjunction of the two, the political and the theological, to explore the difficulties involved in each. It is tempting to understand "the political" as a narrow set of ideas, for example, about sovereignty or about an amorphous notion of social change. It is similarly tempting to understand "the theological" as a narrow set of ideas concerning God's relationship to himself and to the world or about divinely sanctioned moral imperatives. But political and theological ideas are much more complex and not separable from political and religious practices, institutions, cultures, and histories. To consider but one example, love is not only an attribute of God in Christian theology but also a human virtue. Recent work has studied the political implications of this virtue when practiced, for example, at a school board meeting.[12]

Although there has been some discussion of political theology outside North American and European contexts, there has been strikingly little discussion of race and political theology. Perhaps the reason is that race seems especially restricted to a particular historical and cultural context; theology, of course, is rather misleadingly supposed to be in some sense universal. Further, the religious ideas most often discussed in the context of political theology, God's attributes and workings in the world, seem independent of racial considerations (with the notable exception of the religious ideas of certain new religious movements and, of course, black theology). Similarly, it is hard to imagine a racial politics in any sort of generic sense; racial politics has to do more with political practice than political theory. At most, politics and theology both have to grapple with difference, and it is here that race may enter the discussion. Race is one difference among others, and there is no reason to suppose that racial difference would be treated any differently than regional difference, linguistic difference, or gender difference. Investigations of political theology in a particular context might grapple with issues of race, but investigating race, it would seem, has little to say about political theology in general.

Yet political theology in the narrow view, associated with the work of Schmitt, is intimately connected with questions of race. Schmitt's association with National Socialism, and the centrality of the concept of a people rooted in the earth to his thought, forces the issue.[13] That race disappears when political theology expands from a narrow to a broad sense is troubling; perhaps it suggests that, even in the broad sense, political theology is haunted by race. Indeed, National Socialist Germany is the turning point in Aimé Césaire's narrative, the Jew his first example of the racial other. The political theology that authorized colonial atrocities was exposed in its raw barbarism by the Nazis. Césaire writes that Hitler would "reveal to the very distinguished, very humanistic, very Christian bourgeois of the twentieth century that without his being aware of it, he has a Hitler inside him, that Hitler inhabits him, that Hitler is his demon."[14] The excrement already coating Christianity starts to stink in Europe itself.

Césaire's reflections point toward a tension between the narrow and broad senses of political theology subtler than the labels suggest. Might the broad sense of political theology effect a universalizing of the Christian simply by asking the questions that it poses? This need no longer be a "white" Christianity—Césaire's project is to polish away that whiteness—but it may remain a Christianity nonetheless. Scholars of religion have pointed to the very specific, very Protestant heritage of their object of study; Marxists and feminists have made analogous observations about politics. Yet with the political and the theological conjoined, political theology often escapes such worries.

If political theology is understood as arising in a European, Christian context, expanding outward more recently to other contexts, and maintaining a pretense of universality, then race and political theology may be intimately, inextricably bound. J. Kameron Carter's recent work has tracked how the figure of the Jew initiates the European-Christian racial imagination, laying the foundation for understanding colonial others and, in the North American context, understanding African American racial difference.[15] The academic enterprise of genealogy is intended to explore precisely this: how the image of a "scholarly toolkit" elides the political struggles that give rise to, and shape, each "tool," how one who employs tools is an unwitting partisan in these struggles. Inquiries into race and political theology can be seen as genealogical inquiries, uncovering these forgotten struggles and allowing the scholar to become a witting participant—and perhaps dissolving the image of the dispassionate scholar bringing political theology in her trusty toolkit to the data.

In addition to the narrow and broad senses of political theology is what might be called a sectarian sense of the phrase. Political theology in this sense is just the branch of theology that deals with political questions. Theology, uncharitably, is as phantasmal as alchemy or astrology, a pseudo-academic field founded on beliefs in the supernatural. More charitably, theology is a second-order religious discourse, a conversation about what Christians ought and ought not say or do. In either case, theology is opposed to secular academic inquiry, is opposed to, among other things, the secular study of religions. When political theology is understood as the branch of theology concerned with politics—for example, when it is understood as reflection on what Christians ought and ought not say or do in politics—it seems to have no place in the secular academy. It is an activity of believers, for believers.

Although there is an active conversation about political theology as a branch of theology, this sectarian sense of the phrase certainly does not characterize the bourgeoning conversations about political theology in the academic humanities. But the sectarian sense of the phrase is not altogether isolated. The academic journal *Political Theology*, originally subtitled *The Journal of Christian Socialism*, has increasingly featured secular academic discussions of political theology. But the very distinction between these two conversations, like that between theology and secular religious studies, brings with it questionable assumptions. Once personal belief is no longer taken as the core of religiosity, as soon as the importance of community and ritual and culture and tradition are acknowledged, what it might mean for theology to be by and for believers becomes obscure. If, for example, religion is more like a language and theology more like a grammar, the supposed distinction between secular conversations about political theology and sectarian, Christian conversations quickly recedes.[16]

Carl Schmitt himself complicates the distinction between secular and theological inquiry into political theology. Schmitt was a Catholic in a Protestant-dominated German academic landscape, and he was distanced from the Catholic Church after divorcing his first wife and remarrying. His nostalgia and hope mix faith and scholarship.[17] Even though it is well known that Schmitt wrote about race and about political theology, how these two themes are connected and how they are connected to Schmitt's other famous concept, of the existential enemy and friend, are less frequently discussed. Out of this silence, there arises a general sense that Schmitt considered the figure of the Jew as that of the existential enemy and commended the Nazi mistreatment of Jews because it involved the exercise of sovereign authority in a Godlike sense, that is, because it involved the ability to suspend the law. That Schmitt concluded a 1936 speech by quoting from *Mein Kampf*, "By fending off the Jew, I struggle for the work of the Lord," gives this interpretation significant persuasive force.[18]

But this attempt at adding cohesion to Schmitt's theoretical writings and political activity overlooks the complications of his character. An outsider aspiring to intellectual importance, rapidly achieving and rapidly losing influence within the Third Reich, frustrated by his postwar internment and never willing to recant his far from clear-cut wartime views, exercising a quiet but broad influence after the war from his provincial home while revisiting his earlier works, Schmitt was certainly not the dogmatic figure he is sometimes portrayed to be. His instincts were certainly conservative but more creatively than rigidly so. His personal diaries exhibited an unnervingly crude anti-Semitism, dovetailing all too well with his public wartime condemnations of "Jewish" jurisprudence, yet like that of any committed intellectual his work, at its best, exhibits an analytical rigor that allows for independence from the day's conventional wisdom that his diaries so easily echo.

Schmitt's work consists of two apparently independent moments, bound together by political theology. The first moment emphasizes the importance for politics of a people, a group rooted in a location. In the opening lines of *The Concept of the Political* we read that "the state is a specific entity of a people."[19] On a nearly opposite topic, Schmitt suggests that the partisan is properly telluric, coming from and living off the earth.[20] In his reflections on international law, Schmitt begins by describing how "the earth became known as the mother of law," how "the fertile earth contains within herself, within the womb of her fecundity, an inner measure."[21] This Schmitt takes as the starting point for his account of a European legal order, one that rejects both Soviet and American hegemony.

The second moment in Schmitt's work, which at first seems directly opposed to the first, emphasizes the existential. It is the political that makes the state possible, and the basis of the political is the distinction between friends and enemies. There is no feeling of hatred directed at political enemies and no feeling of warmth directed at political friends. The distinction between political friends and political enemies cannot be reduced to economic or moral or cultural affiliation. It is, paradoxically, pure antagonism, uncontaminated by feelings or reasons. Politics consists in helping one's friends and harming one's enemies. Politics is war by other means. Liberalism, and parliamentary democracy, suppresses the political, purporting to provide a venue for political discourse while actually eliminating the space for the existential enmity constitutive of the political. Specific values are advanced under the guise of being universal conditions for politics (reasonableness, free communication, and so on). In his theory of the partisan, Schmitt suggests that political commitment sets the partisan apart from criminals or vagabonds. And in his theory of international law, Schmitt distinguishes *nomos*, which comes about through the dividing or appropriating of land, from law, rules that order society. Schmitt does not call for a reunion of law and *nomos*; in fact, he acknowledges that from the earliest times the two have been split. The land and the people rooted in a land are a necessary but not sufficient element of politics. A second, existential moment is necessary.

These two moments in Schmitt's work appear to be precariously maintained simultaneously without explanation or justification. It is in his account of political theology that this apparent tension is resolved. Schmitt famously asserts, "All significant concepts of the modern theory of the state are secularized theological concepts."[22] As deism gained popularity, with its understanding of a withdrawn God and a world governed by the law of nature accessible to humans, the monarch retreated, leaving a constitutional state governed by laws. The whims of the monarch no longer affected the laws of the state, just as God no longer was thought to act in the world through miracles. In the early nineteenth century, as God's relationship to the world transformed from one of transcendence to one of immanence, sovereign authority came to be understood as held collectively by citizens, the ruler and the ruled the same, the state an organic entity.

Schmitt's claim about the relationship between political and theological concepts is not simply a claim about history. It is also a claim about the current political vocabulary. To understand the meaning of sovereignty, one should start by thinking through what theologians have to say about God's authority. To understand the meaning of political community, one should start by thinking through what theologians have to say about religious community, about the Christian Church. The church has two faces, visible and invisible. It is a collection of sinful humans, and it is also holy, the Body of Christ. There is no worldly explanation for these two identities; it is a mystery.[23] Christians go awry when they forget about this duality, when they focus on either the visible church or the invisible church. Indeed, this is the same paradox at the heart of Christian faith: that Jesus is the Christ, that God can become man.

The two moments of Schmitt's thought are bound together by this mystery. A state grows from a people, but the political is a prerequisite for a state. A people is rooted in a land and at the same time is constituted by existential friendship and by shared existential enmity directed outward. A partisan is at once rooted in his land and committed to political ideals. *Nomos* and positive law are jointly, and separately, the foundation of international law. Schmitt's targets are those who would quash the mystery. He opposes those who would locate political enmity in worldly factors, such as cultural or class difference. He opposes those who would offer a political system supposedly capable of mediating all competing interests in a society. In cases such as these, the church visible and the church invisible are confused—or rather, their political analogues are confused. To put it strongly, taking perhaps too much liberty, race and politics are linked, according to Schmitt, by political theology.

Yet Schmitt is not the necessary starting point for contemporary discussions of political theology. Schmitt's work has been complicated over the years, and new questions about the racially inflected relationship between the political and the theological have emerged. The chapters that follow explore the openings created for conversations about race when the canon of political theology is shaken up, when new figures (Du Bois, Baldwin, Shakespeare) are permitted entry, when priority is given to figures previously considered secondary (Stapel, Brunner), and when the political landscape shifts to the contemporary (Israel, the United States). This is not an entirely new project: the past several decades have seen a variety of reformations of political theology, a few of which will be surveyed here.

Immediate reactions to Schmitt's work were varied, although discussion of race has often been limited to condemnations of Schmitt's anti-Semitism. In the wake of the Second World War, political theology became the label of a German theological movement that took Schmitt's work as a starting point but complicated it, intending to purge racist possibilities. Erik Peterson, an early leader of this movement, emphasized that the connection between political sovereign and God began before Christianity, and that Christianity actually complicated this connection by positing a Trinitarian God.[24] That one person of the Trinity was crucified by the Roman (political) regime further complicates this relationship. Work by Jürgen Moltmann, Johann Baptist Metz, and Dorothee Sölle explores the political significance of a suffering God. For these theologians the Holocaust looms large, and the memory of suffering is seen as a potent political resource. Secular modernity has little experience grappling with suffering, but Christianity has much experience grappling with the crucial nexus of suffering and freedom.[25]

Schmitt gives center stage to the secularized theological concept of sovereignty, but some have worried that a focus on sovereignty reinforces the status quo. Political theological inquiry that follows Schmitt would result, at most, in the conclusion that the form sovereignty takes would need to be reformed; what if a more radical critique is desired? Is there a way to call sovereignty itself into question? The theological vocabulary that separates the time of world and the end of time offers resources for such a critique. In light of the *eschaton*, worldly dealings matter little, and worldly powers tremble. To invoke the *eschaton*, to speak of the *eschaton*'s rapid approach, and to invoke he who will bring about the *eschaton* are ways of invoking a higher power, of undercutting sovereign authority.

Schmitt himself, in his later work, found a political role for eschatology, although it was a role with limited critical potential. With the end of time would come the Antichrist; it is only through a restrainer, a *katechon*, that the Antichrist is held back.[26] The Roman emperor was viewed as the *katechon*, according to Schmitt, holding back barbarians and allowing the present era to continue. This role transferred, in the Middle Ages, to the Holy Roman Emperor, and later, the English monarch played the role, overseeing colonial possessions and guarding them against the uncivilized forces of the Antichrist. In this way, Schmitt portrays the *eschaton* as something to be feared; he portrays the sovereign as a necessary defender against apocalyptic calamity.

In contrast to, and in dialogue with, Schmitt, Jacob Taubes presents an alternative history of eschatology that recovers its critical political potential.[27] What Taubes dubs "apocalypticism" involves both a destruction of the worldly order and the creation of a "new covenant." Further, the imminence of the end of time motivates frantic political action. Taubes emphasizes the connection between exile and apocalypse. God is alienated from the world, and man is alienated from himself. These separations will be healed at the end of time: the alien will return; man's exile will end. Taubes's history of eschatology begins with Jewish exile, with the biblical book of Daniel. Eschatology is peculiarly Jewish, foreign to the Greco-Roman world, posits Taubes, and this difference is crucial for understanding rebellion against Roman rule. It is also a context crucial for understanding the development of Christianity, and Taubes portrays Paul not as the founder of universalism but as a Jewish rebel against imperial Rome.[28] Eschatology arises from a particular context that commitment to the *eschaton* does not supersede. This is what allows Taubes to separate political and religious universalism, and the promise of political theology is the recovery of the political potential of the latter. In a quite different sense than for Schmitt, race remains at the center of political theology.

It is tempting to oppose the Christian Schmitt to the Jewish Taubes, the former finding God walking on earth and the latter asserting that the Messiah is yet to come. This is precisely the sense in which Jacques Derrida embraces Judaism (though one may worry whether Judaism portrayed in this way already buys into the supersessionist logic put forward by a dangerous form of Christianity). Derrida's later work linked the indeterminacy of meaning with the promise of meaning, linked the porous and always already problematic concepts of the day with the only hope possible, that such anxieties would fade in an indiscernible future. In light of the *eschaton*, the present is ruins; Derrida's work exposes the present as ruins. Sovereignty, political and theological and even authorial, names the regime of the present beckoning critique; democracy names eschatological politics, promised but never achieved in this world.[29] Yet in Derrida's eschatological vision, the specificity of race—beyond a crude caricature of the Jew—seems to be lost, dissolving into the rest of Derrida's all too serious play of texts.

The defining power of the sovereign, for Schmitt, is the power to decide on the exception, the power to suspend the law. Michel Foucault's later work emphasizes the power of the sovereign to decide over life and death.[30] American gubernatorial pardons are a reminder of how closely these two positions are linked. It is the head of state government who can decide when to suspend the law and permit a person condemned to death to continue living. Yet this is the sort of example that Foucault suggests can be misleading. The power of the sovereign to kill is highly visible and dramatic, all the more so in centuries past, but it distracts from a pervasive, pernicious aspect of our modern world: sovereign power over life.

By power over life, Foucault means the regulation of life. For Foucault, norms constitute the object they purport to merely regulate. What life is, and what counts as life, increasingly becomes the business of the state in modernity. Characteristically, Foucault tracks this increase across multiple domains, including medical writings, architectural plans, census questions, and, most famously, incarceration. The citizen is no longer an object to be commanded but a body whose biological existence is a matter of interest for the state. It is in this context that race emerges, among the technologies of "biopolitics" that the modern state, particularly in the nineteenth century, devises and employs. As the state becomes increasingly interested in fertility, mortality, and health of populations, racism became "the basic mechanism of power" to the extent that "the modern State can scarcely function without becoming involved with racism at some point."[31] Racism separates those over whom sovereign power over life is exercised and those over whom sovereign power over death is exercised (it is tempting, but much too easy, to call this a division between friends and enemies). With the death of the other, life becomes more healthy, more pure. Foucault here means death, like life, in the broadest sense. Those who are racial others are exposed to physical risks, expelled, deprived of social and political life—culminating in Nazi Germany.

Foucault's account of biopolitics provides an account of race that, at least on the surface, moves away from political theology. Indeed, when Foucault writes of modern anti-Semitism, he describes a transformation of "old religious-type anti-Semitism" into state-sanctioned racism in which the Jew functions as a generic form of the racial other.[32] Giorgio Agamben has attempted to restore the link between biopolitics and political theology by tracing, across an impressive array of contexts, the figure of the sacred man, *homo sacer*.[33] More precisely, what Agamben tracks is the logic of the exception, which he takes to be a privileged motif of (at least) Western society. An exception requires the law but also makes the law possible. Agamben identifies a number of figures, beyond the sovereign, who have this peculiar role with respect to the law—he writes of outlaws, of werewolves, and of those imprisoned in concentration camps. What is notable about all of these figures inhabiting the exception, Agamben argues, is that they are considered sacred and that their bare life (as opposed to their social persona) is at issue. In this, biopolitics and political theology are joined. For Agamben, unlike Foucault, bare life and holy life have been joined throughout the history of Western society; Auschwitz is not strange but a new manifestation of an old phenomenon. But whereas Foucault emphasizes the specificity of race, as a modern construction, race fades in Agamben's narrative as the paradox of the legal exception is individuated onto specific figures.

Growing as it did out of Marxist and early poststructuralist theory, postcolonial theory has as times been suspicious of religion, viewing it as a tool of the colonizer, an opiate of the colonized. Recent work has suggested just the opposite: there is a subversive potential in the religions of the former colonies that has been ignored (or even theoretically colonized) by secular, that is, post-Christian, Western scholars. When the religious ideas and practices of the former colonies are no longer understood on a "world religions" model, forcing them into the peculiar shape of Protestant Christianity or, more generously, of Abrahamic faiths, taking seriously those beliefs and practices can dramatically humble Western scholars. In fact, such religious ideas and practices can be used as a tool for achieving such humility. Dipesh Chakrabarty proposes leaving "gods and spirits" with agency in historical narratives to remind the Western reader, and writer, of the pervasive and futile violence that her attempted translation enacts.[34] Saba Mahmood understands her anthropological account of pious Muslim women in Cairo as calling into question Western assumptions about ethics and politics that govern the secular modern state (as well as the more complicated quasi-secular, quasi-modern Egyptian state).[35]

Yet proposals such as Chakrabarty's and Mahmood's still view secular modernity as a Western construction, one that is to be critiqued from the perspective of the global South. Other recent work has argued that modernity should not be understood as a European creation but as a coproduction of Europe and its others. Modernity emerged as Europeans encountered the peoples of the Americas, Africa, and the Pacific. Furthermore, the transformation from a provincial but ostensibly universal worldview to a planetary worldview happened on both sides of the encounter, as both sides realized that their view of the cosmos would have to change to incorporate those they met. These worldviews were at once philosophical, political, and religious. The way that they transformed, according to Jared Hickman, was to invent race.[36] The way for a worldview thought to be universal to maintain its potency once humans from another corner of the globe dropped by or turned up was to give each group a role in the cosmos. In other words, groups turned into races as part of a political theological perspective— race was born from a transformation of political theology, and it was born Siamese twins, one European and the other in the rest of the world.

This narrative is elegant and compelling, but is it really describing political theology? In other words, can a worldview (if there is such a thing) be so easily associated with political theology? Hickman thinks that it can, because both have to do with "ultimate sense." But such a definition appears to revert to a watery Protestantism, where religion is just beliefs about matters of ultimate concern. The novelty of "political theology" allows it to be deployed without worrying about the genealogical criticisms that have been leveled against the categories of religion and politics. Perhaps this temptation to repeat such theoretically colonizing maneuvers is what prompted Edward Said to advance his notion of "secular critique." By this Said does not refer to secularism in the dogmatic sense, nor does he refer to secularism as the complement to religiosity. As Gil Anidjar recently wrote, Said's secular criticism "must be read as a critique of Christianity, secularized or not."[37] Secularism, as ideology, is invented by Christianity. Paradoxically, political theology at its best is secular criticism, attentive to text and context, ever vigilant of ideologically inflected concepts, the friction between text and ideology exposing both—that is, making both vulnerable. Holding a privileged position among ideologies is the Christian and post-Christian. Césaire, ultimately, returns to a cleansed Christianity, perhaps a secular Christianity.

TO MAKE VULNERABLE the political and the theological through engagement with text and context is the intellectual labor of political theology. Critique and defense are the tools of the polemicist and the demagogue. The vocation of the academic, in contrast, is to expose what is taken for granted, to make vulnerable. Race, from Jews to African Americans to colonial encounters, is a particularly sensitive site of exposure and a catalyst for engagements with political theology. Too often the vocabulary of political theology has been limited, confined to narrow, diluted, or sectarian senses. The essays that follow expand that vocabulary through a concern with race. In order to allow for focused but also comparative inquiry, a particular focus of these chapters is on how Jewish and African American thought inflects political theology.

The first two essays have familiar settings but less familiar protagonists. What does it mean when Otto Brunner or Wilhelm Stapel, instead of Carl Schmitt, inaugurates discussions of political theology? Like Schmitt, Brunner and Stapel were mid-twentieth-century thinkers associated uncomfortably closely with National Socialism. Vincent Pecora shows how Brunner joins a romanticized image of the medieval household with aspirations to a postmodern, postbourgeois social order. Christoph Schmidt presents a provocative case for the limitations of secular liberalism—but demonstrates how this critique, as made by Stapel, was closely associated with intellectual paranoia concerning Jewish theocracy.

J. Kameron Carter retrieves strains in the thought of that towering figure of twentieth-century Protestantism, Karl Barth, that provide resources for ideology critique. By retrieving Barth's radical side, Carter is able to show

how that towering figure of twentieth-century African American intellectual life, W. E. B. Du Bois, a trenchant critic of religion, may in fact share political theological instincts with Barth. Du Bois as a religious thinker is also the theme of Jonathon Kahn's essay, but the political theology Kahn finds in Du Bois is that of a pragmatist. Kahn explores what it might mean for a pragmatist to have a political theology, and the consequent aporias, through a reading of the disappearing figure of the Jew in Du Bois's masterpiece, *The Souls of Black Folk*. Although Du Bois has (until recently) often been read as a religious skeptic, Howard Thurman is often read as a quintessential African American religious liberal. Corey Walker retrieves an unexpected Thurman, one whose concern with the texture of black religious life opens up critical imagination—and a freedom rather unlike the fetishized freedom of liberalism.

What role could the Muslim, figured in the European imagination, have in configuring political theology? Gil Anidjar and Daniel Boyarin take *Othello* as a site at which to address this question. Anidjar tracks figures of the double: the king at once theological and secular, *Othello* about a Moor and *The Merchant of Venice* about a Jew. What forces bind and loose these doubles? Boyarin finds an erotic force binding and loosing, and exchanging, political-theological figures of the Muslim, in particular, Othello. Othello's hidden penis troubles our comfortable differences: racial, religious, gender, and sexual.

The precarious position of the Jew in postmodern times is the topic of the next two essays. Bonnie Honig pairs the early twentieth-century Rosenzweig-Scholem exchange with the Walzer-Said exchange of the 1980s. In each, tensions between ethnic and religious identity push the limits of dialogue, and Honig suggests that these tensions force us to consider what a model of justice that takes the theological seriously might look like. These are also the tensions that Martin Land and Jonathan Boyarin explore in their lively, informal conversation. Thinking together, across continents, Land and Boyarin question what the ethnic-religious figure of the Jew presents today. In a sense, where Honig's Jew is neither ethnic nor religious, a figure of paradox impenetrable by dialogue, Land and Boyarin present a Jew who is both ethnic and religious, and in the process bring those terms into question—and revel in dialogue.

George Shulman, in this collection's final essay, displaces political theology from Europe to America. The concepts of prophecy and redemption are at the heart of American democratic politics, he argues, and the flourishing of democracy depends on acknowledging dependence on political theology. Prophets serve as reminders of this oft-forgotten dependence, and it is the prophet's unique, and uniquely democratic, vocation to speak in an idiom accessible to all: to prophesy in the vernacular. Shulman's essay pushes us to ask about the role of rhetoric—that is, speech intended to persuade—in political theology, how rhetoric mystifies and reveals.

Notes

This collection was originally conceived in cooperation with Gregory Kaplan. It was completed with the support of Emory University's James Weldon Johnson Institute and Syracuse University's Department of Religion. Among those who assisted with the project are Molly Bassett, Christina Bennett, Amos Bitzan, Emily-Jane Cohen, Clara Totenberg Green, Joshua Lupo, Richard Tran, Isaac Weiner, and Leah Weinryb-Grohsgal.

1. Aimé Césaire, *Discourse on Colonialism*, trans. Joan Pinkham (New York: Monthly Review Press, 2001), 48.

2. Ibid., 49.

3. Aimé Césaire, *Notebook of a Return to the Native Land*, trans. Clayton Eshleman (Middleton, CT: Wesleyan University Press, 2001), 16, 4, 6, 8.

4. Ibid., 9, 12, 20, 24.

5. Ibid., 35, 37, 38, 22.

6. This idea is developed by Bonnie Honig as "Jewish political theology" in *Emergency Politics: Paradox, Law, Democracy* (Princeton, NJ: Princeton University Press, 2009).

7. Talal Asad, *Genealogies of Religion: Discipline and Reasons of Power in Christianity and Islam* (Baltimore: Johns Hopkins University Press, 1993).

8. William T. Cavanaugh argues forcefully against this claim in *The Myth of Religious Violence: Secular Ideology and the Roots of Modern Conflict* (Oxford: Oxford University Press, 2009).

9. For example, José Casanova, *Public Religions in the Modern World* (Chicago: University of Chicago Press, 1994).

10. Charles Taylor, *A Secular Age* (Cambridge, MA: Belknap Press, 2007).

11. Carl Schmitt, *Political Theology: Four Chapters on the Concept of Sovereignty*, trans. George Schwab (Chicago: University of Chicago Press, 1985), chap. 3.

12. Charles Mathewes, *A Theology of Public Life* (Cambridge: Cambridge University Press, 2007).

13. Raphael Gross, *Carl Schmitt and the Jews: The "Jewish Question," the Holocaust, and German Legal Theory*, trans. Joel Golb (Madison: University of Wisconsin Press, 2007).

14. Césaire, *Discourse*, 36.

15. J. Kameron Carter, *Race: A Theological Account* (Oxford: Oxford University Press, 2008).

16. For a compelling account of religion as a "cultural-linguistic system," see George Lindbeck, *The Nature of Doctrine: Religion and Theology in a Postliberal Age* (Philadelphia: Westminster Press, 1984).

17. Gopal Balakrishnan, *The Enemy: An Intellectual Portrait of Carl Schmitt* (London: Verso, 2000); Jan-Werner Müller, *A Dangerous Mind: Carl Schmitt in Post-war European Thought* (New Haven, CT: Yale University Press, 2003).

18. Müller, *A Dangerous Mind*, 39.

19. Carl Schmitt, *The Concept of the Political*, expanded ed., trans. George Schwab (Chicago: University of Chicago Press, 2007), 19.

20. Carl Schmitt, *Theory of the Partisan: Intermediate Commentary on the Concept of the Political*, trans. G. L. Ulmen (New York: Telos Press, 2007).

21. Carl Schmitt, *The Nomos of the Earth in the International Law of the Jus Publicum Europaeum*, trans. G. L. Ulmen (New York: Telos Press, 2006), 42, italics omitted.

22. Schmitt, *Political Theology*, 36.

23. See Carl Schmitt, *Roman Catholicism and Political Form*, trans. G. L. Ulmen (Westport, CT: Greenwood Press, 1996).

24. For a comparison of the views of Schmitt and Peterson, see György Geréby, "Political Theology versus Theological Politics: Erik Peterson and Carl Schmitt," *New German Critique* 35:3 (Fall 2008): 7–33.

25. For an overview of this work, see Rebecca S. Chopp, *The Praxis of Suffering: An Interpretation of Liberation and Political Theologies* (Maryknoll, NY: Orbis Books, 1992); Sara K. Pinnock, ed., *The Theology of Dorothee Soelle* (Harrisburg, PA: Trinity Press International, 2003); John Milbank, "Political Theology," in *Encyclopedia of Christian Theology*, ed. Jean-Yves Lacoste (New York: Routledge, 2005), 1251–1253.

26. Schmitt, *The Nomos of the Earth*, 59–60; for discussion, see Günter Meuter, *Der Katechon: Zu Carl Schmitts fundamentalistischer Kritik der Zeit* (Berlin: Duncker und Humblot, 1994); Heinrich Meier, *The Lesson of Carl Schmitt: Four Chapters on the Distinction between Political Theology and Political Philosophy*, trans. Marcus Brainard (Chicago: University of Chicago Press, 1998).

27. Jacob Taubes, *Occidental Eschatology*, trans. David Ratmoko (Stanford, CA: Stanford University Press, 2009).

28. Jacob Taubes, *The Political Theology of Paul*, trans. Dana Hollander (Stanford, CA: Stanford University Press, 2004).

29. Derrida's extended response to the work of Schmitt can be found in *Politics of Friendship*, trans. George Collins (London: Verso, 1997).

30. See especially Michel Foucault, *The History of Sexuality: An Introduction, Volume 1*, trans. Robert Hurley (New York: Vintage, 1990); Foucault, *"Society Must Be Defended": Lectures at the Collège de France, 1975–1976*, trans. David Macey (New York: Picador, 2003).

31. Foucault, *"Society Must Be Defended,"* 254.

32. Ibid., 88–89.

33. Giorgio Agamben, *Homo Sacer: Sovereign Power and Bare Life*, trans. Daniel Heller-Roazen (Stanford, CA: Stanford University Press, 1998).

34. Dipesh Chakrabarty, *Provincializing Europe: Postcolonial Thought and Historical Difference* (Princeton, NJ: Princeton University Press, 2000).

35. Saba Mahmood, *Politics of Piety: The Islamic Revival and the Feminist Subject* (Princeton, NJ: Princeton University Press, 2005).

36. Jared Hickman, "Globalization and the Gods, or the Political Theology of 'Race,'" *Early American Literature* 45:1 (2010): 145–182.

37. Gil Anidjar, "Secularism," *Critical Inquiry* 33 (2006): 52–77, 62. Said writes of "secular criticism" in *The World, the Text, and the Critic* (Cambridge, MA: Harvard University Press, 1983).

CHAPTER I

POLITICAL THEOLOGY AND THE CASE OF OTTO BRUNNER

VINCENT P. PECORA

Otto Brunner's *Land und Herrschaft: Grundfragen der territorialen Verfassungs-geschichte Südostdeutschlands im Mittelalter* (1939) blended Carl Schmitt's ideas (especially the friend-foe opposition as the basis of the political) with W. H. Riehl's nineteenth-century account of the medieval Germanic family, tribe, and nation.[1] Brunner posits the unique nature of the premodern Germanic *Volksgemeinschaft* (people's community), from which he imagined a distinctly postmodern political order arising under Hitler. Medieval Austria's *Land* (territory), *Volk* (people), and *Herrschaft* (lordship or sovereignty) constituted for Brunner a necessary template for the Third Reich, which supplanted the contractual authority of the *Rechtstaat* (modern liberal state). The putatively recoverable deep structure of familial, clan, and regional relationships stands in for the idea of race. What I have elsewhere called a "household of the soul" that shapes much political resistance and nostalgia in the nineteenth and early twentieth centuries—a fundamentally Aristotelian, aristocratic, and anticapitalist image of proper (noble) familial relationships and gens-based symbolic economies—is at the same time a racial household, for it rests on the assumption that authentic political life arises from the family writ large, either in the Hobbesian, top-down, monarchist "throne and altar" fashion of Joseph de Maistre, or in the pre-Hobbesian, bottom-up, *völkisch* populism of Brunner (who focuses directly on *Haush-errschaft*, or household lordship, as the basis of the German *Volk*).[2] Schmitt insists on the force of secularized religious (Roman Catholic) structures of thought as the intractable bases of the sovereign decision that implicitly founds and explicitly preserves the law. Such a decision is an echo of divine authority, without which neither monarchic nor republican sovereignty can survive crises. By contrast, Brunner radically collapses the secularizing distinction between religious moral background and rationalized civil politics that the modern state requires by returning to notions of land and lordship—of *Landrecht*, a sense of law and right welling up from the land—that predate the *Rechtstaat* and through which modern racial politics becomes far more salient.

BRUNNER's *Land und Herrschaft*, published in 1939, 1942, and 1943 (revised), and newly revised in 1959 minus the conclusion, is an example of *Blut und Boden* thought, and there was no shortage of such texts before and during the Third Reich. *Blut und Boden*—blood and soil, race and rural community, an Aryan body returning to the land for corporal rejuvenation and reaffirmation of sacred bonds—was a significant element of Nazi propaganda early in Hitler's reign and a crucial part of the apotheosis under the Reich of the Germanic *Volk*. The term *Volk* had at least two, usually reinforcing but at times distinct, meanings: a people as a cultural community with long-standing traditions of custom and law—what sociologists call an *ethnie* today, equivalent in ways to premodern usages of the term "nation"—and a people defined by a biologically measurable racial composition.[3] Whereas the first meaning of *Volk* had widespread appeal well before the rise of Nazism and during the Third Reich, the second meaning attracted a narrower but more politically aggressive group of writers and theorists. The latter, racial meaning became dominant once Hitler consolidated power. *Blut und Boden* obviously refers to the racial definition of the *Volk* but also to the rural, agricultural basis of that definition. Hence, the expression *Blut und Boden*, however effective as propaganda, raised certain problems once the Reich began intensive rearmament and war preparations in 1934. The cities, with their heavy industry and ready work forces, were a crucial part of National Socialism's drive for lebensraum and the irredentist project of reuniting all Germanic peoples. Urban energy, advanced technology, and centrally organized bureaucratic state apparatus were fundamental elements of Hitler's war machine.[4] By 1938, Hitler was actively denouncing the mystical and occult elements that had defined much *Blut und Boden* and *völkisch* thought.[5] What he needed instead were public representations of *Volksgemeinschaft* that could be materially and ideologically controlled, as in the spectacular state-sponsored party rallies at Nuremberg after 1933.

Walther Darré, appointed Reich minister for nutrition and agriculture in 1933, melded the cultural and political projects of *Blut und Boden*. Darré's *Das Bauerntum als Lebensquell der nordischen Rasse* (The Peasantry as the Life Source of the Nordic Race, 1929) and *Neuadel aus Blut und Boden* (New Nobility out of Blood and Soil, 1935) made him the perfect mix of rural idealist, practical bureaucrat, and anti-Semite. Darré's thinking had roots in that of Karl Haushofer, a WWI general and geographer often named as a source for the idea that the putatively high population density of German cities could be relieved by colonial expansion (an idea that may have had credibility for Haushofer because of the Monroe Doctrine and "manifest destiny"); and in that of Friedrich Ratzel, whose essay "Lebensraum" (1901) popularized the term as part of his science of "biogeography" following upon the Darwinian Ernst Heinrich Haekel (for whom ontogeny famously recapitulated phylogeny). Further back, one finds nineteenth-century geographer Karl Ritter, whose *Die Erdkunde im Verhältniss zur Natur und zur Geschichte des Menschen* (The Science of the Earth in Relation to Nature and the History of Mankind, 1817–1859), was a grand elaboration (nineteen volumes, unfinished) of theories found in Montesquieu and Alexander von Humboldt about how the physical environment shapes human communities. Darré's thinking was racist and anti-Semitic. But Haushofer, whose wife was Jewish and whose son played a role in the plot to assassinate Hitler, was likely not. Ratzel was an imperialist, and his notion of lebensraum depended on a Darwinian process by which healthier populations reinvigorated weaker nations on their borders. And Ritter was a cosmopolitan preevolutionist philosopher, opposed to the slave trade of his time, whose work could suggest a colonizing, racist mentality only via distortion.

The literary expressions of *Blut und Boden*, which perhaps had greater popularity than the scholarly work and were tinged with romantic mysticism, may actually begin with a Norwegian. Knut Hamsun, whose *Markens Grøde* (Growth of the Soil, 1917), translated quickly into German as *Segen der Erde* (The Blessing, or Abundance, of the Earth) and into Yiddish, emerges in Viennese writer Jean Améry's account as the model for subsequent German "peasant" novels.[6] *Growth of the Soil* was largely responsible for Hamsun's Nobel Prize in Literature in 1920. Hamsun became a staunch promoter of the Nazi cause, as did other *völkisch* novelists of the Weimar years, such as Hanns Johst and Hans Grimm. But Friedrich Griese, whose novels *Feuer* (Fire, 1921), *Winter* (1927), and *Das letzte Gesicht* (The Final Vision, 1934) meditate on sacred connections to one's ancestors and to eternal processes of death and regeneration rather than on modern racial politics, traded in nostalgia for a time predating industrial capitalism, with its crowded, multiethnic cities, horrific machine-driven wars, and crushing economic depressions. Griese celebrated a time when unsophisticated rural populations did not feel manipulated by educated elites, when families functioned as extended households, and when relative independence and self-help were (at least imaginatively) the order of the day. The Nazi use of the term *Volksgemeinschaft* was adopted, one might add, from Weimar's Social Democrats, "who, after World War I, had tried unsuccessfully to link it to the new democracy."[7]

This recovery of an ancestrally rooted, rural, and robust yeomanry should *not* be understood as a specifically German phenomenon in earlier decades. It is trans-European, with deep roots in the nineteenth-century British Empire. Adventure novelists such as Frederick Marryat, Charles Kingsley, Robert Ballantyne, George Henty, and H. Rider Haggard championed a seaborne empire built around a *völkisch* resistance to multiethnic urban decay and a *völkisch* embrace of traditional rural values, of kinship and soil.[8] Haggard, barrister by training, produced a parliamentary "blue book" on Salvation Army colonies in North America and England (*The Poor and the Land*, 1905) as well as a study arguing that Britain could relieve urban overcrowding, unemployment, poverty, and the threat of anarchy, and arrest the decline and depopulation of its countryside, by repatriating people from the cities to the country (*Rural Denmark and Its Lessons*, 1911). (Chairman Mao later had the same idea—with disastrous results.) Joseph Conrad, the great chronicler of deracinated adventurers and maritime empire in decay, periodically sang hymns to the primacy of the *Land*. "Each blade of grass has its spot on earth whence it draws its life, its strength; and so is man rooted to the land from which he draws his faith together with his life."[9] Despite the divergent uses to which sociology and fiction about the value of blood and soil were put in different national settings, we need to be disabused of the idea—an idea promoted by Nazi ideologues themselves—that there was anything uniquely German about such sentiments.

Brunner's *Land und Herrschaft* should be read today, despite its claims to Germanic specificity, less as an example of *Blut und Boden* thinking than as a remarkably complex and detailed elaboration of how a family of ideas—including land, household, extended kinship, local sovereignty, and an individual's right to violent self-help in the redress of wrongs—was interwoven in a broadly European, politically complex reaction to an increasingly secular, urban, technologically driven, and socially administered modernity. Moreover, we should understand Brunner's contribution in the context of modern political theology, that is, as an attempt to mend the supposed aporias in the nineteenth-century liberal nation-state between disavowed religious background and democratic secular foreground, between what Schmitt called "the omnipotent God" and the "omnipotent lawgiver," or between "theology" and "the theory of the state," by returning to a singular, integrated, and organic whole. It is a version of—or perhaps a response to—political theology that has uncanny resonances with the political theology of the present day.

The excellent existing translation of *Land und Herrschaft* into English in 1992 is based unfortunately, for my purposes, on the fourth edition of 1959. As the translators point out, Brunner's alterations in 1959 were a response to the embarrassing resonances after 1945 of his earlier formulations. Brunner omitted his conclusion, which makes a direct connection between his account of medieval Austria and the German Third Reich. He deleted references then current among other *völkisch* thinkers (Ernst Huber, Hans Freyer, Ernst Jünger) to the idea that what Schmitt called the "total" or "welfare" state of the early twentieth century, in which private interests became politically organized in and by the state, had already dissolved the nineteenth-century distinction between laissez-faire state (law and administration) and society (Marx's *bürgerliche gesellschaft*, ruled by economic interests, religious

beliefs, and class "ideologies"), thus ushering in the Third Reich's specifically German reintegration.[10] Brunner saw the European nineteenth century, both its state-versus-society distinction and conceptual framework, as
anomalous for German consciousness. The subtitle of the 1943 edition reflects his embrace of irredentist *Ostforschung* (research on the East), aimed
at justifying German desires for more lebensraum and the 1938 *Anschluss*,
or unification, of Germany with Austria: the earlier subtitle refers to *Südostdeutschlands* (Southeast Germany) rather than the 1959 *Österreichs* (Austria).
An "ardent" pan-German Austrian at the University of Vienna before the
war, Brunner supported the *Anschluss* when it came.[11] Raised a Catholic,
he was listed as a Protestant when married in the 1920s, survived Hitler's
Reich, and, though officially retired in 1948 for six years, found, like so
many of his colleagues, a respectable postwar academic appointment, at the
University of Hamburg from 1954 to 1973.

His work has been described as an ignored precursor to the later French
Annales School. While Marc Bloch, Lucien Febvre, and Fernand Braudel
invoked "structural" history, Brunner's revision of earlier "constitutional
history" (*Verfassungsgeschichte*), blending legal and social history, pointed
to the "conceptual history" of an age that distinguished between the analytical categories of modern historians and the *Grundbegriffe* (fundamental
concepts) of the past. Brunner's was less a history of society, laws, or ideas
than of what the Annalistes later called the *mentalité* (the larger consciousness) of a time and place. Brunner's description of his method as "folk history" (*Volksgeschichte*) became in the postwar edition the more palatable,
au courant structural history (*Strukturgeschichte*). Whether Brunner's work
influenced the Annales School is difficult to assess; Kaminsky and Melton
cite one vague quote from Braudel in 1972 as evidence.[12] More important
is Brunner's elaboration of the worldview of late medieval Austria, which
definitively severed its developmental connection to post-Hobbes, monarchical, and nation-state histories of the early modern period, the political
theology espoused by Maistre, and the liberal nation-state of the nineteenth
century. Brunner posited, though not in the later terms of Michel Foucault,
a historical rupture between medieval and early modern perspectives rather
than the inevitable, evolutionary, Hegelian continuum assumed by previous
historians.

Brunner was thus profoundly *anti*-Hegelian, both in refusing the constitutional monarchy that Hegel posited as the culmination of universal
history, and in rejecting the dialectical process of overcoming and yet
preserving the contradictions driving conceptual and historical development. (This is not a trivial point, since commentators on the era still emphasize the Hegelian roots of *völkisch* thought.) For Brunner, the liberal
state that flourished in the nineteenth-century unification of Germany
under Bismarck is as much a historical mistake for Germanic civilization
as Christianity had been for Europe as a whole in Friedrich Nietzsche's
eyes. Though Brunner does not cite Nietzsche, the comparison is not gra-
tuitous: like Nietzsche's, Brunner's political theology refuses the "secularization" of Christianity unfolded by Hegel's dialectical-historical optimism.
Instead of the masking and sublimation of religious ideals in monarchical
and then liberal theories of sovereignty, Brunner recovers late medieval
Austrian forms of right—peace, kinship, friendship, honor, loyalty (*Treue*),
retribution, and blood-vengeance—sanctioned by the "Good Old Law,"
that is, Old Testament Law, and by the perennial sense that all law is rooted
in God (and in "immemorial custom," or *êwa*), so that "God, honor, and
Right" are synonymous (*LL*, 116–119; *LH*, 153–158). Only toward the end
of the medieval period, Brunner argues, did the institutionalized church
succeed in repressing nonstate violence attached to the "Good Old Law."

The subsequent gap separating natural and positive law, which would
become important for early modern ecclesiastical and later modern legal
theory, did not correspond meaningfully to the mentality of the medieval
consciousness. The "conviction of Right" in medieval Austria was simply
the law of the community. It was "'the community's conviction about
what is right and legitimate, the conviction that dominates the heart of
every individual with elemental power,'" so (unlike the governance of the
liberal state) there was "no contradiction between law and justice" and
Right was the product of an "enduring order" (*LL*, 119; *LH*, 158).[13] Although this conviction was most fully encoded in a medieval Christian
worldview, it was also for Brunner essential to ancient Greco-Roman and
pagan religious/ethical worldviews. Belief in that "enduring order" permeated the cults of Germanic tribes, for which law "belonged to an ontological order grounded in religion" and in "the thought of Christian

late-antiquity, in which the Augustinian concern with the idea of *justitia*, of legitimate power, of just war (*bellum iustum*), had become a central problem" (*LL*, 123; *LH*, 164). Such conviction one would find, for example, in the Aristotelian phrase αὖ ἕνεκα (that for the sake of which), describing the telos, the purposiveness, of nature. "Therefore action for an end is present in things which come to be and are by nature"; and again: "It is plain then that nature is a cause, a cause that operates for a purpose."[14] Later Christian natural law theory, rooted in Aquinas's understanding "that the natural law is nothing else than the rational creature's participation of the eternal [divine] law," is then for Brunner perfectly congruent with classical conceptions of law in nature.[15] Though precepts of Christian morality play little role in his history, Brunner's ethical-political concept of *Land* follows directly from ancient and medieval Christian perspectives on the order of nature and of the *Volk* attached to it. Brunner obviates the aporia posited by political theology—the disavowed debt owed by the positive law of the liberal state to its religious foundations, by human law to eternal justice—because in his conception of the premodern Austrian political order, such distinctions do not exist.

Brunner so fully adopted Schmitt's definition of "the concept of the political" as "simply the friend-foe relationship" that even the distinction between *Macht* (might) and *Recht* (law or right) "was essentially a problem posed by the nineteenth century" (*LL*, 2n4, 2; *LH*, 3n1). Brunner further argued that state sovereignty over Austrian territory was not fully achieved until the 1848–1849 constitutions, "which abolished lordship and provincial estates" (*LL*, 149; *LH*, 202). The audacity of his claim about the medieval identity of might and right should not obscure the logic that it possessed in Brunner's thinking, on which it based a twentieth-century pan-German Reich that recovered pre-nation-state political realities. Brunner's book focuses on medieval Austria, primarily between the twelfth and sixteenth centuries. It argues that premodern Europe had notions of land, law, and licit violence ("lawful" feuds) that were not precursors to the modern nation-state, which would appropriate to itself alone the right to all legitimate or lawful violence. For Brunner, Schmitt's definition of the political implied that medieval Austria had notions of *Recht* and ways of distinguishing legitimate from illegitimate violence that could not be understood using the terminology of the nineteenth century and its liberal state constitutions. Instead, Schmitt's friend-foe distinction pointed Brunner to the practice that best defined licit, yet nonstate, violence in premodern "Southeast Germany"—*Fehde* (the feud).

The legitimacy of the medieval feud is fundamental to Brunner's separation of the secularized nation-state's political theology from the integrated, organic, and corporatist political theology of late medieval Austria and the Third Reich. Within medieval Christendom, war is the feud writ large—that is, in princely terms (*LL*, 33; *LH*, 44). Feuds commonly occurred among lords and knights, one party seeking redress of wrongs against property or person. Such feuds would obligate the extended households and clans to participate. Even though peasants and burghers normally did not exercise the right of feud, they were not completely excluded. The right of self-defense of the house, defined as extending to the drip line of the roof, was for Brunner the basis of the feud's legitimacy. Lawful, communally sanctioned violence unleashed by feuds—the violence that Brunner calls "self-help" (*Selbsthilfe*) (*LL*, 13; *LH*, 20)—thus needs to be distinguished from acts of brigandage and illegitimate coercion that occurred independent of the private redress of wrongs. *Recht* is to be enforced not only or primarily by existing sovereigns or their agents—kings, princes, lords, magistrates—but rather by *Herrschaft* rooted in the patriarchal medieval household. All forms of lordship are then versions of a *Hausherrschaft* (household lordship), emanating from the *Land*. "Concepts such as peace, feud, and retribution must be understood in their original context, that of friendship based on kinship. These basic concepts undoubtedly governed Germanic thought to a profound degree; otherwise, one could not explain why, in the historical memory of the early Germanic and medieval world, the great political events of the period of migrations were so completely transposed into the sphere of clan discord and blood vengeance [*Sippenzwist und Blutrache*]" (*LL*, 25; *LH*, 32–33). While Brunner acknowledges a distinction between blood revenge and feud, both derive originally from the right to vendetta quite apart from any state authority and positive law.

The feud's legitimacy as a means of retribution and restoration of communal peace is the key to Brunner's emphasis on the primacy of *Land*, of premodern notions of legality deriving from habitation on that *Land*, and of the household that represented the political kernel of premodern notions of sovereignty. Brunner actually sees the resort to self-help as a possibility sanctioned by all legal systems: "Every legal order recognizes a certain measure of self-help, if only in extreme cases. Even a modern state might conceivably sanction a greater use of the feud between its subjects, as a form of self-help, since no legal order can ever fully dispense with self-help, say, in the form of self-defense" (*LL*, 13; *LH*, 20). Brunner's formulations of self-help as self-defense might have seemed innocuous when they appeared in his 1959 edition. But in earlier editions, published just after Kristallnacht and the advent of mob violence against Jews and Jewish property, such language implicitly justified actions that were technically extralegal by the standards of the modern German nation-state, though legitimate enough in terms of medieval notions of "feud" and "self-help." Only with the Enlightenment's outlawing of the feud, which reduced it to mere *Faustrecht* (the law of the fist), did positive law, modern citizenship, and the "absolutist" state—that is, the state defined by its monopoly on all legitimate violence—arise. "Our modern concepts of state, justice, and law are incompatible with this sort of self-help, and it is therefore extremely difficult to describe that older world as it was" (*LL*, 91; *LH*, 121). Brunner's contribution to political theology is precisely the recovery of a medieval "constitution"—a conception of the unity of *Recht* and *Macht*—that is not describable in the "absolutist" terms of modern constitutional history.

Central to Brunner's medieval constitution was his finding that the terms *terra* and *territorium*—the Latin terms for the *Land*—were in common use before the twelfth century, "when they could not mean 'lordship over a territory'" (*LL*, 155; *LH*, 210). That is, *Land* as a form of legal community—a *Rechtsgemeinschaft*—preceded, both historically and logically, the territorial lord. The implications of this claim are far-reaching: the seemingly autochthonous, natural, and nonabsolutist legal community, derived from the intimate sovereignty of *Hausherrschaft*, became for Brunner the basis of all other forms of medieval territorial sovereignty. To speak of land and lordship is to speak of a condition in which *Recht* is the telos of the land and not of the lord, a telos endorsed simultaneously in tribal custom, classical philosophy, and Christian religious belief. "The nature of a *Land* is not to be derived from territorial supremacy, but rather vice-versa" (*LL*, 161;

LH, 219). Quite opposed to the modern, absolutist, Hobbesian formula of the social contract, in which sovereignty is invested solely in the sovereign, whose role is arbitrarily assigned by deliberation among parties with antagonistic, or feuding, interests, Brunner's medieval sovereignty is a natural efflux of the land itself, in which *Recht* and *Macht* have not yet been sundered and then artificially sutured by contract, and in which whatever notions of sovereignty do exist—from householder to territorial lord to prince—are *consequences* of the communal *Landrecht*, not the source of it. "As for the law of the *Land*, it was originally nothing but the law of the tribe (*Stamm*) and of the people . . . of tribal and ethnic law in the early Middle Ages . . . and this as early as the time when 'the Teutons' [*Germanen*] first appears as a historical name" (*LL*, 157; *LH*, 214–215).[16] For the early Germans, *Land* designated "at once a political and a legal entity" (*LL*, 156; *LH*, 211). The natural, implicit law of association of people who tilled the soil became the law of that land, so "tribal and ethnic law became territorial law; 'people' and 'land' were now interchangeable" (*LL*, 158; *LH*, 215).[17] The election of a king by the associated tribes of the *ethnie* assumed that the king drew his authority from the tribal laws of individual territories, the allegiance of which he needed to procure on a territory-by-territory basis. Medieval *Herrschaft* was the consequence of territorial self-consciousness. *Herrschaft* was founded on *Landrecht* and wielded authority only on condition that it harmonized with territorial law, and was always at risk of feud and overthrow if such law were violated.

It is in this sense of a people (*Leute*) rooted in and by a *Land*—where the terms did not describe the political "state" in general but quite specifically the *Germanic state*, apart from all others—that Brunner's political theology implicates modern notions of race. The term *Rasse* (race or breed, in the sense of breeding dogs or in the sense of eugenics), commonly used during Brunner's lifetime, occurs rarely in *Land und Herrschaft* and most often in the conclusion. Instead, like other *völkisch* thinkers, Brunner relies heavily on the terms *Volk* (people, nation, but also race in a premodern sense) and *Stamm* (literally stem or trunk, and by implication race, but commonly a term for stock, breed, tribe, clan, or family). One could argue that Brunner's terminological choice is hardly significant in the final analysis. In 1939, Brunner's readers would have had no difficulty reading *Volk* as the desig-

nation for both the German people with its putatively long cultural inheritance and the Aryan race biologically distinguished from Slavs, Africans,
Gypsies, and (above all) Jews. The supposed *Sonderweg* (special path) of the
Germans, exemplified in Brunner's treatment of medieval Austria, would
have been explicit, and it implied the demand for racial separation. Nevertheless, Brunner's conception of Germanic *Land und Leute*, in addition to
its indisputable link to Nazi racial thinking, depends on the belief that premodern notions of family, clan, tribe, and people, however impossible to
recover, may yet provide political guidance in the modern age—or more
precisely, once the modern age of the nation-state has come to naught.

Though Brunner relied on earlier German historians for his material
and on the ideas of other *völkisch* theorists and conservative jurists such
as Schmitt for many of his ideas, the issues raised are hardly unique, *pace*
Brunner, to Germanic culture. The Roman notion of the *gens*—family,
clan, tribe, community, but also premodern race, with the sense of a line of
descendants (as in *Stamm*) and a territorial region (as in Brunner's *Land*),
and with deeper roots in the Greek notion of the household community,
or *oikos* (house, temple, household, household property and economy, family, servants, race, home)—is crucial for nineteenth- and twentieth-century
Western culture, and in particular to its conception of alternatives or resistance to the consolidation of hegemony by bureaucratic, capitalist nation-
states.[18] In *Ancient Law* (1864), British legal historian H. S. Maine makes
the essential argument connecting (1) the premodern family, as opposed
to the modern individual; (2) premodern "forms of reciprocity in rights
and duties which have their origins in the Family" and are supplanted by
the notion of "Contract"; and (3) the premodern "Village Community,"
which is formed "on the model of an association of kinsmen" and should
be compared less to the "Roman Family" than to the "Roman Gens or
House," that is, "the family extended by a variety of fictions of which the
exact nature was lost in antiquity."[19] Though politically conservative, Maine
agreed that the passing of the old gentes and village communities was good
for civilization's progress. Drawing on Barthold Georg Niebuhr's *History
of Rome* (1827–1828) for descriptions of the gens and on Baron August
von Haxthausen's *The Russian Empire* (1847–1852) for the likeness of village communes in Russia and India, Maine believed that the persistence of

Haxthausen's village and land-based communities had no direct parallels in the West, and he largely followed Herbert Spencer's argument that homogeneous societies necessarily evolved into heterogeneous ones.

But not all who followed Maine's reasoning about the historical significance of the gens were convinced that its passing was either necessary or entirely good. Drawing on his travels in Russia, Haxthausen went in a different direction, adopted by *völkisch* thinkers, which was guided by nostalgia for a time when nobility and serfs were one people united by common ancestry in a particular soil.

> Formerly, when the nobles were not so numerous,—when they still constituted one people with the serfs, little differing from them in manners, education, and ideas,—when serfage comprised solely the cultivation of the soil,—before the old village communes, in which lies a great principle of true and regulated freedom, were broken up by the partitions that dissolved and destroyed them,—serfage was no unnatural, destructive, or unsuitable condition; perhaps indeed, for the political development of Russia, it was necessary.[20]

After Maine, this nostalgic elaboration of household and community, *Land und Leute*, would be developed by American anthropologist L. H. Morgan in *Ancient Society* (1877), which would have a decisive influence on Karl Marx's late work and Friedrich Engels's investigations of family and state.[21] Morgan thought he had discovered reproductions of the Roman gentes in North America's Iroquois Confederacy (following upon the work of Numa Denis Fustel de Coulanges). Morgan's may be the first and most significant post-Darwinian, evolutionist account of the gens as civilization's point of origin—a primal, clan-based, and communal institution more foundational than the patriarchal households of ancient civilizations, though evolved beyond the savagery and promiscuous horde posited by earlier nineteenth-century thought.

Although Morgan believed that Iroquois society was a preterritorial "*social organization*, founded upon gentes, phratries and tribes" predating in evolutionary terms "*political organization*, founded upon territory and property," his account of the gens is at times indistinguishable from Brunner's discussion of feud, self-help, household, people, and land.[22] Morgan's gens, which Brunner understood as medieval *Landrecht* based on household sovereignty, also entailed "reciprocal obligations of help, defense, and redress of injuries."[23] Whereas the modern individual looks to the state to maintain his rights, with a "corresponding abatement of the strength of the bond of kin," the individual in the gens finds there "a powerful element for mutual support. To wrong a person was to wrong his gens."[24] Where Brunner emphasized the ethnic relevance of a pre-liberal-state confederacy of "individual territories" in medieval Austria to the emerging post-liberal-state triumph of the Third Reich, the more Hegelian Morgan believed that the pre-state Iroquois Confederacy could be a salutary model for a post–Civil War America: "a revival, in a higher form, of the liberty, equality and fraternity of the ancient gentes" would serve as antidote to the "dissolution of society" that threatened when "property is the end and aim."[25] Morgan was no more a socialist than was Maine, but it is easy to see why Marx and Engels were attracted to his work. Morgan's ideas also responded to the recently destroyed plantation economy of the American South, where the clans and gentes had been precisely the conceptual basis of regional agrarian life free from the dictates of the nation-state and soon enshrined in the myth of the lost cause. Both Brunner and Morgan argued that pre-liberal-state social organization, based on household and tribe, clan and gens, could repair or supplant the liberal nation-state.

In *Land und Herrschaft*, the nostalgic conceptions of ancient and primitive societies developed by Haxthausen and Morgan (as well as by Engels) play no role in Brunner's thinking, despite obvious points of convergence. Brunner refers only once, in a footnote, to the work of Maine and Tönnies, whose *Gemeinschaft und Gesellschaft* is the grand synthesis of the previous half century of social theory in this vein and who reproduces Maine's distinction between status and contract, village commune and liberal nation-state. This neglect is perhaps not surprising, given the socialist aura surrounding the work of Morgan and Tönnies, especially if we accept the reasonable observation that Hegelian historicism, which envisioned modern, constitutional society as a dialectical outgrowth of primitive collective institutions, split into two factions in the nineteenth and twentieth centuries. In Lawrence Krader's formulation, the right wing stressed the earlier collectivity "as the womb of the nation" (providing a basis for what has been called a "primordialist" theory of national origins), while the left wing insisted on collectivity "as the womb of all mankind," thus implying internationalist socialism.[26]

Brunner's notions of *Land* and *Herrschaft* were putatively specific to Germanic political theology. He reproduced the conservative nationalism of earlier historians such as G. L. von Maurer and Otto Gierke, even as he challenged Gierke's view that the medieval "association" was the precursor to a modern juristic personality or corporation (*LL*, 196; *LH*, 271). In contrast, socialists such as Karl Kautsky, Karl Wittfogel, and Eduard Bernstein treated the primitive collective as the basis for international collectivism. This sort of neat dichotomy will take us only so far, however; it breaks down completely in certain important cases. Morgan, though admired by Engels, thought his work had a special national relevance for the United States; the political implications of Tönnies's work were notoriously ambiguous; and even the late Marx himself, in his notes on Morgan, "somewhat unexpectedly . . . inclined towards those of the Narodniks, who believed that the Russian village community could provide the basis of a transition to socialism without prior disintegration through capitalist development."[27] The idea of the gens proved to be particularly malleable after Maine and Morgan, informing a range of political perspectives despite Brunner's conceit that his medieval social forms were peculiarly Germanic and proto-Nazi.

What Brunner added to earlier European and American discourse on the meaning and perhaps recovery of the ancient gentes was his focus on the *Land*, an element that had received only superficial attention. The "village commune" of Haxthausen, Maine, and the Narodniks was obviously agricultural, but the terra itself had none of the deeper political theology it would acquire in Brunner's text. Moreover, each territory within the collection of Germanic territories functioned as a *Land* in its own right, and for Brunner this meant that the standard historical account by which various fragments of an inchoate region were united under—and because of—personal dominion, or "unitary territorial lordship," was incorrect. Instead, the association of disparate lands in the hands of one "count," as in the Tyrol, was simply one side of a more complicated process. "The documents of 1282 show quite clearly that there had been a process of fusion which had reached the point of creating something new, not a lordship (*dominium*) but a *Land* (*terra*). For from 1289 [1282 in the 1943 edition] on we find frequent references to the Tyrolean territorial law and above all to a community living by it—'the community of the county of Tyrol,' the 'people of the *Land*' (*landleute*; *terrigenae*), the bearers of Tyrolean territorial consciousness" (*LL*, 190; *LH*, 262). In each territory, it was "judicial power in territorial law, not the lordship of a prince, that created a *Land*" (*LL*, 193; *LH*, 267). The legal order of a *Land* was the "Good Old Law," that is, a view of right that "identified positive law with the moral and religious order," so that the individual's "subjective sense of his rights became his 'justice' and 'honor.' In such a world sovereignty could not be an issue, for Right transcended ruler and people, territorial prince and territorial community" (*LL*, 195; *LH*, 270). Individuals lawfully resorted to self-help—the feud—to settle disputes; even the execution of justice in a court of law was often resolved by the parties themselves.

At the heart of the seigneurial domain was the house, or rather the household, with its extensive network of ties extending beyond family into the larger clan and dependent subjects. The oath of loyalty binding lord and subject, the *Treue*, created mutual obligations and duties (Max Weber called them "liturgies"[28]) as well as personal ties based on a sacred order: "the peasant thereby entered into a definite condition or 'status' that involved the whole man in a bond sanctioned by religion" (*LL*, 217; *LH*, 301). This *Treue* is no "contract," in the modern sense, and it can be legitimately dissolved by either side for failures to observe it; it is a sacred bond that cannot be conceptualized adequately in modern legal terminology. Brunner refers in a footnote to Schmitt's, Maine's, and Tönnies's distinction between status contracts and the contracts of bourgeois liberal society in general (*LL*, 217–218n71; *LH*, 310n2). But Brunner remains convinced that the sacred order of the *Treue* and the household emerges from the unique nature of medieval Germanic consciousness and the *Land* supporting it.

There were, however, two exceptions to the bond between lord and subject and to the broader sacred bond uniting those who cultivated and ruled the land with the land itself. These were the "resident aliens" (*Gäste*), people who lived *on* the *Land* but were not *of* the *Land* ("ohne zum Lande zu gehören," without belonging to the *Land*): Jews and those who were "in transit on the roads" (*LL*, 314; *LH*, 436). Excluded from the "customary law of the *Land*" as non-Christians, the *Jüdischheit* had no sovereignty over the land and no political rights. They enjoyed "limited toleration," due only to the protective power of the prince, to whose *fisc* (treasury) they belonged as property (*LL*, 314; *LH*, 436). The second group was more diverse, since many were classified among "the underworld of 'dangerous people' and vagrants" and were seen as a direct threat to the peace of customary law (*LL*, 315; *LH*, 437). Christian pilgrims, traveling merchants, and itinerant minstrels or "gleemen" had legal recognition. In one sense, the protection afforded Jews and vagrants was no different from that extended to those subject to church authority or to the burghers and administrators of market towns—all nominally enjoyed the prince's protection. But whereas some "protection" was part of the customary law of the *Land*, with its reciprocal duties and obligations guaranteed by the *Treue* for Christians who actually belonged to the *Land*, the protection afforded Jews and vagrants (in the latter case, it is impossible not to read "Gypsy" or "Romany" behind Brunner's *Landstreicher*) was merely a function of the prince's and the community's generosity, since Jews were subject to "extraordinary taxation pushed to the limit of their ability to pay," and vagrants considered dangerous "were subject to capital punishment whenever they were captured" (*LL*, 314–315; *LH*, 436–437). (Hamsun's 1927 novel, *Landstrykere*, captures the existential spirit of his own itinerant, rootless existence as a young man, something very different from what Jews and Gypsies experienced but bearing the same label.) The relevance of the medieval Austrian constitution to the Third Reich crystallizes only at this point, in two brief paragraphs of a five hundred–page book with few signs of overt anti-Semitism or racism in its picture of the customary "peace" achieved by *Land und Leute*.

Brunner's argument sharply rebukes the "estates" perspective of previous scholarship—the idea of a divinely prescribed order of men, as in Aquinas's tripartite division of *optimates* (highest rank), *populus honorabilis* (better or honorable people), and *vilis populus* (common people) in Italian city-states, and in the "clergy, knights, and peasants" of medieval sermons (*LL*, 329; *LH*, 457–458). The fundamental order for Brunner was not that of the estates but of "church and world, the distinction between the ecclesiastical and secular orders, each of which, however, comprised all members of Christian society" (*LL*, 330; *LH*, 459). This medieval constitution held until the sixteenth century, when lordly power became something to be limited, as if it were a tyrannical imposition on people and territory, so that the collective or individual resistance offered by the feud came to be understood instead as a struggle against absolute authority. "Collective resistance now meant something else, namely a claim by the community that the rights of sovereignty lay with it and not with the prince—something close to the radical Calvinist doctrine of resistance to tyranny" (*LL*, 363; *LH*, 502–503). For Brunner, the historical triumph belonged to princely absolutism, to a modern order of justice in which the absolute right to legitimate violence lay with the sovereign alone, whether prince, monarch, or national assembly. The commonwealth of Thomas Hobbes originates in this transition to the liberal nation-state. The "Good Old Law" of the land—and the underlying "religious order, identical with 'justice' (*Gerechtigkeit*)" that obligated the members of the *Land*-community—disappeared. The "peaceful 'civil' (*bürgerlich*) society" that superseded it henceforth denied "legitimate coercive power" to all but the absolute sovereign (*LL*, 364; *LH*, 503), and the modern nation-state, with its sharp distinction between private society and public politics, was born.

In its emphasis on historical rupture, Brunner's argument opposes that of Ernst Kantorowicz's *The King's Two Bodies: A Study in Medieval Political Theology*, which appeared in 1957, two years before the revised fourth edition of *Land und Herrschaft*. Kantorowicz's political theology posits an unbroken history of doubled sovereignty, simultaneously metaphysical and physical, based on the incarnation of a divine, eternal Christ in human, mortal form and running from the Middle Ages through the Elizabethans, with vestiges that can still be found in the time of Louis XIV and George III. Though Kantorowicz does not treat postmonarchical political orders, he does imply that modern abstractions such as "the state" or "the corporation" share many characteristics of Frederic Maitland's "twin-born majesty"; his study demonstrates "how, by what means and methods, certain axioms of a political theology which *mutatis mutandis* was to remain valid until the twentieth century, began to be developed during the later Middle Ages."[29] The conservative Kantorowicz, some of whose early work had itself found favor in National Socialist circles, seems to have the "horrifying" political theologies of the twentieth century in mind in his preface, where he suggests that "the idols of modern political religions" may be illuminated by his medieval scholarship.[30] Kantorowicz's history is a theory of continuous secularization, however uneven and potentially reversible it may have been geographically. By contrast, Brunner's history after the sixteenth century is largely the story of an anomaly or mistake: the disintegration of a once whole *Landrecht* into the class conflicts of a liberal nation-state ill suited to Germanic consciousness.

What remains vaguely legible in the body of his revised text is clear in Brunner's purged conclusion. The difficulty in creating a unified German nation-state in the nineteenth century was itself the surest sign that the German people "did not want and could not give up on the Germanic roots of the German social order. . . . For Reich and *Land* (territory) are original forms of Germanic political alliances. It seems to me questionable whether we have today gained fully sufficient insight into the inner structure of the Reich. Ultimately this depends on the essence of the idea of the Reich itself, which retains the ability to spread beyond its original core and to form narrower and wider layers" (*LH* 508). This Germanic *Sonderweg*—the fact that the "pre-state society of the tribe . . . contains the germ of the nation as institution"—is the reason for the "political superiority of the Germanic peoples as compared to the other Indo-Germanic peoples such as the Slavs" (*LH*, 511–512). "Des christlichen Universalismus" is a central part of this superiority and its expansion, though universalism also threatens to become "boundless" (*Grenzenlose*) (*LH*, 514–515).

For the Germans of the National Socialist era, the great nineteenth-century question of the "'state as institution'" (*Staat als Anstalt*) is meaningless, dependent on the false assumption that the German nation found its origins only in the liberal opposition between state and society (*LH*, 518). What actually happens with the rise of the modern nation-state is the creation of a bureaucracy designed to administer territory within an absolutist political framework. While Brunner acknowledges that the modern German Reich could itself be seen as an administered territorial state, with a state apparatus managing its political order and presenting all the dangers of statism—a special irony, given how often the Third Reich has been seen as an example of statism—he insists that the modern Reich is rather an "alliance state" like that of medieval Austria, where the people and not the state are the true bearers of the Reich (*LH*, 519–520). Brunner's conception of the Reich as an alliance of peoples resistant to an institutional state bureaucracy definitively separates his work from the Hegelian conception of the state as the unified, rational/dialectical representation of the eternal spirit of a people, a conception that had its fullest flowering in J. G. Fichte's *Addresses to the German Nation* (1808).[31] Brunner's rejection of this Hegelian unfolding of spirit into nation-state complements his rejection of the nineteenth-century consolidation of liberal, capitalist Germany itself. The shift from alliance state to institutional-territorial state is the great historical drama of Brunner's research, one that also involves a shift from barter to monetized (that is, capitalist) economy.

Brunner's modern Reich is constituted by a multitude of territories, from the northern Germanic peoples to Austria and the east, and the idea of the German Reich includes its ability to spread itself politically. "It seems to me that both the impulse to expand and the bond with the most intimate circles of the homeland are original functions of the Germanic nature" (*LH*, 523). This Germanic nature persists despite the lack of any institutional-state continuity because of the bond between people and land that underwrites all Germanic sovereignty. "The perhaps historically most operative factor is Germanic loyalty, which is no less essential for us today, just as it pervades all older formations" (*LH*, 525). If Brunner acknowledges that returning to the medieval formula of *Land und Herrschaft* is not fully possible for the modern Reich, it is only because of the degree to which industrialism has supplanted agriculture. "Yet the basic political concepts of the Third Reich, *leadership and ethnic community*, are finally to be understood only on Germanic foundations" (*LH*, 526). Brunner's political theology is the historical framework within which these "germanischen Grundlagen" acquire their meaning.

THOUGH BRUNNER'S ACCOUNT of the *Landrecht* of medieval Austria was designed to provide a basis for the political theology of the Third Reich, his understanding of the actual political structure of Nazi Germany left much to be desired. I want to emphasize instead the degree to which Brunner's representations of the *Volk*, of the greater *Land* they considered their rightful place in a divine order, and of the forms of justice they considered to be rightfully at their disposal, were elements of a detailed and scholarly historical conception that allowed otherwise extremely accomplished intellectuals—Brunner among them—to support the indisputably institutionalized state racism and violence of Nazism.

However, Brunner's Nazi affiliation arose not simply from ideological misconception. Though Hitler's patience with *völkisch* philosophers decreased markedly with the war effort, and though he skillfully manipulated old racial prejudices, it would be wrong to call German xenophobia, anti-Semitism, and resentment over the humiliations of WWI and its aftermath the invention of political elites bent on causing havoc. Brunner's research did not merely respond to a gang of newly risen demagogues. Rather, his work illuminates a powerful and persistent family of historical concepts organizing his argument: *Land, Haus, Herrschaft, Fehde, Treue,* and finally *Recht* (especially the unwritten divine right and law built into the nature of things). Whatever Germanic uniqueness Brunner imagined his key concepts to have, and however much he slighted or ignored the trans-European and American work of Niebuhr, Haxthausen, Maine, Fustel de Coulanges, Morgan, and Tönnies before him, his cluster of primal social realities had an almost equal power over the imaginations of non-Germanic thinkers by the middle of the nineteenth century. The "household of the soul" that formed putatively indissoluble sacred bonds among soil, family, gens, and finally nation was not originally "Germanic," and it is hardly Germanic today. But it *was* a German writer—Friedrich Nietzsche—who provided the most trenchant account of what "homecoming" might have meant for modernity. "Individual philosophical concepts are not anything capricious or autonomously evolving. . . . [Philosophers'] thinking is, in fact, far less a discovery than a recognition, a remembering, a return and a homecoming to a remote, primordial, and inclusive household of the soul, out of which those concepts grew originally: philosophizing is to this extent a kind of atavism of the highest order."[32] The Platonic character of Nietzsche's insight is linguistic—he finds a "family resemblance" in Indian, Greek, and German philosophizing—but it is also racial: "The spell of certain grammatical functions is ultimately also the spell of *physiological* valuations and racial conditions. So much by way of rejecting Locke's superficiality regarding the origins of ideas."[33] Nietzsche's dark comedy aside, his claim that thinking eternally returns to a philosophical urtext or *Grund*—a sacred *topography*—is quite tragic in the case of Brunner. Nietzsche's claim is equally tragic in the afterlife of political theology in Brunner's mode since 1945. But in neither case was this homecoming uniquely German.

Modern nation-states have derived legal citizenship either from a notion of consanguinity (*jus sanguinis*, or right of blood) that may include the right of return for descendants abroad, as was the case in Germany up to the year 2000 and in much of Europe, or a notion of geographical origin or birthright (*jus soli*, or right of the soil), as in France, the United States, Canada, and much of Latin America.[34] (Increasingly, it is some combination of both, as in the UK, Australia, and New Zealand.) But most modern nation-states, of whatever sort, combine such legal foundations with cultural assumptions of a dominant religious tradition, however much tolerance or intolerance of other religions they may exhibit. (France's republican *laïcité* is more rigorous in subordinating church to state than American secularism, for example, yet its tolerance of religious pluralism is also less thoroughgoing.) Whole "civilizations"—European Christendom, the Islamic world, the Hindu subcontinent, the Orthodox Slavic peoples, the Buddhist East—are sometimes invoked as distinct entities, regardless of the bases of citizenship within given nations. Whatever method is used to establish legal citizenship, ethnicity is rarely ignored. Race and religious difference have been invoked to deny civil rights to those possessing citizenship by birthright (as in the case of Jews throughout Europe and African Americans in the United States); even citizenship derived from consanguinity has been challenged by prejudices based on communal affiliation, religious confession, seemingly minor ethnic differences, or all three (as in the birth of the Irish Republic, dividing northern Scots-Irish Protestants from southern Irish Catholics). Brunner's vision of a medieval Austria opposed to the absolutist territorial bases of the modern nation-state posits a *Land*, a *Volk*, and a religious tradition underlying the "Good Old Law" that refuse the distinctions defining and often troubling the liberal state. For Brunner's premodern Austria and postmodern Reich, not only does modern "citizenship" not exist but differentiating between consanguinity and birthright, "blood" and "soil," makes no sense. Opposed religious traditions cannot create tensions within a shared *Landrecht*, since there is neither a religiously plural civic community nor the possibility of community itself outside a specific religious tradition. Yet, to a remarkable degree, the integrated society Brunner recuperates, where land, people, and religion are organically inseparable, did not at all disappear as one might have expected in the wake of the Nazi debacle.

One of the first advisory resolutions (181) approved by the General Assembly of the United Nations recommended the partition of Palestine (then a British mandate), thus establishing a modern political sanction for the State of Israel. (Israel unilaterally declared its independence soon after, obviating efforts to implement resolution 181, which was largely ignored thereafter.) The vote was an understandable (though hardly unanimous) response by the newly created community of nations to the Holocaust, but it resulted in an ironic and unintentional reaffirmation of much of Brunner's political theology all the same. Israel is a modern nation-state built upon a sacred, scripturally authorized connection between *Volk* and *Land*, based on a sense of *Recht* that emanates equally from text and *Land*; on a recuperation of the rural household and gens, accomplished initially through the rural-socialist ideal of the kibbutz and later through the rural-populist notion of settler communities; on an attempt to fill in the aporia between the positive law of the liberal state and the religious law of the *ethnie* by giving the rabbinate a large say in family and sumptuary regulations; and on a belief that the *ethnie* belongs to the land in ways that alien or transient groups (most obviously Palestinian Arabs) do not. The "feud" has not reappeared as part of Israel's internal politics—though the settler community's political relationship to the state and the assassination of Yitzhak Rabin point in this direction—and the degree of attachment to land and to religion varies considerably within Israel's population, however much the governing elite honors them. Nevertheless, since 1948 Israel has lived in a state of feud with its neighbors, in which the irreducibility of state-versus-nonstate violence has been accepted on all sides. One of the most torturous and lasting effects of the problem of *völkisch* thought in the first half of the twentieth century has been the seemingly intractable return to *völkisch* solutions in the wake of its putative demise.

Only with the recent uprisings in Tunisia, Egypt, Bahrain, Yemen, and Libya have the patron-client regimes of much of the Arab-Islamic world been challenged, and the consequences are far from clear. Much of the region has been mired for decades in conditions that seemingly offer a choice only between decadent dynasties and dictators serving Western interests and a fundamentalist return to the medieval *Landrecht* animating Brunner's critique. On the one hand, the *umma* (global Muslim community), the greater part of which is not Arab at all, theoretically transcends all modern nation-state boundaries. The traditional theological understanding, widely accepted in the West, holds that Muslims are a people of the book, not of a specific territory, and are ideally detached from any sense of *Land* or *Landrecht*, just as the advent of Islam is routinely conceived as politically supplanting an earlier Bedouin tribal life-world. In reality, the pre- or anti-state, communally legitimated *Fehde*, attached to a specific understanding of Arab-Islamic *Land*, has been central to the political life of radical Islamist thought since the demise of socialist pan-Arabism, the entrenchment of repressive despot regimes, and the failure of the nation-state ideal in Islamic regions, whether nominal "republics" such as Egypt or dynastic monarchies such as Saudi Arabia.

Recent scholarly work on the medieval beginnings of various Arab-Islamic polities challenges the received view that Arab nationalism's attachment to specific territories was no more than an eighteenth-century consequence of colonial Arab societies emulating the West, a view embraced in the work of Bernard Lewis among others.[35] Zayde Antrim has demonstrated, for example, that the notion of a "homeland"—or *watan*, a word that initially expressed Bedouin "affective attachment to land" in Arab-Islamic literature from the ninth and tenth centuries—also occurred in the literature of twelfth- and thirteenth-century Syria "in conjunction with statements of political loyalty and religious belief and, in so doing, referred to plots of land other than and broader than birthplace, ancestral home, or residence."[36] It is a word that remains embedded in the modern concept of *wataniyya* (nationalism). Nevertheless, it may be that Antrim's tentative suggestion of continuity between her broader conception of medieval Arab-Islamic notions of homeland and the modern nation-state is itself vulnerable to Brunner's critique. The political theology of twelfth- and thirteenth-century Arab-Islamic attachments to territory may be significant and opposed to conventional views of the political primacy of an expanding Islamic *umma* (rather than ancestral territory) in this period, while still representing a political affiliation distinct from, and perhaps contrary to, the modern nation-state. From the Taliban to al-Qaeda to a multitude of related groups, modern expressions of a divinely sanctioned *Landrecht* by radical Islamists opposed to the Western nation-state emulated by Kemal Ataturk in Turkey and Gamal Nasser in Egypt are less an incoherent "terrorist" anomaly than a recursion to a medieval political theology that Brunner's work does much to clarify. The "war on terror" is an awkward response to the initiation of a religious/territorial feud on the part of militant Islamists who are, as Osama bin Laden made abundantly clear, concerned with notions of sacred *Land* and *Landrecht* (however inconsistent these may be with the nonterritorial *umma*) that have been violated by Western militaries and are deeply opposed to the nation-state ideal.

The persistent open wound of stateless Palestinian refugees, who seem to have had a *Land*, in Brunner's sense, built around clans, gentes, tribes, lords, and a sense of *Landrecht*, but never any recognizable state, has generated a near-permanent condition of *Fehde* that has been generalized in the region. While agents of this feud have taken refuge with the Taliban in a nonstate called Afghanistan and in the tribal areas of Pakistan—itself a failed nation-state anachronistically designed as a religious *Land* for a religious *Volk*—their militancy is of a piece with *Selbsthilfe*, with the violent, nonstate, yet "legitimate" redress of wrongs. Whatever formal theology may decree, *Land* and the sense of right that accompanies it are at the material heart of what has been mistakenly called a "clash of civilizations." As the case of Brunner makes clear, Western Christian civilization has been just as willing as militant Islam in the modern period to embrace and at times violently defend its sense of a distinct and religiously anchored *Landrecht*.

The idea that modern Islamist jihad is based in part on pre-nation-state notions in which positive law and religious *Landrecht* do not conflict, and in which non-Muslims would be subject to the same proscriptions as non-Germanic peoples in Brunner's account (including transient populations who have no rights at all), is supported in the description of *dhimma* provided by Abdullahi Ahmed An-Na'im.

> According to the *dhimma* under traditional interpretations of Shari'a, when Muslims conquer and incorporate new territories through *jihad*, People of the Book (mainly Christians and Jews) should be allowed to live as protected

communities upon submission to Muslim sovereignty but cannot enjoy equality with Muslims. Those who are deemed to be unbelievers by Shari'a standards have not been permitted to live within the territory of the state at all, except under temporary safe conduct (*aman*). The pretext of necessity (*darura*) is often cited to justify the failure to enforce such Shari'a principles, but the rationale for that notion is limited and short-term. Those who claim that justification must also strive to remove whatever conditions force them to fail to observe what they believe to be Shari'a obligations. They cannot invoke necessity as a permanent justification for their failure to enforce the *dhimma* system.

I am not, of course, suggesting that this system should be applied today, but I wish to show that it is now so untenable that even the most ardent advocates of an Islamic state do not seriously consider applying it in the present local and global realities of Islamic societies. The recent case of the Taliban in Afghanistan is perhaps the exception that proves the rule.[37]

The special tax on Christians and Jews—*jizya* (poll tax)—under the *dhimma* system, levied in return for "protection," replicates the tax levied on Jews in the Christian territories of Brunner's medieval Austria, while those "unbelievers" who were not "people of the book" are treated no differently than Brunner's vagrants (and the Third Reich's Gypsies).[38] Idealizations of the *umma* as a "people of the book" (and not of the land) may seem opposed to Brunner's notions of sacred territory, but An-Na'im has no difficulty assimilating the Taliban to notions of *dhimma* that precisely capture Brunner's sense of *Land* and *Landrecht*.

The long-standing incommensurability between state and *Landrecht* in the region, between liberal bureaucracy and patron-client networks that are often religiously defined as well, is often the consequence when empires retreat. It is surely one of the intractable conditions that allow groups such as the Taliban fertile ground for survival. The superposition of a faux *Rechtstaat* on a religious-tribal order, based on its own political-theological *Landrecht*, became more or less commonplace in the Arab-Islamic world, in Syria under the Assads, Egypt under Mubarak, Libya under Qaddafi, Iraq under Saddam Hussein, and in the dynastic rule of the Saudi families. This is not to say that a new *Rechtstaat*, a new liberal nation-state, will never succeed in places such as Iraq. But it does imply that Western nation-states have persistently misrecognized a different mode of "justice" in such regions as no more than irrational or criminal violence.

There is now substantial research to show that terrorist activity itself is often feudlike in its triggers: the terrorist's desire for "justice" has been sparked by the politically instigated death of a relative or friend, a fellow member of his gens, or, as the "black widows" of the Caucasus region have shown, a husband. John Horgan has argued, based on studies of terrorist acts committed by the Irish Republican Army and al-Qaeda, that the perpetrator generally believes that the violence is inherently lawful and not criminal; that the violence often has internally prescribed limits; and that the support of a larger group or gens, often kin, is usually needed to complete the act.[39] I certainly do not wish to suggest that all such violence, whether it emerges from radical Islamism, from the Catholic-Protestant struggles of Northern Ireland, or from the neighbor-against-neighbor conflict that characterized so much of the Balkan wars in the 1990s, can be reduced to the concept of "feud" as defined by Brunner or to the friend-foe opposition described by Schmitt as the basis of the political. In such cases, it would be impossible to ignore the effects of centuries of imperialism and modern nation-state geopolitics—including the "terror" that nation-state militaries can rain down on defenseless populations—as root causes, or to excuse the self-serving manipulation of strong religious and tribal affiliations by liberal nation-states (as in the US-Soviet proxy war in Afghanistan in the 1980s). But much that appears simply "criminal" or part of the abstract and nearly meaningless politics of "terror" from the perspective of the liberal state may be following the logic of a certain internal political theology that should not be ignored.

Finally, it would not be hard to apply much of what Brunner discusses to the rise of an arms-bearing, antistate, *Landrecht*-inspired, self-help-oriented, religious, and clannish figure such as Sarah Palin in American politics. Regional resistance to the central state originating in colonial America has acquired, since the Civil War, a racial character in the idea of states' rights, a resistance embodied most recently by gun-toting "Tea Party" adherents whose ideas of self-help neatly echo Brunner's emphasis on *Selbsthilfe*. It is only partially accurate to categorize the growth of rural, religiously infused, and often racist resistance to secular federal bureaucracy over the past half century as one more example of American faux populism, as though we fully understood what the term "populism" itself meant, or what longer historical narratives have to tell us about the nature of rural political resistance in Western nations. Michael Kazin has persuasively argued that the transformation of left-populism to right-populism in America occurred with the end of WWII—the patriarch of radio populism, Father Charles Coughlin, began by supporting Roosevelt's New Deal and ended by supporting Huey Long and Hitler.[40] But like most historians of the United States, Kazin does little to link this shift to deeper currents of European thought that are echoed all too well by the history of American notions of *Landrecht*, especially in the American South and West, both before and after the Civil War.[41] (American historians, in this sense as in so many others, have often been more than willing to grant America its own *Sonderweg*.) Unlike much of the *völkisch* thought of his time, Brunner's work is anything but mystical or obscurantist. It is highly rational and informed, and that is what makes it useful for grasping what twentieth-century conservative populism represented in its deeper recesses and over the long haul, even in the United States.

The most important academic lesson to be drawn from *Land und Herrschaft*, however, concerns our current understanding of "political theology" itself, which, especially in leftish Western academic appropriations of Schmitt's work after 1945, has been embraced as proof of the contradictory nature of the liberal nation-state, as the key to explaining why its putatively secular and rational foundations always and necessarily return to their underlying religious, authoritarian, and violent roots. From Walter Benjamin's "Critique of Violence," which rejects both the earlier natural law tradition and the positive law of the nation-state, to the work of Giorgio Agamben, for whom the inevitable denouement of the nation-state is totalitarian Nazism, to the "Red Tory" revanchist theology of John Milbank and the delirious Christian Stalinism of Slavoj Žižek, a certain strain of academic theory has emphasized that the nation-state after Hobbes rests on an absolutist basis—a monopoly on violence—that its own constitutional presumptions must constantly disavow.[42] Ironically, Brunner's own deeply conservative, National Socialist thinking is in complete agreement with such indictments. Yet what Brunner demonstrates at the same time, albeit unintentionally, is that the attempt to find a final solution to the aporia of the liberal state's political theology—its seemingly endless and irresolvable process of secularization—may be far worse than the aporia itself. For just this reason, Brunner's book should not be relegated to the dustbin of outdated historical projects. Nor should it be dismissed as another example of mystical *Blut und Boden* claptrap. It is neither. It is, instead, a roadmap that orients us in the present, seemingly exceptional, historical moment as if this moment were neither a small, dialectical glitch in the inexorable progress of rationalization and modernization nor just more disavowed evidence of the eternal repetition of a religious history we should, yet cannot quite, escape, but rather an example of what Martin Heidegger called *Verwindung* (and Gianni Vattimo tendentiously translated simply as "secularization"): history as a process of distortion, one that is also a "going-beyond" and perhaps an acceptance, but always a consequence of errant gestures of recollection, transformation, and (on occasion) emancipation that represent the deeper story of modernity's often disturbing theological politics.[43]

Notes

1. Otto Brunner, *Land und Herrschaft: Grundfragen der territorialen Verfassungsgeschichte Südostdeutschlands im Mittelalter* [Land and Lordship: Fundamental Questions on the Territorial Constitutional History of Southeast Germany in the Middle Ages], 3rd ed. (Brünn: Rudolf M. Rohrer Verlag, 1943); subsequent references to this German text are designated *LH*. The only English translation of Brunner's text is of the revised 1959 edition: *Land and Lordship: Structures of Governance in Medieval Austria*, trans. Howard Kaminsky and James Van Horn Melton (Philadelphia: University of Pennsylvania Press, 1992), hereafter designated *LL*. The 1943 conclusion has been translated by Heidrun Kubiessa and Vincent P. Pecora in *Genre* 43:1–2 (2010): 13–26. See also W. H. Riehl, *Land und Leute* (vol. 1); *Die bürgerliche Gesellschaft* (vol. 2); and *Die Familie* (vol. 3) of *Die Naturgeschichte des Volkes, als Grundlage einer deutschen Social-Politik* (Stuttgart: I. G. Cotta'scher, 1854–1855).

2. Vincent P. Pecora, *Households of the Soul* (Baltimore: Johns Hopkins University Press, 1997).

3. The least reductive use of the idea of the *ethnie* as the foundation of modern nationalism is to be found in the work of Anthony D. Smith. See especially *National Identity* (London: Penguin, 1991), *The Ethnic Revival* (Cambridge: Cambridge University Press, 1981), and *The Ethnic Origins of Nations* (Oxford: Blackwell, 1986).

4. For the link in Germany after WWI between racial mystique and technological rationalization, see Jeffrey Herf, *Reactionary Modernism: Technology, Culture, and Politics in Weimar and the Third Reich* (Cambridge, MA: Harvard University Press, 1984).

5. See Frank Trömmler, "A Command Performance? The Many Faces of Literature under Nazism," in *The Arts in Nazi Germany: Continuity, Conformity, Change*, ed.

Jonathan Heuner and Francis R. Nicosia (New York: Berghahn Books, 2006), 111–133, reference to 123.

6. Ibid., 119. On Hamsun and the peasant novel, Trömmler's excellent overview cites Jean Améry, *Bücher aus der Jugend unseres Jahrhunderts* (Stuttgart: Klett-Cotta, 1981), 28.

7. Trömmler, "A Command Performance?," 120.

8. See Pecora, *Households of the Soul*, 77–106.

9. Joseph Conrad, *Lord Jim*, ed. Thomas Moser (New York: W. W. Norton, 1996), 135.

10. See *LL*, 138n146. See also Howard Kaminsky and James Van Horn Melton's rich (though far too apologetic) "Translators' Introduction," in *LL*, xxii–xxiv. For a good discussion of the problems of translating Brunner's work, see Thomas A. Brady Jr., "Whose Land? Whose Lordship? The New Translation of Otto Brunner," *Central European History* 29:2 (1996): 227–233.

11. See Kaminsky and Melton, "Translators' Introduction," in *LL*, xvi.

12. Ibid., xxvi.

13. Brunner is quoting C. von Schwerin, "Der Geist des germanischen Rechts," in *Germanische Wiedererstehung*, ed. H. Nollau (Heidelberg: K. Winter, 1926), 205.

14. Aristotle, *Physics*, in *The Complete Works of Aristotle*, ed. Jonathan Barnes, rev. Oxford translation, 2 vols. (Princeton, NJ: Princeton University Press, 1984), 122a7–8, 199b32.

15. Thomas Aquinas, *Summa Theologica*, trans. Fathers of the English Dominican Province, 3 vols. (New York: Benziger Brothers, 1947), parts I–II, Q. 91, A. 2.

16. Both the 1943 and 1959 editions use the word *Germanen*, not the more ethnographic *Teutonen*, and in neither case is the word in the translation's scare quotes. The translator's choice of "Teutons" would be trivial were it not for the fact that Brunner would likely have wanted the resonance with the *Germania* of Tacitus, a text that played a large role in German education during the rise of nationalist sentiment in the early twentieth century.

17. The last sentence here—"'Volk' und 'Land' können alternative gebraucht werden"—appears only in the 1959 edition.

18. See Pecora, *Households of the Soul*, esp. 201–212 on the gens and 3–25 on the *oikos*. Karl Rodbertus was largely responsible for reintroducing the idea of the *oikos* to European thought in the mid-nineteenth century (see Rodbertus, "Untersuchungen auf dem Gebiete der Nationalökonomie des klassichen Alterthums, II: Zur Geschichte der römischen Tributsteuern seit Augustus," in *Jahrbücher für Nationalökonomie und Statistik 4*, ed. Bruno Hildebrand [Jena: Friedrich Mauke, 1865], 341–427). But debate over its role in Greek society and over its existence continued in the work of Karl Bücher and Eduard Meyer. The idea holds an important place in Max Weber's account of ancient economics (see Weber, *Economy and Society: An Outline of Interpretive Sociology*, ed. Guenther Roth and Claus Wittich, trans. Ephraim Fischoff, Hans Gerth, A. M. Henderson, Ferdinand Kolegar, C. Wright Mills, Talcott Parsons, Max Rheinstein, Guenther Roth, Edward Shils, and Claus Wittich, 2 vols. [Berkeley: University of California Press, 1978], 1:381). For more contemporary accounts, see M. I. Finley, *The Ancient Economy* (London: Chatto and Windus, 1973); and William James Booth, *Households: On the Moral Architecture of the Economy* (Ithaca, NY: Cornell University Press, 1993).

19. Henry Sumner Maine, *Ancient Law: Its Connection with the Early History of Society, and Its Relation to Modern Ideas* (Tucson: University of Arizona Press, 1986), 163, 256.

20. Baron August von Haxthausen, *The Russian Empire*, trans. Robert Farie, 2 vols. (London: Chapman and Hall, 1856), 1:112.

21. See Lewis Henry Morgan, *Ancient Society* (Tucson: University of Arizona Press, 1985). Marx invokes the Roman gentes, based on his reading of Niebuhr, in the *Grundrisse* (see Marx, *Grundrisse der Kritik der politischen Ökonomie* [Berlin: Dietz, 1953], 381–382), but his interest in this ancient super-clan-like social formation is more evident in Marx, *The Ethnological Notebooks of Karl Marx*, ed. Lawrence Krader (Assen, Netherlands: Van Gorcum, 1972), esp. 80–81, where the "*attitude* to the land, to the earth as the property of the working individual" means that the working individual "has an *objective mode of existence* in his ownership of the earth." Even more significant is Morgan's contribution, via Marx's notes, to Engels's work on the origin of the family, the title of which invokes Morgan's own research: Friedrich Engels, *Der Ursprung der Familie, des Privateigentums und des Staats im Anschluss an Lewis H. Morgans Forschungen* (Hottingen-Zürich: Schweizerieche Genossenschafts-buchdruckere, 1884).

22. Morgan, *Ancient Society*, 62.

23. Ibid., 76.

24. Ibid.

25. Ibid., 552. For Brunner's discussion of territories within medieval Austria (such as Lower Austria, Upper Austria, Styria, Carinthia, and Carniola), see *LL*, 165–192; *LH*, 226–265.

26. Lawrence Krader, "Introduction," in Marx, *Ethnological Notebooks of Karl Marx*, 71. For one of the founding sociological statements of the "primordialist" explanation of national identity, especially in "new," twentieth-century nation-states, see Clifford Geertz, "The Integrative Revolution: Primordial Sentiments and Civil Politics in the New States," in *Old Societies and New States*, ed. Clifford Geertz (New York: Free Press of Glencoe, 1963), 105–157.

27. Eric Hobsbawm, "Introduction," in Karl Marx, *Pre-capitalist Economic Formations*, trans. Jack Cohen (London: Lawrence and Wishart, 1964), 49–50 (a translation of Marx, *Grundrisse*, 375–413).

28. See Weber, *Economy and Society*, 2:936.

29. See Ernst H. Kantorowicz, *The King's Two Bodies: A Study in Medieval Political Theology* (Princeton, NJ: Princeton University Press, 1997), 3, 5, xviii.

30. Ibid., xviii.

31. See Johann Gottlieb Fichte, *Addresses to the German Nation*, trans. R. F. Jones and G. H. Turnbull (Westport, CT: Greenwood Press, 1979).

32. Friedrich Nietzsche, *Beyond Good and Evil*, trans. Walter Kaufmann (New York: Vintage Books, 1989), sec. 20.

33. Ibid.

34. See Rogers Brubaker, *Citizenship and Nationhood in France and Germany* (Cambridge, MA: Harvard University Press, 1998).

35. See Bernard Lewis, *Islam and the West* (Oxford: Oxford University Press, 1993), 168, and *The Political Language of Islam* (Chicago: University of Chicago Press, 1988),

40–41. See also Ami Ayalon, *Language and Change in the Arab Middle East: The Evolution of Modern Political Discourse* (Oxford: Oxford University Press, 1987), 52–53.

36. Zayde Antrim, "Watan before Wataniyya: Loyalty to Land in Ayyūbid and Mamlūk Syria," *Al-Masaq* 22:2 (2010): 173–190, quote on 174. For further discussion of the concept of *watan*, see Ulrich Haarmann, "Watan," in *Encyclopedia of Islam*, 2nd ed., ed. P. J. Bearman et al. (Leiden: E. J. Brill, 2005). For previous work on the notion of prenational Arab-Islamic attachments to broad, if necessarily obscurely defined, territories, see Jamal Abun-Nasr, *A History of the Maghreb in the Islamic Period* (Cambridge: Cambridge University Press, 1975); Haim Gerber, "Palestine and Other Territorial Concepts in the 17th Century," *International Journal of Middle East Studies* 30 (1998): 563–572; and Thabit Abdullah, *A Short History of Iraq, from 636 to the Present* (London: Longman, 2003). I am indebted to the workshop organized by Steve Tamari and Okasha El-Daly on the topic of premodern attachment to lands in the Islamic Middle East and North Africa for pointing me to this research.

37. Abdullahi Ahmed An-Na'im, *Islam and the Secular State: Negotiating the Future of Shari'a* (Cambridge, MA: Harvard University Press, 2009), 31.

38. Ibid., 70.

39. John Horgan, *The Psychology of Terrorism* (New York: Routledge, 2005).

40. Michael Kazin, *The Populist Persuasion: An American History* (New York: Basic Books, 1995).

41. For a longer discussion of Brunner and American populism, see Vincent P. Pecora, "Introduction to Otto Brunner," *Genre* 43:1–2 (2010): 1–10.

42. See Walter Benjamin, "Critique of Violence" (1921), trans. Edmund Jephcott, in Walter Benjamin, *Selected Writings, Volume 1: 1913–1926*, ed. Marcus Bullock and Michael W. Jennings (Cambridge, MA: Belknap Press of Harvard University Press, 1996), 236–252; Giorgio Agamben, *Homo Sacer: Sovereign Power and Bare Life*, trans. Daniel Heller-Roazen (Stanford, CA: Stanford University Press, 1998); John Milbank, *Theology and Social Theory: Beyond Secular Reason* (Oxford: Blackwell Publishing, 1990); and Slavoj Žižek, *The Fragile Absolute: or, Why the Christian Legacy Is Worth Fighting For* (London: Verso, 2000).

43. See Martin Heidegger, *Identity and Difference*, trans. Joan Stambaugh (New York: Harper and Row, 1969), 36–37, 101; and Gianni Vattimo, *The End of Modernity: Nihilism and Hermeneutics in Post-modern Culture*, trans. Jon Snyder (Cambridge, UK: Polity Press, 1988), 179.

CHAPTER 2

"THE POLITICIZATION OF HEAVEN"

Wilhelm Stapel's Political Theology of Nationalist Sovereignty

CHRISTOPH SCHMIDT

Point, Line, Sphere: From Theogeometry to Theobiology

"When God passes over man, it is like a sphere rolling over a straight line. The sphere only comes into contact with the line at a mathematical point, and this point carries the entire sphere but does not encompass it. Through revelation, the divine touches humanity at one point, but humanity does not encompass the divine in revelation."[1] With this geometrical image from the 1518 treatise "Resolutiones disputationum de indulgentiarum virtute," Luther describes the relationship between God and man, salvific and human history, which initiated a revolution in the church of his age. Four hundred years later, the theologian and journalist Wilhelm Stapel (1882–1954) picks it up as a vivid image for his revolutionary program against modern liberal Lutheran theology, the secular idea of culture, and the democratic idea of the state. The aim of this "conservative revolution" is the restoration of dogmatic Lutheran kingdom theology,[2] which Stapel wants to achieve on racist-biological foundations. If, according to Luther's image, revelation and history intersect at only one point, without salvific history ever turning into real history, then God and the kingdom of God move, at first, an infinite distance away from one another—beyond ethics and politics. It is not hard to see that Stapel juxtaposes this emblem of theological geometry against modernity, in which the kingdom of God and human history are supposed to merge into one another at a utopian telos.[3] The vanishing point of their modern conversion can thus only be another point of contact, in which the sphere of God will roll over the line of human history.

One could say, then, the journalist speaks here as an eschatologist: Wilhelm Stapel, similar to the radical right-wing Protestant theologians Friedrich Gogarten and Emanuel Hirsch,[4] recognizes in the project of modernity, which he describes with the term "secularization," an implicit political theology that frees itself from orthodox Protestant theology and its church but also articulates the claim that it can realize the true ethical-humanistic content of this religion, Christian love of neighbor, in a this-worldly kingdom of God free from all domination. The equation of this "secular messianism" does not balance because the utopian idea of a kingdom of God on earth presupposes a political state of *Herrschaftslosigkeit* (state without domination), which the brutal violence of the First World War factually contradicted, but is ideally and principally based upon an illusionary anthropology of the "good man." Stapel now wants to contrast this implicit political theology of the Enlightenment conception of secularization with an explicit political theology, which derives from the orthodox dogmatic premises of Protestant theology (the absolute sovereignty of God and the insurmountable original sin) first the "realistic" and then the biological political consequences for a theory of sovereignty. Against secularization as the ideological principle of *Herrschaftslosigkeit*, Stapel wants to erect an "antisecular front," which actually marks the ruling agents who set secularization as the enemy of theology and politics.

Stapel, who had been publishing the monthly journal *Deutsches Volkstum* since 1919, had early on "exposed" the idea of Jewish theocracy behind this secular messianism, which he simply denounces as the ideal of a merely this-worldly political theology within a long, modern philosophical tradition.[5] Stapel attributes this idea of theocracy to a Jewish racial instinct in order to construct the Jewish racial enemy, who only wants to advance its own desire for dominance behind a display of criticizing sovereignty. It can be shown that this Jewish enemy actually is an image of the liberal Jesus who, undogmatized and humanized in the liberal theology of the nineteenth century, becomes the representative of a universal ethics of autonomy but, by being historicized, now belongs to the Jewish people and represents its political messianism.

Against the modern synthesis of rational theology and universal political ethics, of the kingdom of God and society, which is symbolized in the political ethics of the liberal Jesus, Stapel now not only constructs a political theology on the basis of his own Germanic racial identity but also pursues political theology in general to its supposedly biological-racial roots. In this manner his political theology constitutes both an explicit strategy against the concealed politics of secular theocracy and itself executes, behind the setting of its antisecular rhetoric, precisely what Stapel accuses the enemy of: secularization. Here, however, theology is no longer transformed through ethics but through biology into exclusively secular politics—that of racial sovereignty. This secular politics now constructs itself as an absolute vanishing point of the conversion of salvific history and human history as eschatological goal of all history: kingdom theology becomes the political theology of the Führer-state.

In the following account of Wilhelm Stapel's political theology on racial foundations, I pursue this implicit transformation of theology through politics to biology. This countersecularization is always based upon the correlation of Führer and enemy so that Stapel's biopolitical theology entails the construction of the Jewish enemy as a theological, political, and biological enemy. This enemy indeed bears the conspicuous traits of that liberal Jesus who so "angered" the theologian Stapel. The liberal Jesus as universal ethicist, who emerges from the ranks of the Jewish people, symbolizes for Stapel this Jewish enemy and elucidates the role Stapel attributes to the Jewish enemy in his construction of secularization.

The reconstruction of Stapel's antimodernism as the form of a fundamentalist countersecularization and his politicization of Paul's theology on radical right-wing foundations are significant in the context of current discussion about secularization, especially the rediscovery of Paul's political theology. Against Nietzsche's discovery of the political dimension of Paul's theology as "typical Jewish-rabbinic" and especially aimed against the Roman Empire,[6] Erik Peterson has theologically turned Nietzsche's negative critique into a positive one and thereby essentially shaped the contemporary discussion about the political theology of Paul from Jacob Taubes to Giorgio Agamben.[7] Thereby, the dark chapter of the radical right-wing politicization of Paul, characteristic of Wilhelm Stapel, Friedrich Gogarten, and Emanuel Hirsch, has tended to be neglected, even though it seems to overshadow at each step the contemporary political theology of Paul.

The Antisecular Front

"I will force this age to return to God or to perish" (CS, 211), Stapel proclaims with the same pathos that he so admires in Johann Gottlieb Fichte's *Addresses to the German Nation*.[8] Stapel, after all, was a member and supporter of the Fichte Society. Similarly to how his role model, after the Prussian defeat of Napoleon, draws the German nation as a genuinely national-linguistic *ethnos* from the baptismal font, which is supposed to represent the true spirit of freedom since Luther, Stapel, in the historical moment of the Wilhelmine Empire's catastrophic defeat, wants to remind the German nation of its political-theological mission, which he now links to the name of Luther. "Great victor over the nations, noble Germania, you will ascend to the audacious throne, ruling over all kingdoms. Then truth will return with great glory. . . . You will lead us again to the highest sovereignty, and the holy Trinity will sanctify the Germans" (CS, 7). Stapel wants to erect an antisecular front against the liberal culture and its ideology in order to revive the Prussian-Protestant kingdom theology, and he evokes a bizarre comparison: "One will respond to the dream of an empire . . . with this objection: it is a dream of impotence; it is wishful thinking with which the subjugated unaccountably intoxicates himself. . . . Theodor Herzl also did not dream the Zionist dream at the climax of Jewish history. He seized this thought in an hour of humiliation" (CS, 7).

On the basis of salvific providence, Stapel finds the salvation of the political nation actually prefigured for the first time in an exemplary way in Jewish history: "When Israel abandoned Yahweh, God punished Israel, as one can read in the Old Testament. When we abandon the Reich, God punishes us, as German history shows. That is the German testament" (CS, 10). However, Stapel identifies modern secularization with that universal and antinational ethics that weakened the political-theological potency of the German Reich-nation; indeed, he senses in it a form of political messianism that he has always ascribed to the assimilationist Jewry. "Our question is posed at a time when the secularization of the state, scholarship, art, culture, morality, law, etc., has been carried out, and indeed at a time when one can see through this process of secularization" (CS, 12). "Secularization"—Stapel can recognize it only as a monolithic block that will develop its own discursive imperialism—in reality amounts to a conspiratorial political-theological strategy, which pretends to transform the principle of Christian love of neighbor and enemy into the political constitution of a humanist global society but in truth implements a Jewish this-worldly theocracy. This theocracy is supposed to be the ideological mask of the secularizing and assimilating Jewry against the German Reich, its theology, and its sovereignty. Whereas the Zionist acts as a role model of political-theological reflection on national-collective foundations, the assimilating German Jew represents the double plot of the enemy: he allegedly wants to eliminate the ethnic difference of Germans by himself assuming a leading role in the secularization and liberalization of culture. "The social instincts of Jews aim at a theocracy that tries to expand itself over all of humanity. God's justice, the messenger of which Jewry is, is supposed to order and define all of humanity. For in areligious Jewry the theocratic disposition lapses, but the social instinct stays the same. . . . God's justice turns into the justice of man, not the justice of the state or even of a lord (as among the Germanic peoples)" (AS, 96).

Thereby, Stapel has "seen through" the occluded sense of secularization in order to now establish his own plan of action for an antisecular front in three steps: (1) The restoration of Protestant-dogmatic theology is a prerequisite for (2) the restoration of ethnic differences, the sense of which it is to substantiate the political primacy of the German people, which is destined for dominion over the other European peoples because of this political-theological disposition, in order to (3) eliminate the principle of Jewish theocracy, which competes with the German kingdom theology, on the basis of this correlation of theology and nationhood. To the extent that Stapel transforms his political theology on racial foundations into a political biology, his distinction between Zionist-nationalist and assimilationist-antinationalist Jewry, occasionally present in National Socialist circles, recedes completely, insofar as "Zionism . . . wants to bring about the kingdom of heaven on earth, understood as a kingdom without war, through propagandistic dissemination of Jewish morality." The either-or of a religious worldview and secularization is finally transformed through the either-or between German kingdom theology and Jewish theocracy into an either-or between two national racial principles. "Race is soul and spirit; therefore it is also blood and body. For the racial spirit constructs the racial body for itself. . . . Race exists. Because it exists, it also determines the way in which religion appears" (*CS*, 17). If the foundation of religion therefore always has to be sought in biology, then this does correspond to Stapel's own account of secularization and his attempt to adjust this theo-biology to the requirements of the National Socialist party program. Also, the oscillation between theology and biology through the gate of politics is always aimed not only at biologizing theology for the National Socialist case of emergency but also at facilitating the retreat into "pure" theology. Thus, after the war, Stapel will appear in the Federal Republic as a serene theologian who directs his reflections "On Christianity" exactly in the solemn, trivializing tone of the liberal Lutheran theology of Friedrich Daniel Schleiermacher "to the Thinking among Its Despisers."[9]

A Trinitarian Analogy: From the Love of Neighbor to the Obedient Victim

If the critique of sovereignty, which is inherent to secularization, amounts to a concealed will to power of the Jewish people, then Stapel demands a "serious discussion" about the principle of sovereignty. In principle, Stapel detects only the ambivalences in the term "secularization," which are always inherent to it, but in fact Stapel hypostasizes, distorts, and apocalyptically inflates them to stark antitheses. Man's "leaving his self-caused immaturity," already postulated in the German Enlightenment—above all by Gotthold Ephraim Lessing and Immanuel Kant—designated detachment from the sovereignty of the orthodox-dogmatic theology of Protestantism and its church, as well as the claim to erect the true eschatological content of religion, the kingdom of God, on the basis of the love of neighbor.[10] A second ambivalence has always been inscribed into this ambivalence, insofar as the foundation of the kingdom of God was assumed to presuppose either a utopian or a realistic anthropology. In its utopian version, represented particularly by Lessing, the principle of original sin would be abolished with the end of sovereignty.[11] In the more realistic version, represented by Kant, overcoming the "radical evil" in human nature could only be imagined as a never-ending fight over the kingdom of God.[12] Insofar as enlightenment, in the end, always already constitutes a political theology of the kingdom of God on earth, it comprehends itself as the third gospel, following the Old and the New Testaments. However, a third ambivalence has always already been designated: Which role were Jewry and Christendom supposed to play precisely in this eschatology of the Enlightenment? When Lessing, with the succession of the three realms of Jewry, Christendom, and the Enlightenment, establishes a doctrine of succession through respective suspensions, he simultaneously wants to balance it through the spiritualist principle of the transmigration of the soul,[13] so that every human being is supposed to be Jew, Christ, and enlightened at the same time. In this manner, Jewry and Christendom at least intentionally act as equal agents of this modern eschatology. In contrast, Immanuel Kant stated a radical difference between these two religions, which considers, so to speak, their respective "secularization capacity." Whereas Judaism aims only at an external political-legal theocracy,[14] Christianity symbolizes a religion of the "heart" and of pure inner ethical revolution, in which Kant recognized the presupposition for all external historical revolutions.

Stapel's either-or constructs his antisecular front against the backdrop of these ambivalences of the Enlightenment, when he now articulates, against the third gospel of Enlightenment, his national "German gospel" as explicit political theology, which discards the utopia of the kingdom of God on earth along with its utopian anthropology as a political construction of Jewish racial theocracy. Thus, if the symbiosis of society and the kingdom of God, and thereby the German-Jewish cultural symbiosis, is to be destroyed, Stapel dissolves this symbiosis into its premodern elements and substances. Church and state are dissociated from one another, and Jewry and Germanness are differentiated as original national substances and are to be separated from now on.

Stapel's revision of modern circumstances thus aims at clarifying factual power relations. The term "sovereignty" is at first substantiated from the theological perspective in order to then derive from it the actual political consequences. "Like Jesus, so Paul, too, recognized and called upon the

Roman Empire's legal sovereignty, whose citizen he was. Moreover, Paul gave a metaphysical justification of state power as such (Rom. 13:1), translated very felicitously by Luther as *Obrigkeit*, and thereby obligated Christianity once and for all" (*CS*, 33). According to Romans 13:1, it is supposed that the *Obrigkeit* "is from God" and that the state, as far as it is sovereign, cannot be evil. Thus, sovereignty is "good," and its goodness involves not only domination of "evil," "sin," and "hostility" but also that it definitely may be "non-Christian," that is, for Stapel, "pagan sovereignty." If man stands "in his totality under original sin," then Stapel overstates the principle of original sin in the sense of the Protestant tradition as a case of insurmountable indignation against God in order to reject the autonomy of ethics and morals as such a rebellion. For these ethics of secular modernity always presuppose a moral conscience of the autonomous human being, who reckons on being able to elude the law of original sin in this way—as if conscience "was not expelled from paradise" (*CS*, 21). Each this-worldly alternative to sovereignty over sin necessarily succumbs to the totality of sin, so the function of a true law can only be sovereignty over sin. In such an unequivocal attribution of the law, it does not matter, for Stapel, which law or which state facilitates the sovereignty over the sin. Sovereignty as such comes from God. "Paul . . . derives the rights of the *Obrigkeit* from the rights of God; he gives reasons for the duty to obey the state . . . , because it protects the good on earth in the interest of God . . . , and imposes a just punishment on the evil. . . . The Roman state he looks at officially had a pagan religion, and therefore the believers, who actually see evil only outside their own cross, are supposed to venerate a divine in it" (*CS*, 38–39).[15]

Indeed, the commandment of love of neighbor and, in its wake, the commandment of love of the enemy are supposed to rank so highly and heavenly that they cannot have anything to do with worldly law and state order. As pure and sublime expressions of otherworldly salvation, both stand above and beyond each law and political principle of order that govern the matters of this world under the scepter of sovereignty. The Protestant radicalness of the theology of grace, which negates any justification through human work and law, is not only turned over, according to Stapel, in a radically secular way, but simultaneously entails a devaluation of the Jewish law as a purely political law and a valorization of heathen law, which as such can fulfill the requirements of sovereignty and order. In this context, Stapel develops his own tenet of *nomos*, which he unfolds, according to Paul and Luther, in its political consequences. Being instituted by the worldly *Obrigkeit*, *nomos* is an instrument against the uproar, indignation, and enmity of man, and it thus always articulates what Stapel and Carl Schmitt called the political principle of the distinction between friend and enemy.[16] Any form of human sovereignty already fulfills the requirements of a defense against the enemies of the God-given order.

In this way, religion and politics are at first radically distinguished from one another. Love of neighbor no longer functions as a basic principle of a utopian constitution; however, at the same time, this separation initiates a new form of legitimizing politics through theology: each form of government, even the completely secular-pagan one, is from God. Thus, love of the enemy needs to be removed from fusion with political circumstances when this relies on the distinction between friend and enemy. Stapel wants to prove these correlations by dint of Schmitt's explanations of the terms "public enemy" and "private enemy" in the case of Jesus's Sermon on the Mount.[17] "With regard to the term 'love of the enemy' one usually disregards that Jesus does not speak about the political enemy, the 'polemos,' but about the private enemy, the 'echthros'" (*CS*, 41). Already for Schmitt, this philological operation serves to radically criticize the attempt to elevate love of the enemy to a principle of universal "politics of friendship." As is well known, according to Schmitt, the sphere of the political works only in compliance with the principle of distinction between friend and enemy and thus always already comprises the church itself, insofar as the church necessarily acts publicly as political power. Stapel, however, even deprives the principle of love of the enemy of its private license insofar as love of the enemy is supposed to count only for the kingdom of heaven or the immediate discipleship of Jesus.

The martyrdom of Christ becomes the absolutely singular case of love of the enemy, which may be of importance only in a theological dramaturgy without any political implications. On earth, it cannot be effective; in heaven, it becomes superfluous. Thus, love of the enemy becomes effective only at the unique moment when earth and heaven touch each other, at the cross. Even here, religion and politics are to be torn so far apart from one another that Christ's death on the cross becomes important only to inner salvation and the beyond. Though the martyrdom of love occurs in the midst of political circumstances, it may no longer have anything to do with these circumstances. It factually designates only that "geometrical point" at which revelation and human history touch each other, without any transformation of human history to be expected from this event. Therefore, Christ's death on the cross at first corresponds only to the inner-Trinitarian logic, according to which the Son of God subjects himself to God the Father out of pure love. "Here, however, the will of God and thus also that of the Son was that the Son of God be subject to Pilate, that he be sentenced by him . . . , die and resurrect" (*6K*, 28).

With this translation of the crucifixion into the immanent heavenly dynamics of the Trinity, not only is Pilate degraded to an instrument of the Trinitarian dramaturgy who does not possess any free will, but this interpretation unveils very quickly a highly concrete and eminently political sense. The Son of God's obedience out of love corresponds to the inner-Trinitarian correlation, and Stapel recognizes in the religious correlation between Father and Son the original pattern of political obedience: "And even the Son of God does not stop recognizing the Father as Lord, for Father and Lord are the same. The Son of God is not identical with God the Father, and he also is obedient to him" (*CS*, 48). When Stapel further confirms this statement with Paul's Epistle to the Philippians 2:8, "He became obedient unto the death of the cross," he implicitly always aims at a political-theological analogy of God's sovereignty and political sovereignty, but he exaggerates this analogy over the inner-Trinitarian correlation, which loses any ambiguity in the context of the following explanations about Luther's comprehension of *Obrigkeit*. If Luther's theory of the state actually presupposes a "metaphysics of paternity," Stapel reasons that the political "leaders, beyond right and law," always are "fathers (*patres*)" (*CS*, 97). When Stapel excludes agape, love of neighbor, and the enemy from the political sphere and thereby rejects any utopian dimension to the political sphere, he simultaneously institutes this love again as a political principle of absolute obedience. Whereas Ludwig Feuerbach attempted to secularize the Trinity of God, Son, and Holy Ghost in the sense of an ideal dialogical-communistic community,[18] Stapel proposes a secularization with the opposite premise, which constructs the Trinity as drama of absolute subordination.

Similar to how Christ subjects himself to the Father and thus becomes the model of political obedience, the political, which as counterprinciple is contrary to the love of neighbor and thus constitutes the principle of the distinction between friend and enemy, eventually also changes into the political role model of a religious analogy: "Like the state fights with its enemies, God would fight with his heavenly hosts" (*CS*, 170). The political distinction, which ought to be valid only for the profane sphere, is now itself metaphysically-theologically hypostatized such that the state that is organized in a sovereign manner is supposed to serve what Stapel designates as the "politicization of heaven." "Because now the contrast between friend and enemy mirrors the metaphysical contrast between heaven and hell, on the one hand, the first falling away from God has quasi-politicized heaven, and, on the other hand, the falling creation breaks apart into contrasts. For this reason, the falling away and the breaking apart cannot be effected by man, but only by God. Thus, all human attempts to moralize away the contrast between friend and enemy, to depoliticize the world . . . are a sign of corruption. The expelled creature who has fled, who has concealed (secularized) herself from God and now believes that there is no God, arrogates herself in her pride to achieve what is up to God" (*CS*, 171).

Therefore, the political enemy is not only the enemy of the existing order, or the enemy of enmity, who has secularized love of the enemy, but he is always already the theological, absolute enemy whom a state that is designed according to the principles of a political anthropology of original sin does not only have to recognize, to distinguish from the friend, and to fight against, but also to annihilate. Thus, Stapel writes: "By wanting to become the friend of all human beings, he becomes God's enemy" (*CS*, 171).

Here, the suspicion is confirmed that the political theology Stapel strives for executes, against the secular messianism of the kingdom of God on earth, its own countersecularization, which transforms the commandment of love of the enemy into a model of absolute obedience and institutes this obedience as divine judgment over the liberal forms of secularization. Antimodernity proves again to be an alternative secularization, a secularization with a reversed premise, if now the state actually becomes the eschatological judgment over believers and unbelievers. "Thus, we have accounted for the metaphysical element of the state, which is falling away from God and by virtue of which the state is brought under that judgment to which every creature is subject" (CS, 131). Indeed, humans can be atoned for only by God, but practically, the state itself becomes more and more a sacrosanct institution of judgment and atonement through liberal secularization. The victim of Christ turns into the model of political violence; the state, into the institution of the last judgment.

This secularization of the theology of original sin is supplemented with the theological tenet of eros and *nomos*, which Stapel tries to deduce from Paul and from an orthodox Lutheran perspective. With the removal of the actually divine love, agape, from the circle of creation, postlapsarian creation would have had to fall back into nothingness and chaos had God not provided worldly love, eros, in lieu of heavenly agape. Eros comprises sexual love, friendship, and communal instinct. "Thus, man and woman did not fall out with one another, but eros kept them together. Thus, brothers and friends did not fall out with one another, but brotherly love, *philia*, kept them together. Thus, also, the community of the state became possible, namely, by dint of the *nomos*" (CS, 173).

Eros, *philia*, and *nomos* are the ordering powers of creation, given after the fall, which are to take the place of the spiritual-heavenly agape. From now on, all human acting is subject to these natural principles that Stapel tries to substantiate by appealing to Luther. "If there were not father and mother, husband and spouse, who bring forth and educate children, the state could not exist. Thus, out of the house the city spreads, which is nothing else than a lot of houses and families. The families turn into a principality, and the principality into a Reich" (CS, 87). This naturally forming order of the political is always already depicted in language, morals, and the history of a people, which develops a kind of "cult community" and articulates its specific "law of life." In this reduction of the political to the conditions of creation and nature, not only is a genuine moment of pagan-cultic religiosity supposed to have developed, but also the subsumption of these natural conditions under the term "law of life" poses a necessary delineation of, and a possible enmity between, the different "laws of life." Moreover, the term "law of life" always already facilitates, beyond its anchoring in an exegesis of Pauline theology, a biological-racial foundation of the political.

"The *nomos*, as Paul says, has arrived, . . . it has been added for the sake of sin (Rom. 5:21)." Insofar as each community constitutes its law of life, based upon eros, *philia*, and communal instinct, so it marks a difference to the other laws of life but is valid especially against the backdrop of this difference and thus, on a basic level, at first without any difference. There is no difference between *nomos* and *nomos*. Against the backdrop of the Lutheran critique of justice through works, no salvific function at all can be attributed to any *nomos*, and thus also not to a Jewish *nomos*. Likewise, all *nomoi* receive their dignity by facilitating social and political order. Certainly, God proclaimed "the law of life to one people personally," namely, "to the people of Israel at Mount Sinai" (*CS*, 174), but insofar as this law, like all laws, can be erected only against sin, it is not different from the other laws of life in any way. According to Stapel, *nomoi* receive their proper dignity by orienting themselves toward the "birth of the Son of God," that is, toward fulfillment in Christ. "Thus, the non-Jewish Christ does not need the Jewish law, because one can also become aware of one's sin and impotence without the Jewish law" (*CS*, 178). The "difference without differences," by virtue of which the merely political validity of the *nomos* is established against every salvific function, thus creates immediately a new, fundamental difference between the *nomos* that is oriented toward Christ and the *nomos* that cannot orient itself toward Christ, or rejects this orientation because it wants to fulfill itself in a secular or theocratic manner. "Paul erects grace against the law. However, he does not say that the law is without any significance for becoming Christ. It contains a *dikaioma* since it is from God." This *dikaioma* designates the justification that the law receives by virtue of guaranteeing order, but especially by being oriented toward the face of God and not wanting to fulfill itself. The law that forms itself from eros to the *nomos* is necessarily the law of life of a particular people, whereas the law of agape, of the love of neighbor and the enemy, is transcendental law, which can be fulfilled only through God or, for Christians, through Jesus Christ. (Therefore, it is subject to the dynamics of a radical politicization as a principle of obedience and subordination to God the Father, as noted earlier.) Since there can be no continuity from eros/*nomos* to agape, any attempt to derive an ethics of universal completion from agape and the love of neighbor designates a rebellion against the sovereignty of God. On the basis of this radical antithesis of eros and agape, both the peculiar double legitimization and the degradation of the Jewish law follow. As merely political law, it cannot become a "messianic" or universally ethical law; the attempt to nonetheless elevate it to such a law amounts to a false usurpation of salvific history, the hidden sense of which can only be the deployment of its own sovereignty beyond the borders of its own law of life.

However, the racial retreat to the *nomos* as a particular law of life, if it simultaneously orients itself toward the "face of Christ," is indeed supposed to open up this racial law of particular sovereignty for the possibility of a universal mission of sovereignty over all peoples, because one people that orients itself toward the face of Christ is supposed to disclose to other peoples not its own law but only the universal dimension of sovereignty through transcendence. By becoming Christ, the *nomos* receives its "metaphysical consecration" as *dikaioma zoes*, which Stapel translates with Paul as "eternal justification of life through Christ." The metaphysical consecration of the political *nomos* at first consists in limiting the *nomos* to the dimension of the people and in its opening for Christian transcendence, which is supposed to now assign to the particular *nomos* the mission of sovereignty over the world. Whereas the Jewish law thus confuses the orders of politics and transcendence and wants to universalize its own particular law, the Christian-justified *nomos* is supposed to set another order of immanence and transcendence, which facilitates, especially since it insists on the particularity of the *nomos*, universal sovereignty through transcendence, without the other particular laws needing to be suspended.

Thus, Stapel's tenet of the *nomos* proves to be the core of an anti-Judean political theology, which, even before it constitutes itself biologically, postulates a basic theological conflict between legal interpretations, the actual sense of which lies in a putative will to sovereignty over the world. The German nation denies to the Jewish nation its putative will to sovereignty over the world, which it deems to be able to recognize in the assimilationist form of Jewry as a conspiracy against the national German *Volksgeist* (spirit of the people), in order to now institute for the German nation the rights of its own mission as Reich and its sovereignty over Europe.

When eros as principle of creation becomes the basic element of *nomos* and of the law of life of people and the state, it becomes the basic principle of the political in the sense of a distinction between friend and enemy. This basic principle receives its final consecration from a Christology that, as we have seen, has revealed its actual political function in the confession to the subordination of the Son to the Father, of the people to the sovereign. Thus, eros symbolizes an opening for agape, which, understood in a Christological way, appears in Stapel's work as judgment over the enemy and corresponds to the Trinitarian analogy as well as to the "politicization of heaven." At the same time, however, the creationist principle of eros always already discloses the option for a last secularization as biological principle. Stapel's theology proceeds via the "politicization of heaven" increasingly to the sphere of worldly secularity: with a radical anchoring of all human circumstances in the totality of creation and original sin, which is characteristic of Stapel, Stapel's theology can be transformed into a political biology. In the definition of the law of life, especially in the *dikaioma zoes*, which Stapel reads in Paul, such a biological transformation of the term "life" is always already implied. Only secular science can biologically misunderstand this religious and metaphysical term of "life"; only the secularist Stapel can carry out this "turnaround" of theology into biology as a basic racial principle. Indeed, here too, Stapel prepares this secularization through the term "the political." The more unequivocally Stapel articulates the political consequences of his theology of sovereignty and original sin, the more unequivocally the former becomes biologically convertible. However, this always already corresponds to his freeing of the state and of sovereignty from any theological obligation: the state can indeed be non-Christian; it can be, as Stapel has extensively expounded with regard to Romans 13:1, a pagan state. It is *nomos* and sovereignty that theologically legitimize this state.

This process of biologizing the political thus occurs in parallel with the politicization of the theological. The way Stapel now employs, again in a completely unhistorical manner, Luther's theory of the state for his political purpose of legitimizing the Führer-state is blatant. On the basis of the concealed Trinitarian analogy, Stapel expands, by using Lutheran terms, the parallels between Father and Son in the sense of a doctrine of the Father as Lord and Führer. When "the political" is always already thought from the perspective of sovereignty in terms of personal domination and is supposed to consist of three elements, "power of the order, struggle, and authority,"

Stapel repeatedly invokes Luther's legitimization of the absolute kingdom as paternity. The king as father is not only the lord of the law; he always already stands above the law, in order to reign over his subjects as "father," not only according to the wording of the law but also according to grace, which goes beyond law.

Stapel quotes Luther to explain the correlation of sovereignty and order from a Christian theological perspective: "In the state, one has to be especially certain that there are good and prudential men rather than that laws are made" (*CS*, 87). However, not only this prudence, which is oriented to the law, is required for the father to live up to his task of bringing his subjects to reason, which again means that his subjects do not attack one another like "wild animals" and cause chaos. The king also stands above the law in order to factually "make human beings out of wild animals" and preserve human beings "so that they do not become wild animals." Both moments, the absolute sovereignty above the law and the domination over the anarchical life of the subjects (and the wildness attested to the latter by Luther) constitute in Stapel's reconstruction a higher entity in which "the political" is united with a unique total will. By virtue of exercising "authoritarian power over the minds, the will of the political lord appears as will, which fulfills a divine task" (*CS*, 128); however, it amounts to that *volonté générale* (general will) the lord represents because the people "does not know what it wants." With direct regard to Adolf Hitler, Stapel articulates the law of life of the people as symbiosis of life and will, whereby the people "only [have] the instinct," but the "Führer knows what the people want" (*KCSH*, 17).

Whereas Stapel's rhetoric at first stays within the framework of a theology of paternity, which is supposed to institute the Führer as God given, this rhetoric of the Führer takes on a life of its own when it describes the Führer as charismatic original fire. "Such people are a flame that consumes the powerless, the rotten, the putrid" (*CS*, 187). The father turns into the Führer only through his unfathomable magic "of grace," which "makes human beings bend down before him" (*CS*, 187–88). Increasingly, the theological and biological perspectives merge in the "blessed" figure of the Führer, when eros and agape unite in him as the same divine-human principle of sovereignty. In the erotic-intimate symbiosis of people and Führer, which then also has already transcended any *nomos*, unity is brought about that

Christologically proves to be the libidinous subordination of the son and the people under the father and Führer. This erotic-agapean symbiosis corresponds to a theology that is completely reduced to life and the law of life. As the father becomes the Führer, so the son becomes the wild animal to be subjected, which experiences its erotic attachment in the instinctive self-sacrifice for power, sovereignty, and violence. Stapel now consequently substitutes a "biological term of wildness" for Luther's theological-apocalyptic formula of the "wild animals." "The constitutional term 'sovereignty' and the biological term 'wildness' relate to one another in a close spiritual relationship" (*CS*, 221).

Now, Stapel refuses the theogeometry that he had adopted from Luther in the first place: by virtue of carrying out secularization on its own, his political theology also orients itself toward a historical vanishing point of the conversion of theology and biology, which takes the place of the utopian conversion of God's kingdom and society. The sphere of God, which was supposed to touch the history of humankind only in a single point, here too coincides with a vanishing point of the Führer-state and its eschatological war. At the same time, the secularization practiced here functions in both directions: as heaven transforms the political earth into a drama of sovereignty, in order to be itself grasped by this drama in the "politicization of heaven," biologizing theology also already always corresponds to theologizing biology. On the one hand, "the soundness of ethics" consists "in the appropriateness of the ought to the biological state of the community." On the other hand, this soundness of the biological law of life exactly corresponds to what Paul (Titus 1:13) would designate as "soundness of faith."

In the end, the Trinitarian model thus functions as a racial-biological principle of sovereignty and obedience. The father as Führer and the people as loyal son constitute the merely biologically (instinctively) determined totality and identity of a will to violence, which "consumes all the powerless, rotten, putrid," in order to fulfill in this consumption the law of life of the people. This totality follows only the "energetic imperative" of a concentrated instinct, the sense of which is supposed to be "separation" and "shaping the Gestalt." "The power of separation is not actually creative, but it alone can shape the Gestalt of a community by discarding the unassociated, that is, the hostile. The paternal cannot realize itself without separating the foreign from one's own house and servants." Political biology proves to be, in the last instance, the blind violence of homogenizing life as violence against all that is not homogeneous. Biological life is identical with the political principle of the annihilation of the enemy. The Führer, so Stapel already writes in 1932, "must set limits and defend, create space and annihilate. For a life lives only through the annihilation of another life. This implies mastery of feelings and nerves" (*CS*, 187).

The Enemy

Erecting the antisecular front against liberal theology and culture defines the secularist from the beginning as enemy of God and the people. If the Führer/father is now supposed to be destined to take action against "moral corruption," that means at first nothing other than that he is supposed to remove secularization. "Moral corruption, however, is by its nature nothing else than secularization, i.e., secularization of the sacred, rationalization of the metaphysical" (*CS*, 187). This moral corruption designates, purely formally, the transformation of the secularization into a "secular messianism," which transforms the principle of Christian love of neighbor into a universal ethics, on the basis of which a utopian politics is to be set into motion and at the end of which God and the people are to be dissolved into an ideal society of freedom without sovereignty. Stapel writes: "Therefore, denying one's own nationhood is always basically godlessness" (*AS*, 17). The secularist, so Stapel writes in another context, wants to substitute advocacy for war, discussion for weapons, negotiation for battle, and he proves to be the prototype of a theocracy of eternal peace. However, this theocracy is then immediately attributed to Jewish theology, which itself is supposed to correspond to a racial-Jewish instinct, which serves Stapel as the point of departure for his own secularization from theology to biology. Attributed to Jewry is a racial/antiracial instinct that needs to be annihilated because it is supposed to be the law of life.

Exactly at this point, one needs to ask how this clear-cut attribution of secularization to Jewish theocracy comes about, especially since the Enlightenment is, above all, the enterprise of the secularizing German Protestant intelligentsia of the eighteenth-century bourgeoisie, represented by the likes of Gotthold Ephraim Lessing, Georg Christoph Lichtenberg, and Immanuel

Kant. That is not to say that there was no Jewish enlightenment, but it took place, since Moses Mendelssohn, in the framework of the Leibniz-Wolffian enlightenment and then in the wake of, especially, the Kantian enlightenment.[19] Therefore, it is indeed necessary to take Stapel's double reproach "literally," that the secularist universalizes the principle of Christian love of neighbor but wants to eliminate God and the people, in order to unveil a "theopsychology" that is effective and is able to elucidate this delusional identification of secular enmity and Jewry. One may assume that this theopsychology, before being completely translated into the biological, roughly corresponds to what Stapel calls "instinct," in order to then conceptualize on its basis his own theobiology against the theobiological enemy of Jewry. If, at first, one takes Stapel's double reproach seriously, it contains an important cue to a central moment of secularization. So, for example, after publishing the theologically critical writings of Hermann Samuel Reimarus,[20] Lessing moved the person of Christ into the center of his own theoretical writings about the Enlightenment in order to initiate, through the radical dedogmatization of the classical Christology, a process of humanizing Christ, at the end of which Jesus the Man is "revealed."[21] Jesus was to be emancipated from the constructions of the Christian dogma, which now was attributed to Greek myth, in order to elevate his emphasis on love of neighbor to the basic law of radically humanistic ethics for all people, the ultimate sense of which was liberation from sovereignty and authority. This transformation corresponds not only to a this-worldly politicization, universalization, and eschatologization of Jesus's message, a secular messianism, but also to the simple historical deed: Jesus takes off his metaphysical double nature as God-man and now is discovered in a rational-historicized incarnation as Jewish rabbi. Reimarus himself has tried to completely interpret the Jewish Jesus against the backdrop of the Jewish messianism of his age, differentiating between the faith of Jesus and the accounts of the evangelists: "Therefore, it was not his intention to suffer and to die, but to erect a worldly kingdom and to redeem the Jews from their bondage . . . and therein, God has abandoned him."[22] Lessing's distinction between the belief "in Jesus" and the belief "of Jesus" is similar to the differentiation between the Christology of suffering and the ethical-political interpretation of the self-understanding of Jesus.

The accusation that secularization is a secular messianism thus results from an enlightened Protestant critique of the gospels and the late *Leben-Jesu Forschung*, which elevates the figure of Christ to the medium of a universal ethics of human rights; Christ thereby wanted to found "a worldly kingdom," indeed, a theocracy in conformity with a Jewish-messianic understanding. This humanization and secular universalization finally entail, by radicalizing and increasingly dedogmatizing, a historicization that completely merges Jesus with the specific Jewish context of the time before the destruction of the Second Temple. This connection of universal antinational ethics and national-Jewish foundations of liberal Protestant theology now obviously creates a tension, which Stapel "detects" as the nature of secularization and as its "fundamental" contradiction, and which he retrojects to a specific Jewish theopsychology. Through precisely this political theocratization, secularization fulfills the denial of the people and of God. Since Christ, the Son of God, becomes the man Jesus, he loses his divinity and becomes a Jew, who proclaims an ethics beyond "ethnic difference" but interprets the latter in the sense of a specific Jewish theocracy.

Before the attack on secularization turns into an attack on the Jewish people, it is an attack on the liberal Jesus, so the Protestant Enlightenment, which moves the Jewish Jesus into the spotlight of epochal attention, can be discarded. The liberal Jesus is, as it were, the "missing link" by virtue of which "secularization" becomes the hidden work of "the Jew," who wants to come to power through enlightenment. It suffices to read the following lines from Stapel's "Six Chapters about Christianity and National Socialism": "If you, gentlemen, regard Jesus as the son of a Jewish father, as the corporeal son of the carpenter Joseph of Nazareth, then you will not be able to circumvent this consequence: And then piety comes, which despite all racial doctrine does not want to abandon Jesus, and looks for historiographic and ethnographic excuses of such a kind that, in Galilee as an area that a lot of peoples traversed, there was a lot of Aryan blood so that Jesus's appearance and teachings exhibited many un-Jewish traits" (*6K*, 15). By "abducting" Jesus as the central figure of identification for the German Wilhelm Stapel with the Jewish people and withdrawing him from German fantasy, the Jewish people, which brought forth this Jesus, becomes the inevitable enemy who turns out to be the hidden profiteer behind secularization. Love of neighbor as ethical principle becomes a genuinely Jewish complot, a conspiracy, and explains why the assimilationist, secular Jew is elevated to an ultimate enemy—because he is the actual profiteer of the secularization and humanization of the liberal Jesus, who himself represents a Jewish, cosmopolitan ethics. Like the liberal Jesus, the assimilationist speaks a double language: he speaks of universal ethics, but now he means his own ethnic power.

Thus, the antisecular front necessarily aims to redogmatize Christ and to fight assimilationist Jewry; both fronts are aspects of the same project of an antisecular front. Redogmatizing Christ corresponds to the concept of the assimilationist Jew as ultimate enemy. After his reflections about the danger of historicizing Jesus, Stapel then claims: "However, we Christians have been taught by the gospels and the apostles that Jesus is the Son of God. It is the premise of the New Testament that Jesus does not have an earthly father, but only an earthly mother. . . . If, however, Jesus is born from the Virgin Mary, the Son of God, he is not the son of a Jew" (*6K*, 15–16). This political theology of virginity uses the antiethnic formula of classical orthodox dogmatics as a foundation of racial-ethnic politics! Whereas Jesus, in this classical doctrine of dogmatics, no longer wants to be the son of his mother or the brother of his brothers, but calls every human being his mother and brother, and thereby revolutionizes all biological-ethnic relations, Stapel perverts classical dogmatics, as he does in the case of the Trinity, in order to deploy it as a weapon in his fight on the racial-ethnic front against secularization.

If the identity of the liberal Jesus with the figure of the liberal Jew results from the double structure of universalism and ethnic affiliation, which is common to both, for Stapel, both cases illustrate a double strategy of denying ethnic national difference, wherein the affirmation of one's own ethnic difference is articulated. This double strategy corresponds to doublespeak: secularization changes in Stapel's orthodox theological fantasy into original sin, which he symbolically aligns with the snake from the Garden of Eden in a mythical way. "In the Enlightenment, the snake crept out of the leaves of the forbidden tree; in the end she devours the Word of God and inflates herself: I am the true Christ and proclaim peace" (*6K*, 21). The snake as allegory of doublespeaking secularization is a theological symbol of an actual biological law of life, which Stapel deploys to describe secularization as a process of retransformation of the cross, which God the Father erected against the principle of the snake and original sin but now changes again into the principle of the snake. Against the elimination of the snake through the cross, secular modernity as double strategy designates the Jewish enemy as such: the suspension of the cross through the snake.

"Permeated by the thoughts and feelings of liberal justice I left the university as a friend of the Jews. . . . And look: does not the Jew help you to judge yourself thoroughly, to judge you or rather to batter you? So that you constantly need to feel embarrassed about your own insufficiency?" (*AS*, 6). At that time, the liberal philo-Semite Stapel wants to find in his conversations with Jews a heavy spiritual problem, which made him slowly recognize the "underground fight between Germanness and Jewry" (*AS*, 7), the deed that "Jews often deny, even though they do not admit it to themselves, the difference from the Gentiles, which is not only fortuitous but essential, because they do not belong to their own, but to another people" (*AS*, 16). Here, too, it is true: Different from the Zionists, who "affirm a self-contained Jewish people" and "do not want anything other than a Jewish state in Palestine, so that their people have a home and a state structure in the world," the assimilationist is said to deny his racial identity and thus to try to unconsciously impose a strategy of his own displacement upon the German people. However, by doing that, he can follow only an instinct, the theocratic root of which the assimilationist himself cannot grasp and on which Stapel wants to throw light. Whereas the liberal Christ still embodies the bridge between enlightenment and secularity, which makes the "contradiction" between universality and Jewish particularity transparent, these correlations in the secularized assimilationist consciousness are effective only in a concealed way; they function "according to the instinct," and that means at first on the basis of an unconscious theopsychological vitality. Stapel's theory of the instinct always presupposes this form of a "messianic unconscious" and a "theocratic vitality" by dint of which the explicit politics of displacement of the ethnic identity of assimilationist Jewry can become comprehensible for the first time. In Stapel's view, the "instinct" of denying the people is so unique and typical for the Jews that, for him, it is only explicable through the theological dimension that the secularized assimilationist himself can no longer understand. He acts blindly and instinctively, as only a secularized people can act. "The social instincts of the Jew aim at a theocracy that is to spread over all of humanity. The justice of God, of which Jewry is the messenger, is supposed to order and determine all of humanity. Indeed, in areligious Jewry, the theocratic disposition disappears, but the social instinct stays the same" (AS, 93).[23]

From the Roman Empire of the German Nation to the "Imperium Teutonicum"

Führer and enemy form a phantasmagoric correlation, which condition and exclude one another in the construction of two absolutely competing visions of history. The vanishing point of the secular utopia of history is thus not only rolled over by the sphere of the dogmatic construction of Lutheran salvific history but indeed replaced by another secular vanishing point. Where, in emancipatory modernity, ethics and theology, society and kingdom of God are supposed to converge in the telos of history, Stapel poses his own version of a secular conversion of theology and biology. Instinct-driven secular messianism conditions the instinct-driven kingdom theology that replaces and eliminates it. Each represents functions of a fundamental law of life and of an instinct that, because each is absolutely determined by nature and biology, can only confront one another in a war of extermination.

For this reason, the Führer is the ultimate principle of racial sovereignty, which accomplishes its mission in the absolute "political" separation of friend and enemy that now means in a biological act of "discipline" and "selection": "May in our nation gather together the natures that are harsh and willing to be disciplined and push the powerless and undisciplined into contempt that they deserve" (CS, 223). It is the "proud lads," the "marching troops" (CS, 277), that Stapel wants to address directly and encourage at the end of his antisecular appeal to the German nation when he holds out to them the prospect of sovereignty over the world under the Führer: "In your bitterness, the future ferments. God must reward your pride with the Führer, who will make you lords over large territories that you are destined to dominate" (CS, 228).

When Stapel draws, again and again, on the classical kingdom theology, which, according to him, begins with the medieval Catholic "Holy Roman Empire of the German Nation," and the continuation of which he recognizes in the Wilhelmine Empire of German-Protestant sovereignty, so he himself has already long inscribed this kingdom theology into a secular eschatology in contrast to secular messianism. The first medieval Roman Empire transitions through the second Wilhelmine Empire of Protestantism into the Third Reich of the sovereignty of the Führer, in which Protestant theology secularizes itself, whereby it puts to work its eschatology of an absolute conversion of theology and biology. However, the Führer-state is not a simple state but, in terms of the doctrine of *nomos*, an imperium, and as such the completion of the occidental eschatology in the Third Reich. With the Führer-state, the "German people" becomes what it has always already been by nature: "an imperial people" (*CS*, 228). From the beginning, the Germans "took direction not toward a state, but toward a Reich" (*CS*, 228). Stapel's review of the German idea of the Reich from Charlemagne through the collapse of the Wilhelmine Empire in the First World War is to be understood as a preview of a restoration of the Reich on the basis of the theobiological synthesis that he calls "Imperium Teutonicum." "One nation needs to elevate itself highly and brightly above the others; one nation needs to consolidate its authority over the others; one nation needs to set an imperial law and a European *nomos*" (*CS*, 253).

Theological Postscript: or, The Liberal Jesus as Savior and Redeemer

After the war, Wilhelm Stapel was integrated into the new democratic state of the Federal Republic with the help of his theological outfit, now eliminating its biological, secularized form. Following Friedrich Daniel Schleiermacher's "On Religion—Speeches to Its Cultural Despisers" (1799),[24] Stapel published a book called "On Christianity—To the Thinking among Its Despisers" (1951). In the preface, he writes about himself as author from the distant perspective of the third person, who demonstrates to an entire generation how a National Socialist casts off his skin and turns into a democratic citizen: "He did not belong to any political party. Therefore, he also declined the exhortations to join the National Socialist German Workers

Party and bore the consequences. . . . The author wrote the present book in the Second World War and finished it at Pentecost in 1943. He wrote it when he was assured that the political power wanted to abolish Christianity after the hoped-for victory" (*ÜdC*, 9). This biographical reconfiguration, which was followed by exculpation through the denazification process, presented Stapel's own political career in the light of an apolitical neutrality, according to which Stapel resisted, in a quasi-heroic manner, the request to join the party, at which point he became a victim of the Führer-state through the ecclesiastical politics of Hitler. It is not difficult to show that Stapel by this time had quite unequivocally changed his political theology into the political biology that he had always already presupposed implicitly in his prolegomena to the sovereignty of the Führer, and thus remained faithful only to his own law of life of oscillation between theology and politics. Earlier, Stapel had published numerous confessions to racial biology, which also corresponded to his membership (since 1936) in the Institute of the Reich for the History of the New Germany, directed by Walter Frank, and to his collaboration (since 1939) with the Institute for the Exploration and Removal of the Jewish Influence on the German Ecclesiastical Life. Even after 1941, Stapel published a monumental endorsement of racial biology, "The Three Estates—Attempt of a Morphology of the German People,"[25] in which he writes: "The biological type of the human race actually is the connection of predator (individual) and herd (community). This peculiar connection of dominance and herd instinct, this accumulated dominance, this alternating double form of life has made man fear all co-creatures. . . . However, dominance and a spirit of fellowship together lead man to great heights. Each is valuable through the other, and each refines itself through the other" (*DDD*, 301). The theological term "co-creature" is a rhetorical pledge of a biological mechanism that has taken off its theological mask in order not to ascribe to itself an "art of writing" in an "age of persecution."

Stapel's biography functions like so many other German biographies after the Second World War, as attempts at exculpation, but it is more than only opportunistic adaptation. What distinguishes it from its beginnings, the oscillation between theology and biology, Stapel now deploys as a strategy to initiate his own biological-political self-assertion under the guise of a theologian. Politics is the bridge on the basis of which Stapel can transform his theology into biology and his biology into theology at any time. Stapel himself recognized that point early: "That, however, was the peculiarity of the religious worldview, which emerged out of the thought of the divine right of kings," he writes in "The Fictions of the Weimar Constitution— Attempt of a Distinction of Formal and Functional Democracy,"[26] "namely, that it corresponded to the biological matter of facts. In order to clarify the analogies, we have expressed the religious as much as possible in biological terms" (*FWH*, 73).

In his book "On Christianity," Stapel now positions himself on the side of a Christianly substantiated reason, which pretends to be "occidental" and "European," in order to condemn the Bolshevist revolution and the "National Socialist terror" in the spirit of the theory of totalitarianism at that time. The "total war," Stapel writes, was not accidentally the war of "purely pagan magic, the most merciless and most fanatic of all wars" but, as such, "the war of an age that degenerated from the height of Christianity" (*ÜdC*, 182). Retrospectively, Stapel deplores the "inner corrosion of Christianity, the striving to create a particularly racial religion" as "symptom of the decline of Europe" (*ÜdC*, 205).

At the same time, the word *secularization* emerges as a neutral sociological category through which the theologian, now cleansed, explains that "Europe would not have come into being without Christianity" (*ÜdC*, 182). Stapel has made his peace with liberal theology and now begins a short biography of the "historical Jesus" into which he introduces the dogmatic parameters of classical dogmatics that he had once distorted and deformed because of his National Socialist ideology, as time-bound historical forms of a theological consciousness. "We will not fail to recognize the historical fact that these ideas are bound by the worldview of their age. The present worldview (which also is not final, but still in a state of flux, which is often forgotten) is reluctant to accept such things as reality or expression of a deeper truth" (*ÜdC*, 107). Besides, the liberal theologian stands out because of his knowledge of the Hebrew language, with the help of which he relocates the dogmatic Jesus into his originally Jewish landscape in the tradition of the *Leben-Jesu-Forschung*: "It is remarkable that already in Hebrew the name 'Jeschua' (Jesus) contains the notion of Savior and Redeemer.

'Jescha' means help, salvation; 'jascha' means to help" (*ÜdC*, 110). The same liberal Jesus that angered the National Socialist Stapel—whatever this secularized Jesus may have kept as salvific forces—has indeed "redeemed" and "saved" the National Socialist Stapel after the war.

Translated by Simon Kerwagen

Notes

1. See Wilhelm Stapel, *Der Christliche Staatsmann: eine Theologie des Nationalismus* (Hamburg: Hanseatische Verlagsanstalt, 1932), 21 (hereafter *CS*). For a series of works that explain the movement of the Führer-state to a political-theological state, see Stapel, *Sechs Kapitel über Christentum und Nationalsozialismus* (Hamburg: Hanseatische Verlagsanstalt, 1931) (hereafter *6K*), and *Die Kirche Christi und der Staat Hitlers* (Hamburg: Hanseatische Verlagsanstalt, 1933) (hereafter *KCSH*). Besides his political-theological writings, Stapel has published a series of straightforwardly anti-Semitic texts, including *Antisemitismus und Antigermanismus* (Hamburg: Hanseatische Verlagsanstalt, 1928) (hereafter *AS*), and *Die literarische Vorherrschaft der Juden in Deutschland 1918 bis 1933* (Hamburg: Hanseatische Verlagsanstalt, 1937) (hereafter *LV*). About Stapel, see especially Willi Kleinhorst, *Wilhelm Stapel: ein evangelischer Journalist im Nationalsozialismus* (Frankfurt am Main: P. Lang, 1993); Oliver Schmalz, *Kirchenpolitik unter dem Vorzeichen der Volksnomoslehre* (Frankfurt am Main: Lang, 2004).

2. The term "conservative revolution" was coined by Armin Mohler, *Die konservative Revolution in Deutschland, 1918–1932* (Darmstadt: Wissenschaftliche Buchgesellschaft, 1989). With regard to the role of political theology under National Socialism, see Claus-Ekkehard Bärsch, *Die politische Religion im Nationalsozialismus* (Munich: W. Fink, 2002). With regard to the Protestant church in the Third Reich, see Roland Kurz, *Nationalprotestantisches Denken in der Weimarer Republik* (Gütersloh: Gütersloher Verlagshaus, 2007).

3. Cf. Karl Löwith, *Meaning in History: The Theological Implications of the Philosophy of History* (Chicago: University of Chicago Press, 1949); Jacob Taubes, *Occidental Eschatology* (Stanford, CA: Stanford University Press, 2009); Eric Voegelin, *The New Science of Politics* (Chicago: University of Chicago Press, 1952).

4. Heinrich Kessler, *Wilhelm Stapel als politischer Publizist* (Nürnberg: Spindler, 1967); Friedrich Gogarten, *Politische Ethik* (Jena: Diederichs, 1932); Emanuel Hirsch, *Deutsches Volkstum und evangelische Glaube* (Hamburg: Hanseatische Verlagsanstalt, 1934). With regard to Gogarten and Hirsch, see also my *Der häretische Imperativ: Überlegungen zur theologischen Dialektik der Kulturwissenschaft in Deutschland* (Tübingen: Niemeyer, 2000).

5. Baruch Spinoza, *Theological-Political Treatise* (Indianapolis, IN: Hackett, 2001), especially chap. 17; Immanuel Kant, *Religion within the Limits of Reason Alone* (New York: Harper, 1960), chap. 3, sec. 2, identifies Jewish faith with what he calls the "embodiment of merely statuatory laws," which he likens to a state constitution; Johann Gottlieb Fichte, *Attempt at a Critique of All Revelation* (Cambridge: Cambridge University Press, 2010), exacerbates the difference between rational and revelational faith such that he invents a new political anti-Semitism that follows traditional religious anti-

Semitism, as Saul Ascher, "Eisenmenger der Zweite," in *4 Flugschriften* (Berlin: Aufbau-Verlag, 1991), has claimed.

6. Friedrich Nietzsche, *The Anti-Christ* (Cambridge: Cambridge University Press, 2005).

7. Erik Peterson, *Der Brief an die Römer* (Würzburg: Echter, 1997); cf. Barbara Nichtweiß, *Erik Peterson: Neue Sicht auf Leben und Werk* (Freiburg: Herder, 1992); Christoph Schmidt, "Apokalyptischer Strukturwandel der Öffentlichkeit. Von der politischen Theologie zur Theopolitik," in *Die theopolitische Stunde* (Munich: Wilhelm Fink, 2009), 113–42; Jacob Taubes, *The Political Theology of Paul* (Stanford, CA: Stanford University Press, 2004); Giorgio Agamben, *The Time That Remains: A Commentary on the Letter to the Romans* (Stanford, CA: Stanford University Press, 2005).

8. Johann Gottlieb Fichte, *Addresses to the German Nation* (New York: Harper & Row, 1968).

9. Wilhelm Stapel, *Über das Christentum. An die Denkenden unter seinen Verächtern* (Hamburg: Agentur des Rauhen Hauses, 1951) (hereafter *ÜdC*), presents itself, in the title, as a response to Friedrich Schleiermacher, *On Religion: Speeches to Its Cultured Despisers* (1799; repr., Cambridge: Cambridge University Press, 1996), and thereby as confession to the tradition of liberal Protestant theology.

10. Gotthold Ephraim Lessing, "Testament des Johannes" and "Die Erziehung des Menschengeschlechts," especially paragraphs 85–90, in *Theologiekritische Schriften III*, Werke VIII (Munich: Hanser, 1974); Kant, *Religion within the Limits of Reason Alone*, chaps. 2, 3.

11. Lessing, "Erziehung des Menschengeschlechts," 508, where Lessing announces "an age of completion," in which "man will do the good, because it is the good." This formula has to be read against the backdrop of Paul in Romans 7:19: "For the good that I wish, I do not do; but I practice the very evil that I do not wish," i.e., as a suspension of exactly this sinful brokenness of man through a new practical reason.

12. Kant, *Religion within the Limits of Reason Alone*, chap. 1, defines the radical evil, following Paul, as a "moral evil penchant," as "a radical, innate (but nonetheless acquired by us on our own) evil in human nature."

13. Lessing, "Erziehung des Menschengeschlechts," paragraph 90.

14. Kant, *Religion within the Limits of Reason Alone*.

15. How differently actual political theology within dialectical theology, a field in which Stapel evidently would place his own work, can turn out is shown with the example of the most important representative of the return to orthodox Christianity. Karl Barth, *The Epistle to the Romans*, trans. Edwyn C. Hoskyns (London: Oxford University Press, 1968), launches, in the context of Romans 13:1, the chapter "The Great Negative Possibility," a critique of all absolute claims for justice, of the nationalist authoritarian state, as well as of the revolutionary state of Lenin in order to maintain, on the basis of the doctrine of original sin, that a state is required, but this state must be thought democratically because all human beings are sinners.

16. Carl Schmitt, *The Concept of the Political* (Chicago: University of Chicago Press, 2007). Cf. Leo Strauss, "Anmerkungen zu Carl Schmitts Begriff des Politischen," in *Schriften III* (Stuttgart: Metzler, 1997); Hugo Ball, *Der Künstler und die Zeitkrankheit*

(Frankfurt am Main: Suhrkamp, 1984); E. Peterson, *Monotheismus als politisches Problem* (Leipzig: Hegner, 1935); Jacques Derrida, *Politics of Friendship* (London: Verso, 1997).

17. Schmitt, *Concept of the Political*, 28–29.

18. Cf. Ludwig Feuerbach, *The Essence of Christianity* (New York: Harper & Row, 1967), especially chaps. 5–8.

19. Cf. Ernst Cassirer, *The Philosophy of the Enlightenment* (Princeton, NJ: Princeton University Press, 2009). Specifically with regard to the Jewish enlightenment, see Christoph Schulte, *Die jüdische Aufklärung: Philosophie, Religion, Geschichte* (Munich: C. H. Beck, 2002); Shmuel Feiner, *Haskala—Jüdische Aufklärung. Geschichte einer kulturellen Revolution* (Hildesheim: Georg Olms Verlag, 2007). With regard to modern Jewish history in general, see especially Michael A. Meyer, ed., *German-Jewish History in Modern Times* (New York: Columbia University Press, 1996–98).

20. Lessing acknowledged Reimarus with his script "Von dem Zwecke Jesu und seiner Jünger. Noch ein Fragment des Wolffenbüttelischen Ungenannten," ed. Gotthold Ephraim Lessing (Braunschweig, 1778). Here, I follow the depiction of Albert Schweitzer, *The Quest of the Historical Jesus* (Minneapolis, MN: Fortress Press, 2001).

21. Cf. Lessing, *Theologiekritische Schriften III*, Werke VIII. With regard to the intellectual-historical context, see the distinguished reconstruction of Schweitzer, *Quest of the Historical Jesus*.

22. Quoted in Albert Schweitzer, *Ausgewählte Werke in fünf Bänden* (Berlin: Union Verlag, 1971), 3:69.

23. Stapel identifies this destructive instinct with such assimilationist Jews as Heinrich Heine, Gustav Landauer, and Louis Hagen, who "occupy . . . the book market of the other people [non-Jews], thereby empathizing with it, and ridicule the best goods of the others" (*AS*, 20). Louis Hagen is not well known today. A banker and supporter of the arts, born as Louis Levy, he is my great-uncle.

24. Schleiermacher, *On Religion*.

25. Wilhelm Stapel, *Die drei Stände: Versuch einer Morphologie des deutschen Volkes* (Hamburg: Hanseatische Verlagsanstalt, 1941) (hereafter *DDD*).

26. Wilhelm Stapel, *Die Fiktionen der Weimarer Verfassung. Versuch einer Unterscheidung der formalen und der funktionalen Demokratie* (Hamburg: Hanseatische Verlagsanstalt, 1928) (hereafter *FWV*).

CHAPTER 3

BETWEEN W. E. B. DU BOIS AND KARL BARTH

The Problem of Modern Political Theology

J. KAMERON CARTER

As the guns fell silent in 1918 with the conclusion of the First World War, it was unknown at the time that what in fact was being concluded was but the first, painful episode in what one historian has called, summarizing the first half of the twentieth century, an era of "total war." It was then, with the First World War, that "the great edifice of nineteenth-century civilization crumpled in . . . flames" and a new framework for carrying out the Western civilizing mission started to arise phoenixlike from the ashes.[1] With the Treaty of Versailles, the old form of domination through imperial dynasties was giving way to a new political form of Western hegemony: the nation or, more accurately, the nation-state. Indeed, the term "nation" itself was embedded in the name of one of the chief products of the postwar settlement: the League of Nations.

With the First World War and its aftermath as a reference point, I interrogate in this chapter the theological architecture of secular modernity with special attention to the problematic eschatological kingdom-community it has sought to create and the utopian figure as its stabilizing center. This is the figure of Western Man who has operated as an imperial God-Man. In my analysis, I situate the issue of imperialism and the racial imagination at the center of the problem of modern political theology. Insofar as this imperial Man projects a certain kind of divinity—what we might call "imperial divinity"—that legitimates his claim, in the Hegelian sense, to be Master, he functions as a messianic or a Christ figure at the center of an economy of "redemption." As such, Western Man is a new instance of what in classical Christian theology is called "the Christological problem" in that the problem of imperial Man is in fact the problem of the imperial God-Man. He carries out a "soteriological" or "missionizing" project of salvation—the civilizing mission of the West—aimed at ruling the world. My claim is that it is precisely this configuration of the human that came into crisis in the flames of war in the second decade of the twentieth century, and arguably, it is this form of the human that has been working to reconstitute itself, its world, and its divine prowess ever since.

I consider the problem of the imperial God-Man through the eyes of two vitally important twentieth-century intellectuals, who, to my knowledge, have never simultaneously been engaged on the particular issue of modern political theology (or, more broadly, on any issue). They are the African American intellectual W. E. B. Du Bois (1868–1963), a figure well known in diaspora and literary studies and across other fields in the humanities, and the Swiss-German intellectual Karl Barth (1886–1968), one of the most consequential Christian thinkers of the twentieth century. I do not suggest that there was a direct collaboration between Du Bois and Barth, as they were unknown to each other in their virtually overlapping lives. Instead, I will identify a convergence of their ideas—or an analogical collaboration between them—on the problem of modern political theology.

These two thinkers wrote from within different social landscapes but the same world situation—the crisis of the First World War and its aftermath. One was a humanist intellectual trained as a historian and ultimately working as a wide-ranging social theorist of the modern condition from the position of modernity's underside; the other was a theological heir of nineteenth-century European humanistic traditions—particularly that of *Kulturprotestantismus* (cultural Protestantism)[2]—who worked within the bourgeois climate of the Western metropoles of Germany and Switzerland. Yet Du Bois and Barth converged in considering the modern condition and the contemporary problem of the human. This convergence lay in their diagnosis of their historical moment as being located inside a wider theological or theo-political crisis. For both men, then, modernity was a *theological* problem. It was the theological problem of the White, Global Masculine, the problem of imperial Man—a figure that needed to be reimagined if a just society was to be realized. In light of this problem, both attempted to rewrite the terms of modern anthropology and the vision of religion internal to it. By historicizing and theorizing the work of both Du Bois and Barth in terms of the problematic just sketched, I shall call specific attention to the form of the human that their work identifies as anchoring the West's theo-political project of attaining its social fantasy of an *eschaton*—a project that they seek to disenchant or demystify.

Nationalism, Social Fantasy, Representation

For purposes of this essay, I understand "fantasy" in terms similar to those employed in Benedict Anderson's description of the "nation"—thus of nationalism—and even more similar to Étienne Balibar's analysis of the "nation-form." There is nothing natural about a nation. Rather, it is, as Anderson remarks, an "imagining." It is a created or invented phenomenon. Therefore, what distinguishes nations is "the style in which they are imagined."[3] This style has everything to do with the myth of origins or of beginnings mobilized to sustain nations. What is the form by which identity—or the formation of a citizen, *homo nationalis*—comes into being and is sustained? That form is imagination, where the fantasy work of subject formation or "nation building" takes place. Imagination is the psychic space between the state and the constitution of the citizen as a subject of and within the nation; it is the domain in which subjectivity is nationalized and a subject is formed as bound to "the community," the *ethnos*, "the people." Subjectivity, then, is that space where internal and external relations of force meet, and it is at this meeting point that nationalization occurs. Therefore, while the nation is enacted at one level at the political conscious, it is enacted at a deeper level at the "political unconscious."[4] It is here that "the effect of unity by virtue of which the people will appear, in everyone's eyes, as 'a people,'" is produced.[5]

Balibar offers an interesting analogy for the homogenizing processes of subject formation and the production and binding of a subject to a people. He likens the universality of nationalism in the production of the citizen-subject or "the national" to the universal theological or soteriological process by which a Christian is formed as bound to Christ's body and the social form that is church (or, in an earlier era, Christendom). Balibar suggests, in other words, that the making of a national has its analogue in the making of a Christian: citizen-subject formation is analogous to conversion and discipleship.

For Balibar, however, the processes involved in the making of a national or a citizen and those involved in the making of a Christian or a disciple are more than simply analogous. A defining feature of the modern situation is that these processes represent two aspects of a singular, Janus-faced social process: the subject formation of the citizen and that of the Christian have been articulated to each other. Being caught up in the one entails being caught up in the other. Balibar makes this point when, speaking of the nationalization of religious identity in the secular French context, he writes that "national identity [has] more or less completely [integrated] the forms of religious identity."[6] If this is considered not just in the French context but also in the context of the history of the United States and the ongoing effects of its Puritan religious legacy, one sees that the reverse can also be true: religious identity can predominate, absorbing national identity in the making of nationals as well. It is precisely this problem of the articulation of citizen subjectivity and religious subjectivity to each other as a signal feature of the nation-form—with one being more pronounced than the other, depending on the national context and the historical moment—that Du Bois and Barth discern as the symbolic foundation of modern subjectivity.

One final aspect of Balibar's understanding of subject formation within the modern configuration of the nation-form is worth noting. He argues that at the articulating joint between citizen-subject formation (i.e., the construction of a national self) and religious-subject formation (i.e., the making of the "converted" self) in the establishment of peoplehood and (kingdom) community stands the mediating notion of "fictive ethnicity." Because "no nation possesses an ethnic base naturally," its unity as an *ethnos* must be generated—hence, the "fictive" aspect of fictive ethnicity.[7] It is against this background of "fabrication," Balibar writes, that (national) belonging in the sense of "what it is that makes one belong to oneself and also what makes one belong to other fellow human beings" is enacted. This fabrication is the constant production and reproduction of a people.[8] As Alys Weinbaum has noted, this is the "race/reproduction bind."[9] As it is religion that houses the race/reproduction couplet in the making of modern subjects, this is nothing less, in my view, than the bind of religion.

The other aspect of fictive ethnicity at which Balibar hints but does not develop—an aspect that is quite important to my effort to clarify the role of religion in making modern subjects—is the notion of an ideal figure of the nation, a *persona ficta*, a "concrete universal" who anchors the process and thus secures the nation's anthropology. As in the assertion in the US Declaration of Independence that "*all* men are created equal," this anthropology aspires toward universality. Nationalization entails the process of approaching or approximating a concrete universal figure in striving toward subjectivity and visibility, that is, toward nationality. In this way, by serving as a kind of godlike image (*imago dei*) that represents the ideality of the nation, the concrete universal acts as a fictive mediator.

The relationship between this fictive mediator and those striving for citizenship is mimetic; it is a relationship-in-imitation or in-repetition. With regard to this point, I supplement Balibar's analysis with insights from critical theorist Rey Chow, who observes that "the image is, ultimately, not the problem; the *act* of imitating, of copying, is."[10] Echoing the theological notion of *imitatio Christi*, mimesis puts forward the White Man as the original, national figure, the exemplar of a citizen. At the first level of mimesis, one strives to reproduce model citizenry within oneself by imitating the (white) original. When one succeeds, whiteness is a fait accompli in the self. As subjects mimetically approximate the ideal figure or image of the concrete universal, they are bound together into a national community—indeed, into a "family" with this mediator, one might say, as fictive patriarch. Thus, the nation becomes "fatherland" for its subjects as they speak its "mother tongue" and exemplify its "culture."

When the process of imitating the (white) original succeeds, successful nationalization, that is to say, whiteness, is accomplished. The problem arises when colonials (and postcolonials) enter into the mimetic process of citizen-subject formation. Rather than whiteness being fully accomplished, they often produce within themselves an inferior copy of the (white) original that yields failed or suspect citizenship. This failure is then representationally linked to them or becomes visually signified as their racial difference. Indeed, their racial-ethnic difference is precisely what is being produced in this moment of failure to reach universality/nationality. In many ways, this dynamic underlies the current and historical immigration debates both in the United States and in Europe.

For my purposes, the lesson to be learned is that the concrete universal of whiteness, which has served to ground many Western nationalisms, cannot be imagined without the accompanying "failed" nonuniversal, nonwhite particulars. Much, therefore, turns on the figure of the mediator as the concrete universal and the racialized nationalism necessarily linked to this figure: what we discover are the workings of racialization as a feature of social fantasy and subject formation in the making and sustaining of nations.

At a theoretical level, my concern is precisely with this mediating figure, the social imaginary constituted around him, and his imaginary work of securing an eschatological kingdom-community (the nation in global relationship to the West). My specific concern is to examine the West as an *eschaton* that a false mediator, a Christ figure, secures. For, changes notwithstanding, the ideal and utopian figure of a mediator continues to function as the one toward whom "salvation" as a social process aims in the making of modern subjects. Mediation still works on bodies. In approximation to him, subjectivity arises, the citizen is made, or—if subjectivity is denied—citizenship is refused. Extending Balibar's analysis, we face this wider problem of political theology, a project that requires both the quest for a kingdom-community and a certain form of the human (Balibar's "fictive ethnicity") to anchor it.

Considering this problem from the vantage point of its historical display in Germany further develops my argument and provides a transition to my engagement with Karl Barth. Germany's fantasy of nationalism was long in the making and came into crisis in 1914. Five years later at Versailles, when Germany was stripped of its colonial holdings, Germans took themselves to have been emasculated or "feminized" as a Western nation (especially in relation to the victors in the war, Britain, France, and the rising global power, the United States). This sense of crisis was, as historian Claudia Koonz demonstrates in *The Nazi Conscience*, a crisis of masculine national strength, and Adolf Hitler seized upon it in the 1920s to propel himself to power in the following decade.[11] Hitler promised to restore Germany's cultural strength by "defeminizing" the nation and restoring its masculine prowess.

The significance of Germany being stripped of its colonial possessions as a result of the war cannot be underestimated, for the rise of Germany as a modern nation in 1871 is paired with its virtually simultaneous establishment (within a mere thirteen years) by Otto von Bismarck of colonies in southwest Africa, Togo, Cameroon, East Africa, and the Pacific. As these colonies were taken away, so too was part of Germany's national manhood. To appreciate this loss of national manhood is to appreciate not only Germany's emasculation by its powerful opponents but also its being treated as a colony itself: Germany watched as stronger powers divided its territory—its colonial holdings in Africa and its borders in Europe—among themselves. Thus, Germany received the humiliation that it had previously doled out as a colonial power at the Berlin conference in 1884.

Intellectuals like Immanuel Kant, Friedrich Schleiermacher, and G. W. F. Hegel (to name but a few from the worlds of theology and philosophy) partook in this cultural obsession with colonies, which was a central element in the forging of German national identity. The figure that they created was decidedly virile and racially white. Germans imaged a German masculine subject in competition with the other white European subjects who ruled globally and internationally. This figure also ruled in the domestic sphere of the bourgeois family, the seat of the nation's reproduction "at home." In both spheres, at home and abroad, as Zantop shows, this figure was a man of war, a bourgeois warrior subject. The "colony"—in both its global and domestic/bourgeois registers—was a kind of "blank darkness." That is to say, "the 'colony' . . . became the blank space for a new beginning, for the creation of an imaginary national self freed from history and convention—a self that would prove to the world what 'he' could do."[12]

In turning first to Barth and then to Du Bois, I demonstrate that this process was also a theo-political one built on a specific religious anthropology. It was (and, to a large extent, remains) one in which the constitution of the White Masculine as imperial Man was tied to his assuming a messianic and mediatory role in the world, as he accumulated divinity for himself. As imperial Savior, he functioned by "divine right" to establish a utopian kingdom—a kingdom of whiteness, we might say—as the kingdom of God. Those who enter this kingdom can be saved. Yet to be saved is to be made "religious" in the proper way within a properly ordered secular space; those

who cannot or who refuse to enter this "order of things" must be annihilated for the sake of the kingdom. In this chapter I develop this claim
and start to delineate the specific deformation within Christianity's social
imagination that has given the Western civilizing project its Christological
and eschatological or, more simply, its theo-political energy.

Karl Barth, Eschatology, and the Imperial God-Man

From almost the first day of his time as a pastor in Safenwil, Switzerland,
in the first decade of the twentieth century, when as the "Red Pastor" he
worked with unions to improve working conditions for people in the community and in his congregation, Karl Barth was deeply concerned with the
religious dimensions of European bourgeois culture and civilization. Over
time he came to see a connection between the events of 1914 and the inequality and exploitation of workers that he took so seriously as part of his
pastoral work. The significance of the war was that it started to clarify for
him some of the ways in which a deformed Christian world outlook functioned as the unseen architecture of modern bourgeois culture. Thus, the
war, as Barth saw it, was a theo-political and theo-social phenomenon, unseen for what it was because it was shrouded in the illusion of religion. For
this reason, the war and the emerging postwar world had to be demystified.

In a letter to his friend, fellow pastor, and theological conversation partner
Eduard Thurneysen, written but a month after the war started, Barth was already beginning such demystifying work. As if testing out his ideas before his
friend, he suggested in the letter a connection between the war and the discourse of theology. "The unconditional truths of the gospel," he wrote, have
with the war been subjected to a kind of state of exception.[13] That is to say,
they had been "simply suspended for the time being and in the meantime a
German war-theology"—or a theology working in conjunction with or as
the conceptual complement to war—"[had been] put to work, its Christian
trimming consisting of a lot of talk about sacrifice and the like."[14]

Looking back on this period in an essay that was published in 1922
("The Righteousness of God"), Barth further developed the point he had
made to Thurneysen by connecting the war and capitalism in modern liberal society: "Is it not remarkable that the greatest atrocities of life—I think
of the capitalistic order and of the war—can justify themselves on purely

moral principles," he asks, on the basis of a "religious righteousness" that "take[s] flight to Christianity"—in short, on the basis of the one we call God?[15] Barth is clear who this "we" is: "all the distinguished European and American apostles of civilization, welfare, and progress, all zealous citizens and pious Christians" (22). The war, he observes, has been a kind of perverted religious ceremony, with these "apostles of civilization . . . and progress . . . falling upon one another with fire and sword" (22). Moreover, writes the young Barth—who in 1921 had recently become a theology professor at the University of Göttingen—the absurdity of this religious worship, of warfare as social regeneration, is not lost on the non-Western world, for "the poor heathen in India and Africa" look on in "amazement and derision" (22). While we rightly fault Barth for his use of the problematic language of "heathenism" in connection to India and Africa, it is important nonetheless to note that he is positioning the crisis of the West in the interwar years within the frame of global imperialism—this being the frame in which "heathen" and "civilized" have discursive cachet—even if he had yet to develop fully the structures of this frame.

For present purposes, this limitation should not detain us. What is critical to appreciate is Barth's insight about what is operative inside that "religious righteousness" that is the hallmark of the "distinguished European and American apostles of civilization . . . all zealous citizens and pious Christians." Barth understands that what animates "the righteousness of men"—the specificity of the phrase is vital, as he is speaking of Western Man—is the name of the one whom they call "God." It is this God who underwrites the present social arrangement of the righteousness of capitalist society that is at war, thus making this a kind of sacred arrangement. As a young scholar, Barth set for himself the agenda of decoding the identity of this God. In *The Word of God and the Word of Man*, first published in 1924, he demystified this God as "really an unrighteous god," a god for whom "it is high time for us to declare ourselves thorough-going . . . atheists in regard to him" (22).

From his time as the Red Pastor of Safenwil, to the time of his authorship of the Barmen Declaration in the 1930s, to the period from the 1930s to the 1960s during which he wrote the multivolume *Church Dogmatics*, Barth is simultaneously engaged in two tasks. On the one hand, he is reconceptualizing

Christianity's theological imagination so as to overcome "the 'embourgoise-ment' of theology."[16] On the other, he is performing theology as ideology critique, as a critique of modernity's false gods that had come to be reified as "our human righteousness, morality, state, civilization, or religion" (22).

Between the 1914 letter to Thurneysen and the 1922 essay "Righteous-ness of God," Barth wrote the book in which he would begin diagnos-ing this great problem of the war and its aftermath—such diagnostic work would continue throughout his life—and in which he would examine the spiritual or religious side of capitalist civilization and the logic of the the-ology on which it rests. Described as a bombshell that exploded on the intellectual playground of theologians and Bible scholars alike and written in two versions (the first edition of 1919 and the completely overhauled 1921 edition), Barth's commentary on Saint Paul's epistle to the Romans shook things up in a way that a commentary on scripture rarely does. Why did that usually innocuous document, a scriptural commentary, written by a pastor as he sat under a tree, provoke such responses—both favorable and unfavorable—across the intellectual landscape? I contend that the reason is that Barth's book demystified the religious operations of the West and, with the second edition, began to discern how the forces that lead to war—the forces of a false eschatology and a yearning for utopia after catastro-phe—were reconstituting themselves already with the Versailles Treaty and continuing into the Weimar Republic. With his *Römerbrief*, Barth uttered a resounding *Nein* to these operations.

Barth found himself caught inside nationalizing and imperial whiteness. Although he did not fully grasp the shape of this system, he nevertheless made great strides in demystifying one of its central features: its religious anthropology or, more specifically, the deeply troublesome theological sub-strate of this anthropology. Barth discerned that Western Man functioned as a replacement Christ figure or as a problematic "divine" mediator who routed all subjectivity through his being. He was also beginning to under-stand how Christian theology as a discursive practice had come to speak of Western Man in its God-talk. Barth's Romans commentary is consumed by this ethical problem:

> We suppose that we know what we are saying when we say "God." We assign
> to Him the highest place in our world . . . we press ourselves into proximity

with Him . . . [but] secretly we are ourselves the masters in this relationship. . . . And so, when we set God upon the throne of the world, we mean by God ourselves. . . . God Himself is not acknowledged as God and what is called "God" is in fact Man.[17]

From the opening pages of his Romans commentary, Barth's critique is focused, particularly in the section of the first chapter titled "The Night" (which he subdivides into a meditation on "Its Cause" and "Its Operations"). Taking his cue from the language of Romans 1:18, Barth explicates "the wrath of God." This wrath is God's No, which Barth reads as targeted at *the course of this world.* The presentism Barth extracts from passages such as Romans 1:18 leads Mark Lilla in *The Stillborn God* to interpret his commentary as contributing to the political theological sensibility that would eventuate in and legitimate National Socialism.[18] This reading of Barth, I submit, is misguided: Barth's claim is not that God was the active agent of either the war or the postwar realities that would lead to National Socialism, the formation of a Nazi conscience, and finally to Nazi theology. Barth does not, in other words, give divine sanction or warrant to either the war or the postwar situation. He is clear on this point: the wrath of God is God's protest against "the course of the world" (43), a course marked by unrighteousness. Indeed, God's protest, in Barth's view, unveils what lies at the root of the problematic course of the world—*human* resistance to God.

Barth employs a much-talked-about distinction—more precisely, a dialectic—between time and eternity in order to capture the nature of this resistance. It is with a time-eternity dialectic more than anything else that Barth sought to unmask how the West was functioning as an *eschaton* or a utopia. This utopian vision was driving the "course of this world"; it stood behind the war and the emerging postwar situation in Germany and the West *and* in the emerging revolutionary Russian East.

Barth used this dialectic to make the point that the new world of God, which for Barth is uniquely disclosed in the person of the resurrected, but first crucified, Jesus Christ, is not to be confused with the old world of fallen humanity. The former, centered in Jesus Christ, is God's eschatology, God's eternity; the latter is that false eschatology of "world history" and its accompanying political theology of time. This false eschatology of world history is centered in Europe and conceives of those culturally outside Europe as people without history and thus outside time (Hegel).Thus, this false eschatology of world history constructs "anthropology and its objects" in such a way that the West is conceived of as both path and goal of the *eschaton*, or as the "end of history." "End" here does not mean that history has stopped. Rather, it signals the privileging of one current, as it were, within the stream of history (in this case, the Western current) as the measuring stick of history, the benchmark of evaluation for the other, lesser streams. In this way, the West and its modernity *define* History (with a capital *H* to match the capital *C* of Civilization).

However, Barth saw the West not only dominating and defining events in worldly time but also legitimating its domination by appropriating eternity. For when time seizes eternity—thus defining eternity within the series of creaturely objects and concepts—the world has no Other. The result, as a matter of realpolitik, is apocalypse or catastrophe. It is Barth's contention that because of a confusion between time and eternity—with time storming the gates of eternity in an effort to divinize itself as "righteous" and thus stabilize the instabilities of creation and the contingencies of time—a politics of apocalyptic crisis arises. According to Barth, this is the problem of "the course of this world"—or, put differently, the problem of modern political theology.

The goal of the *Römerbrief* was in significant part to name this problem of eschatology and the West's efforts to construct itself as an eschatological kingdom-community. Moreover, Barth sought to rearticulate the relationship of time and eternity and to reconceive the identity of Jesus Christ beyond being an anchoring, messianic symbol to stabilize time in the social processes and production of the West as *eschaton* or Civilization (with a capital *C*). Much of this project is reflected in the well-known passage from the preface to the second edition of the *Römerbrief*:

> If I have a system, it is limited to a recognition of what Kierkegaard called the "infinite qualitative distinction" between time and eternity . . . "God is in heaven, and you are on the earth." The relation between *this* God and *this* human, and the relation between this human and this God, is for me the theme of the Bible and the sum of philosophy in one. Philosophers call this crisis of human knowing the Prime Cause. At the same crossroads, the Bible sees Jesus Christ.[19]

It is against this background that Barth probes the war and the postwar situation as the question of "the course of this world," or, put differently, as the question of what happens when creatures resist the fact that God is God and the creature is the creature. Resistance takes the form of the creature stepping into the place of God. The one who is not God, the "No-God" (*Nicht-Gott*) strives to be "like God" (*sicut deus*), where Godness manifests itself as lordship-mastery. Thus, the course of this world is one now marked by another dialectic—that of mastery-slavery, with divinity itself (eternity) as that which must first be mastered or subjected. Barth was pressing the insight that this theo-logic animates modern nationalism and drives the social fantasy or imaginary of the course of this world. It is this theo-logic that has been introjected into the self in the making of modern subjectivities. This is the theological side of what Foucault has called "the invention of Man."[20]

Such a social fantasy, which Barth came to see as central to the catastrophe of the world, represents a breakdown in the social performance of Christian doctrine, a breakdown that has significant ramifications for difference and identity. Thus, when God becomes a projection of Man, the positive relationship of difference between God and creation is lost; God, the "Wholly Other" (to use Barth's Kierkegaardian language), is now assimilated into a homogeneous totality. As a result, time as "world history" now gets envisioned as a totality, as a false universal, and having become one of the elements in the world system, "God" and the language related to this God—that is, *theology*—function to legitimate and stabilize a world that is in fact unstable and contingent. That God becomes an element of the world reflects the will of this world toward homogeneity and "universality." It follows from this fact that, with God as nothing more than a creaturely projection within the totalizing or universalizing structure of the world, those who now seemingly control or own this God wish to present their project as if it were the single will of God. Where creation does not adhere to this will, those in power will be engaged sometimes in benevolence, sometimes in antagonism, to bring about obedience to the will of God so that what is deemed "aberrant" or heterogeneous is stamped out. Thus, as a false God, the dominant remake the world in their image. In short, the breakdown in the Christian doctrine of God that, following Barth, I am describing—which is also a breakdown of Christian eschatology—is a breakdown of (theological) ethics that manifests, among other things, as political catastrophe.

Later in the *Römerbrief*, Barth redescribes this ethical catastrophe, this situation of conflict or "crisis," using the language of death:

> Death is the supreme law of the world in which we live. . . . [It] is engraved inexorably and indelibly upon our life. It is the supreme tribulation in which we stand. In it the whole riddle of our existence is summarized and focused; and in its inevitability we are reminded of the wrath which hangs over the man of the world and the world of man. So completely is death the supreme law of this world [*oberstes Gesetz dieser Welt*], that even that which, in this world, points to the overcoming of and renewal of this world, takes the form of death.[21]

But what lies at the heart of death? What is its deeper law, its spiritual or hidden side? For Barth, the principles of sin lie inside death. It should be noted that Barth does not understand sin in a pietistic, sentimental, or individualistic sense. Rather, sin is a matter of the political. It is a matter of political theology inasmuch as sin and sovereignty are linked. Sin is "power—sovereign power," Barth says (167). It is "an especial relationship of men to God; and it derives its [false] sovereign power, and even its existence, from this relationship" (167–68).

What is this relationship? Echoing Du Bois's language (as discussed later), it is theft: "Sin is a robbing of God" (168). More specifically, it is "a robbery which becomes apparent in our arrogant endeavour to cross the line of death by which we are bounded" (168)—the line, in other words, of our creatureliness. "In our drunken[ness]" on the booze of divinity, on the wine of the will to power as the will to be like God, we have "blur[red] the distance which separates us from God" (168). With the blurring of this distance, Western Man took on the characteristics of the divine, functioning like a God-Man. Herein lay the origins of *homo religiosus*.

It is in this theoretical context and historical situation of the unfolding of bourgeois/capitalist culture that we must hear Barth's critique of the ideological system of Western Man as a religious figure:

> Wherever the qualitative distinction between men and the final Omega is overlooked or misunderstood, that fetishism is bound to appear in which God is experienced in birds and fourfooted things, and finally, or rather pri-

marily, in the likeness of corruptible man [Romans 1:23] . . . and in the half-spiritual, half-material creations, exhibitions, and representations of His creative ability—Family, Nation, State, Church, Fatherland. And so the "No-Go" is set up, idols are erected, and God, who dwells beyond all this and that, is "given up." (50–51)

Barth demystifies the fetishes of "Family, Nation, State, Church"—in short, the Fatherland—that work in relationship to the Western (religious) self. He sees that what makes the fetishism work as it does is representation (what Chow identifies as mimetic reproduction) that aids and abets misrecognition. Mystification works through representation, through visual image (re)production. These images—and here we recall Balibar's theorizing of the nation-form—posit an ideal in relation to which subjectivity is formed through mimicry of the ideal and inside of which subjection occurs. As Barth insightfully understood, the image operating as the ideal—that is, as the Beautiful and thus as the master over the grotesque, to put it in aesthetic terms—is tied to the making of a slave: "The images and likenesses, whose meaning we have failed to perceive, become themselves purpose and content and end. And *now men have really become slaves* and puppets of things, of 'Nature' and of 'Civilization,' whose dissolution and establishing by God they have overlooked" (51; emphasis added).

With this insight, Barth has penetrated deeply into the order of things. One wishes that he would have meditated longer on the problem of mastery and slavery—especially the slavery side of the problem—in executing his theological project of demystification at this early stage of his thinking. Had he done so, Barth might have seen the global designs—and eventually he does come to see them, as his critiques in the posthumously published *Church Dogmatics* fragments (volume 4, part 4) of capitalism's post–World War II transformations suggest—tied to the production of Western Man as an imperial God-Man.

It is precisely at this point that Du Bois provides assistance, for he too saw the problem of a will to divination—a will to righteousness—as central to the making of imperial Man as an imperial God-Man. He too interpreted the war in theo-political terms. But because he interpreted the situation from the viewpoint of a diasporic or transnational, black Atlantic intellectual and thus from modernity's underside, Du Bois saw with a clarity at crucial points beyond Barth how the problem of modern political theology is bound up with the performance of whiteness. Moreover, he was able to link this problem to Christian supersessionism and to the closely related Christological question of the identity of Jesus Christ as Mediator.

Du Bois and the Political Theology of Whiteness

Between the publication of the first and second editions of Barth's *Römerbrief*, the African American intellectual W. E. B. Du Bois assembled and published a set of writings in various genres—history, sociology, autobiography, poems, and novellas—that sought to interpret the war and its immediate aftermath. This text, *Darkwater: Voices from within the Veil* (1920), was completed after his return from Paris in the summer of 1919 as the global powers met at Versailles to remap the world.[22] Like Barth's *Römerbrief*, *Darkwater* offers a counternarrative of the origins of the war and of the West but also a counternarrative of the origins of the United States within a broader framework of Western Man's will to rule the planet. In other words, Du Bois's text positions the United States within a global ideological system. What is critical for my purposes is that like Barth, Du Bois interpreted this broader system in religious terms that at once complemented and supplemented Barth's analysis in ways that throw into sharp relief what Barth himself was going after at this early stage of his intellectual output.

At the center of the reimagined cartography by which Du Bois renarrates the past that has been overlaid, if not erased, is Africa.[23] That this is the case is most evident in the chapter titled "The Hands of Ethiopia" (previously published in 1915 in *Atlantic Monthly* under the title "The African Roots of War"). This chapter roughly coordinates with Barth's letter to Thurneysen in 1914 in which, as noted previously, Barth too struggled to come to terms with the meaning of the war. Unlike Barth, however, Du Bois lodged the war within an imperial framework with Africa, not the North Atlantic world, at the center. The chief cartographic metaphor in *Darkwater* is just that— water—but modified by the important adjectival qualifier *dark*. Du Bois will tell the story of the current world situation from a "tower, above the thunder of the seven seas" (74); that is, he will consider the war as it relates to the darker peoples of the planet whose identities were once tied to slave ships and are now tied to warships.

Du Bois thus insists that the story of the war precedes 1914. Its more recent history can be traced to the scramble or the race for Africa, which was greatly intensified in the 1880s and into the opening decade of the twentieth century. Yet the story goes back even further. Invoking now the extended history of the war, Du Bois states:

> For four hundred years white Europe was the chief support of that trade in human beings which first and last robbed black Africa of a hundred million human beings, transformed the face of her social life, overthrew organized government, distorted ancient industry, and snuffed out the lights of cultural development. Today instead of removing laborers from Africa to distant slavery, industry built on a new slavery approaches Africa to deprive the natives of their land, to force them to toil, and to reap all the profit for the white world. (80–81)

This new slavery, which is "the beginnings of a modern industrial system" (85), drives "a new imperialism—the rage for one's own nation to own the earth or, at least, a large enough portion of it to insure as big profits as the next nation" (71). This quest to own the earth on the part of the European nations is what marks the new imperialism: "If the slave cannot be taken from Africa, slavery can be taken to Africa . . . menaced and policed by European capitalism" (86).

But it is not just the earth in general over which the European powers worry. Africa in particular was the source of their conflicts; therefore, there cannot be an adequate understanding of the present world crisis, Du Bois claims, without an understanding of its African roots:

> There are those who would write world history and leave out this most marvelous of continents. Particularly today most men assume that Africa lies far afield from our present problem of World War. Yet in a very real sense Africa is the prime cause of this terrible overturning of civilization which we have lived to see; and these words seek to show how in the Dark Continent are hidden the roots, not simply of war to-day but of the menace of wars tomorrow.[24]

What does one see in this mayhem of the white world? Du Bois's answer is telling—particularly for my argument about his convergence with Barth on the problem of modern political theology. The mayhem is religious (73) inasmuch as the war manifests "the utter failure of white religion": "a nation's religion is its life, and as such white Christianity is a miserable failure" (60–61).

Now we encounter a further task of *Darkwater*: by carrying out a carto-graphic renarration of the war and the world it created, Du Bois intervenes in the social fantasy of the West. He presents this war as the latest drama-turgical scene within what he calls the "religion of whiteness on the shores of our time" (56). Explaining the creed of this religion and, in doing so, possibly alluding to a messianic passage from Second Isaiah ("For he shall grow up before him as a tender plant, and as a root out of a dry ground: he hath no form nor comeliness; and when we shall see him, there is no beauty that we should desire him" [Isaiah 53:2, King James Version])—Du Bois asks: "'But what on earth is whiteness that one should so desire it?' Then always, somehow, some way, silently but clearly, I am given to understand that whiteness is the ownership of the earth forever and ever, Amen!" (56). On what basis can Du Bois make this claim as part of his explanation of "the souls of white folk"? Playing on the Genesis stories of the creation of human beings, Du Bois declares himself to be "bone of their thought and flesh of their language." Du Bois can diagnose the pathology plaguing the souls of white folk, in other words, because he is, in many ways, a prod-uct of that pathology and thus a mirror to white folks who "created" him as the Black or "the Negro."

With his clairvoyance, Du Bois declares that at the heart of "personal whiteness" is a will to rule the earth. Moreover, this will to world rule finds its authority in a fundamental and problematic theological act: in a Promethean gesture, white folk who claim divinity assign righteousness to themselves at the same time that they assign unrighteousness and evil to the wretched of the earth. In two compressed sentences that invoke the imagery of lynching, Du Bois states: "Back beyond the world and swept by these wild, white faces of the awful dead, why will this Soul of White Folk,—this modern Prometheus,—hang bound by his own binding, teth-ered by a fable of the past? I hear his mighty cry reverberating through the world, 'I am white!' Well and good, O Prometheus, divine thief!" (74). It is precisely at this point that Du Bois and Barth converge in their diagnosis of the modern situation. Where Du Bois names the self-assertion of the Western Masculine and the ethical situation of religion in the West as a "Promethean gloom" (74), Barth uses the language of "final solution" (a full decade before its use by the Third Reich!): "God does not live by the idea of justice with which we provide Him. He is His own justice. He is not one cause among many; He is not the final solution which we propound to the problem of life" (76).

Their convergence does not stop here: not only do both issue a No to this ethical situation but also both reimagine Christology. More specifically, both reimagine Jesus as that sociopolitical reality that interrupts the political regime of the No-God, the imperial God-Man, and thereby intervenes to redirect the political trajectory of the West. At this point, it is useful to consider Du Bois's Christological intervention in more detail—for in reimagining the identity of Jesus as interrupting imperial and racial longings, he reconceives politics and community at the site of death. In "Jesus Christ in Texas," the short story at the structural center of the book, Du Bois unpacks this reimagining of Christianity's central figure as no longer assimilated to Western Man and his imperial and political-theological ambitions.

Published originally in 1911 as "Jesus Christ in Georgia" but revised for republication in *Darkwater*, "Jesus Christ in Texas" is a life-of-Jesus story. Yet unlike the nineteenth-century lives of Jesus that used the tools of modern historical criticism to reconstruct the historical Jesus—a Jesus who was often a de-Judaized exemplar of Western civilization—Du Bois imagined a Jesus who arrived nameless and unknown, a stranger and a foreigner in Waco, Texas. Recently acquired in 1845 as a result of the US-Mexico War, turn-of-the-twentieth-century Texas becomes for Du Bois an imaginative site at which to dramatize Western imperial designs. Indeed, I suggest that Du Bois's story is a modern retelling of the life of Jesus as recorded by the New Testament insofar as it is a story in which Jesus interrupts and confronts a world structured by racial and imperial domination and in which death becomes the new sociopolitical space of life. Working out what Ronald A. T. Judy has called a "thanatology" or a "writing of annihilation that applies the taxonomies of death in Reason (natural law) to enable the emergence of the self-reflective consciousness of the Negro" of black writing, Du Bois recasts death to be a productive (rather than merely a constricting) space of negativity, a site from which to engage in "the horrible labor of self-recognition."[25] Thus, Du Bois's life of Jesus culminates with the cross of Easter and with a reworked vision of atonement or salvation that moves beyond the vision of stratified social relations that marks Western civilization and its will to own the earth. Du Bois presents his Texan Jesus as illegitimate, and—drawing on Barthian imagery—as "God's Revolution," though largely unrecognized as such.

This theme of recognition is crucial, for the story is built around a series of recognitions and misrecognitions of Jesus, the "stranger," who appears out of nowhere at a prison to confront the guard and eventually the prison owner, a man given no name but only a military title—"the colonel." Du Bois's American prison system, which functions as a surrogate for the system of Western imperialism in relationship to the non-Western world, is not the slave system of old. Rather, it is a new form of slavery built on the criminalization of black bodies.[26] As the guard says to the stranger in the opening lines of the story in speaking of one of the black convicts, "But that nigger there is bad, a born thief, and ought to be sent up for life" (136). But immediately we see that these black convicts are really laborers within a system of white profit. "'The convicts,' [the colonel's business partner] said, 'would cost us $96 a year and board. Well, we can squeeze this so that it won't be over $125 apiece. Now if these fellows are driven, they can build this line within twelve months. It will be running by next April. Freights will fall fifty percent. Why, man, you'll be a millionaire in less than ten years'" (ibid.).

In the corner stands the stranger, softly questioning the colonel—just as the Jesus of the synoptic gospels questioned the scribes and Pharisees—and asking if the prison arrangement is good for the convicts. Feeling compelled to defend himself, the colonel turns to address the stranger; though he does not know who the stranger is, he is struck with a sense of familiarity. By contrast, when the black convict "raised his eyes and they met the eyes of the stranger," a moment of liberation ensues. He recognizes him and "the hammer fell from his hands" (137).

Although further episodes of recognition and misrecognition take place, the only one among the white folks who recognizes the stranger is the colonel's "little girl." It is she who jumps "into his lap and together they conversed in low tones all the way home" (138). The colonel and his wife puzzle over who he is, unable to glimpse him because the lights are low. But when the nurse comes to care for the little child, she switches on the light and "with one accord they all looked at the stranger." They were incensed, because their "practised eyes knew" he was not white. He was "a mulatto, surely; even if he did not own the Negro blood. . . . He was tall and straight and the coat looked like a Jewish gabardine. His hair hung in close curls far down the sides of his face and his face was olive, even yellow" (139).

This scene marks the moment of disruption, a key moment in Du Bois's envisioning of a reimagined Jesus. What is critical for my purposes is that Du Bois does *not* present a black Christ here; to present a black Christ at this moment would be to present a Christ whose identity could be construed as a cultural reflex of whiteness, as performing "the blackness whiteness created."[27] Rather, Du Bois gestures toward a reclamation of the Jewishness of Jesus.

Yet Du Bois presents a quite complex picture, for he identifies the garb of the stranger as Jewish and his body as racially ambiguous. Being neither black nor white but "olive" and "even yellow," as if Asian, the flesh of this Jesus is mulatto and thus occupies an in-between zone at the outskirts of racial purity and its logic and politics. Mulatto functions less as a racial marker and more as a point of ambiguity and even a breakdown of racial classification within the apparatuses of biopower. Although there is no incarnation scene in Du Bois's Jesus story, this moment of Jesus's mulatto identity is ripe for interpretation in relationship to the New Testament birth narratives. These narratives are stories of the ambiguity of identity located at the crossroads of the relationship, framed in terms of love, between Mary of Israel and YHWH, the God of Israel and the Gentiles. As such, these narratives rewrite the relationship between Creator and creature as a positive relation; it is only Joseph—the masculine principle, shall we say—who is set aside. They are stories of a new or re-created relationship between God and humankind—and thereby of the relationships within the social world—that takes place in the birth of Jesus. Re-creation takes place precisely by God judging, setting aside, and decentering a relationship of domination as centered in the masculine. In this act, the relationship-in-difference between Creator and creature and, as a result, the relationships-in-differences within a heterogeneous creation and among human beings are reestablished. The stories of the birth of Jesus Christ, then, present a vision and ethics of love.

Jesus's status as mulatto in Du Bois's "Jesus Christ in Texas" embodies the same impulses precisely in this Jesus's strangeness. In lodging Jesus's mulatto body—a body "that did not own the Negro blood" but with a face that "was olive, even yellow"—inside "Jewish gabardine," the story points to one whose identity disregards the boundaries established in relationship to ideal nationality and fictive ethnicity. He ignores them because he mediates a reality in which no such boundaries exist. This reality constitutes his life as a Jew. It also constitutes his strangeness, a strangeness that lies in his *being* the interruption of the imperial politics of racial and national purity. He interrupts, in other words, the identity-as-homogeneity that is central to the formation of imperial subjectivities (both colonizing and colonized).

Du Bois's Jesus is one who embraces the despised and rejected in the story—or, in the language of the New Testament, the tax collectors and sinners. Dressed in Jewish clothing, he is not known in himself; he is no *Ding-an-sich* (thing in itself). Rather, he is an intersubjective being who exists in his *being-with*—not his being-over or being-against—others (in this case, black folks). He is not just near them—although such nearness is itself significant—but, indeed, with them: he is open to, responsive to, and shares in their suffering. He does so precisely because he shares in their finitude and creatureliness. In other words, his ethics does not begin from sameness as the basis of human being, but from the ability to respond (responsibility) in love and as Neighbor to the suffering that calls out to him from them. This is the content of his being with them as their Neighbor. Having reconceived the identity of Jesus in this story and in this way, Du Bois suggests that such a Jesus can have only a fringe existence within the order of things. He exists as a being-in-responsibility toward the other, even the stranger, in their suffering. This mode of being human is a being-in-love, a new and disruptive form of social and political life, a new politics of theology.

But can this disruptive and marginal mode of existence signified by Du Bois's (and for that matter, the New Testament's) Jesus be further specified? I think it can. The interstitial zone for this disruptive mode of new life is, in fact, death outside the gates of the city, outside the place where boundaries and borders are operative and where identity is performed as enclosure. The death in view in the story of the New Testament Jesus is death on Golgotha, death at the very fringes of a world structured by the violence of purity or homogeneity. Du Bois signals this as well at the dramatic conclusion of his story. Again, it is a scene of misrecognition, this time both aural and visual.

A farmer's wife has just prepared supper for her husband and gone out from the house to visit "a neighbor." But the scene raises the question of whom we take to be a neighbor. On the way home the white wife sees "a dark figure on the doorsteps under the tall, red oak. She thought it was the new Negro until he said in a soft voice: 'Will you give me bread?' Reassured at the voice of a white man, she answered quickly in her soft, Southern tones: 'Why, certainly.'" Because of his voice, the stranger is mistaken for a white man. The white woman befriends, talks with, and gossips to him about her neighbors. The stranger asks her, "Do you like them all?" She hesitatingly says yes, "there are none I hate; no, none at all." The stranger probes further, "You love your neighbor as yourself?" (144–45 [1920]). As she is offering an affirmative response, the stranger directs her gaze to the cabin where there were black folks living. Refusing to recognize them as neighbors and thus as bound to her, she quickly rises up to get away from the stranger and his invasive questions. And as she lights the lamp, she sees that the stranger himself has a dark face. Startled, she runs away in horror and in her mad dash bumps into a black convict who is running away from the chain gang. Her husband, who sees only the end of what has transpired, accuses the black man of attacking—code for sexually assaulting—his wife. The episode then quickly becomes a lynching scene, triangulated between the strange Jesus, an about-to-be-lynched black man, and a white woman, whose domestic purity has been supposedly violated.

A mob quickly assembles to lynch the black man while the white woman is escorted to the safety of the domestic sphere, the symbolic home front of the nation. While in the sexual and reproductive space of her bedroom, she looks out of the window at the dangerous outer world beyond the home where nonwhites dwell and where white men must keep the peace—or make the world safe for democracy when things get out of order and Civilization and Freedom are under assault. As she looks out of her window, gazing upon the black man as he hangs from the tree with his body no doubt doused with fuel—in a similar scene Richard Wright in his poem "Between the World and Me" calls this the moment of "baptism by gasoline"—he is set ablaze. His burning body lights up the night sky in the shape of "a great crimson cross." Gazing at the emblazoned sky, the woman sees the stranger between her and the burning body. Just then, at the moment of the black man's death, there is recognition and thus possibility. In a moment that holds the possibility of a different kind of mediation, one that does not mimetically repeat the logic of the concrete universal and the failed, ethnic nonuniversal, the stranger stands between her and the burning man, his silhouette made one with the outstretched, torch-lit body of the black man. She mouths to herself inaudibly, "Despised and rejected of men" (allusion to Isaiah 53:3), and then through superimposition she sees "the stranger on the crimson cross, riven and bloodstained, with thorn-crowned head and pierced hands" (146). The strange Jesus did not hear her wailing; he is looking at the lynched and crucified black man. His back is to her as "his calm dark eyes, all sorrowful, were fastened on the writhing, twisting body of the thief, and a voice came out of the winds of the night, saying: 'This day thou shalt be with me in Paradise'" (146; cf. Luke 23:43).

This strange Jesus is free of the fear of death. In looking at the dying black man, he embraces his own death symbolically, for he too is seen as nonwhite. By his embracing his own death in nearness to the dying man on the cross, the possibility of a different future is opened up: this is a Jesus who does not fear or shrink before death. Thus, he is free for a future beyond the constraints of what Orlando Patterson has called "social death" so that he can enact a different strategy of death, as Zygmunt Bauman might put it.[28] His death-work is nothing less than the death of death. Were there space, I would theorize this in a Fanonian direction as the affirmation and instantiation in this strange Jesus of a violent, which is to say violating, order of love. Hence, the significance of the words of this strange Jesus in Du Bois's story, words that echo the New Testament (Luke 23:43; KJV): "This day thou shalt be with me in Paradise."

Conclusion: Atonement's Future after Political Theology

In having the strange Jesus utter these words as he faces the one who has just been lynched (and thus as he also faces the mob who has just carried out the deed), Du Bois constructs a Jesus who exists beyond death-bound subjectivity and thus beyond colonized subjectivity. This Jesus is the one who ever looks at and exists into a new life-death strategy of existence. He is the one who looks symbolically into his *own* coming death by looking into the lynched, colonized, or otherwise subjugated subjectivity of the story's black man. The light that is thrown off the burning body casts light on him, and the mob will no doubt see what the white woman saw: the stranger is not white. This strange Jesus thus sees his own death in the death of the lynched black man. He sees his own being as a being-in-response or a being-in-response-ability to another. In this highly compressed concluding scene of the story, we see that something survives modernity's imperialized death contract.

The futurity that concludes "Jesus Christ in Texas" and functions as the basis of a politics of hope puts this story beyond the pale of the false eschatology or vision of utopia that animates the religious logic that has animated Western civil society and that I have meditated on in this chapter. This moment of future potentiality from within the space of death extends a tradition of African American writing that goes from the slave narratives all the way through to the writings of authors such as Richard Wright and Toni Morrison. Drawing on the work of Jacques Lacan but bending Lancan toward the position of blackness, shall we say, Abdul JanMohamed has discerned within these writings a "future anterior" for postcolonial subjects. JanMohamed brilliantly articulates what this means:

> From a psychoanalytic viewpoint, the perspective made available by the structure of the future anterior plays a crucial role in the "cure" of the patient and in freeing him from the tyranny of external determination. And it does so, according to Lacan, because of its function in determining the identity of the subject: "I identify myself in language, but only by losing myself in it like an object. What is realized in my history is not the past definite of what was, since it is no more, or even the present perfect of what has been in what I am, but the future anterior of what I shall have been for what I am in the process of becoming." According to this view, the "truth" of the analysand's life is not simply determined in a mechanical fashion by past events; rather, he is brought by the analyst to a point where he can acknowledge that this truth also *depends* on the future, the nature of which is governed by his evolving desires, knowledge, commitments, and investments and, above all, by his choices. The efficacy of the subject's past history is determining, but that determination is drastically modified and, hence, in turn, determined by the subject's present and future choices and actions.[29]

Here, says JanMohamed, is the "kind of trajectory that [one] who just has experienced his symbolic-death must take up in order to overcome his own determination by the culture of social-death" or the culture set in place by imperial Man (296).

This notion of the future anterior can help us rethink salvation and atonement as a social process that entails rethinking the identity of Jesus as uncoupled from or as crucified unto the West. In other words, the notion is a caesura within the religious logic of the West and of the modern world. Indeed, it is just this caesura or rupture in civil society and in the political ontology or structural order of the West that Aimé Césaire and Frantz Fanon call "the end of the world" and that the latter theorizes under the rubric of "violence."[30] I want to suggest that Barth's interpretation of the "shalt" in his reflections on "Thou shalt love thy neighbor" (a phrase that appears in Romans 13:9) accords with Du Bois's closing scene and with JanMohamed's use of the "anterior future" and further still with Césairean and Fanonian or decolonial eschatology. Barth writes in his Romans commentary:

> Love is "eternal, levelling righteousness" (Kierkegaard). . . . Love is not the EROS that lusteth ever, it is AGAPE that never faileth.
>
> For this reason, then—*Thou* SHALT *love thy neighbour.* Understood strictly as the action of the NEW man, love is duty; and as such, it is protected against caprice and disappointment and misuse. In this *Thou shalt* every divine *Thou shalt not*—*not commit adultery; not kill; not steal; not covet* (Exod. xx.13–17, Deut. v.17)—is summed up! . . . In this *Thou shalt!* there is manifested the flaming sword of death and of eternity. Therefore love is in itself perfect: it is the NEW doing, THE new doing, which is the meaning and fulfillment of all "not-doing." Love is the breath we breathe when, in the realm of evil, we have no breath left.[31]

Barth elaborates on how living into this love means living by a future that disrupts and reorients the present: "Love, because it sets up no idol, is the demolition of every idol. Love is the destruction of everything that is—*like God*: the end of all hierarchies and authorities and intermediaries, because, in every particular man and also in the 'Many,' it addresses itself, without fear of contradiction—to the One."[32] In short, love is the "protest against the course of this world," and Jesus Christ, argues Barth, *is* the telling of this tale that "has occurred, does occur, and will occur."[33] A statement such as this lies at the heart of Barth's effort to rework Christian eschatology in the *Römerbrief* to counter the false, post–WWI utopianism built on a "progress" grounded in the West as *eschaton* (both as goal and path), an *eschaton* secured by the false mediation of Western Man as an imperial God-Man. "A Christianity," Barth writes, "that is not eschatology, completely and without remainder, has absolutely nothing to do with Christ" (314; translation modified).

More work certainly remains to be done in developing this line of argumentation, particularly in rethinking social sacrifice or atonement (to use a more strictly theological vocabulary) and further interrogating the eschatological imaginary internal to modernity's political imaginary. I hope that I have provided an impetus for such future work.[34]

Notes

1. Eric J. Hobsbawm, *The Age of Extremes: A History of the World, 1914–1991* (New York: Vintage Books, 1996), 22.

2. I've offered "cultural Protestantism" as a rather literal or wooden translation of *Kulturprotestantismus*, though it defies easy English translation. *Kulturprotestantismus* represents a synthesis of a mode of interiorized and intellectualized religion of a distinctly Protestant sort and modern progressive elite culture in Germany. This synthesis reached its height during the era of the Wilhelmine Empire (1890–1914). The result of the synthesis was that German Protestantism and German culture functioned in lockstep. Together they were a single social reality and social program. Thus, *Kulturprotestantismus* represents the fusion of religious subjectivity and the subject of civil society in the absence of political subjectivity. The academic and church-based discourses of theology (in Germany, these were not separable) provided the intellectual architecture of this fusion. Thus, theologians and scholars of religion, such as Adolph von Harnack, served vitally in the role of what we would now call "public intellectuals."

3. Benedict Anderson, *Imagined Communities: Reflections on the Origin and Spread of Nationalism*, rev. ed. (London: Verso, 1991), 6.

4. Fredric Jameson, *The Political Unconscious* (Ithaca, NY: Cornell University Press, 1981).

5. Étienne Balibar and Immanuel Wallerstein, *Race, Nation, Class: Ambiguous Identities* (London: Verso, 1991), 93–94.

6. Ibid., 95.

7. Ibid., 96.

8. Ibid.

9. Alys Eve Weinbaum, *Wayward Reproductions: Genealogies of Race and Nation in Transatlantic Modern Thought* (Durham, NC: Duke University Press, 2004), 7.

10. Rey Chow, *The Protestant Ethnic and the Spirit of Capitalism* (New York: Columbia University Press, 2002), 101.

11. Claudia Koonz, *The Nazi Conscience* (Cambridge, MA: Belknap Press of Harvard University Press, 2003).

12. Susanne Zantop, *Colonial Fantasies: Conquest, Family, and Nation in Precolonial Germany, 1770–1870* (Durham, NC: Duke University Press, 1997), 7.

13. Karl Barth and Eduard Thurneysen, *Revolutionary Theology in the Making; Barth-Thurneysen Correspondence, 1914–1925* (Richmond, VA: John Knox Press, 1964), 26.

14. Ibid.

15. Karl Barth, *The Word of God and the Word of Man*, trans. Douglas Horton (1924; repr., New York: Harper, 1957), 18–19. Further references are cited parenthetically in the text.

16. George Hunsinger, "Toward a Radical Barth," in *Karl Barth and Radical Politics*, ed. George Hunsinger (Philadelphia: Westminster Press, 1976), 203.

17. Karl Barth, *The Epistle to the Romans*, trans. Edwyn C. Hoskyns (London: Oxford University Press, 1968), 44.

18. Mark Lilla, *The Stillborn God: Religion, Politics, and the Modern West* (New York: Knopf, 2007).

19. Barth, *Epistle to the Romans*, 10, translation modified.

20. Michel Foucault, *The Order of Things: An Archeology of the Human Sciences* (New York: Pantheon Books, 1970), xxv, 422.

21. Barth, *Epistle to the Romans*, 166–67. Further references are cited parenthetically in the text.

22. W. E. B. Du Bois, *Darkwater: Voices from within the Veil* (Amherst, NY: Humanity Books, 2003). Original edition, 1920. Further references are cited parenthetically in the text (2003 edition unless otherwise noted).

23. See Amy Kaplan, *The Anarchy of Empire in the Making of U.S. Culture* (Cambridge, MA: Harvard University Press, 2002).

24. From "African Roots of War," quoted in Amy Kaplan, *Anarchy of Empire*, 171.

25. Ronald A. T. Judy, *(Dis)forming the American Canon: African-Arabic Slave Narratives and the Vernacular* (Minneapolis: University of Minnesota Press, 1993), 89, 85.

26. Du Bois anticipates the vital work of such contemporary intellectuals as Angela Y. Davis and Michelle Alexander. See Angela Davis, *Are Prisons Obsolete?* (New York: Seven Stories Press, 2003); and Michelle Alexander, *The New Jim Crow: Mass Incarceration in the Age of Colorblindness* (New York: New Press, 2010).

27. Victor Anderson, *Beyond Ontological Blackness: An Essay on African American Religious and Cultural Criticism* (New York: Continuum International Publishing, 1995).

28. Orlando Patterson, *Slavery and Social Death: A Comparative Study* (Cambridge, MA: Harvard University Press, 1982); Zygmunt Bauman, *Mortality, Immortality, and Other Life Strategies* (Cambridge, UK: Polity Press, 1992).

29. Abdul R. JanMohamed, *The Death-Bound-Subject: Richard Wright's Archaeology of Death* (Durham, NC: Duke University Press, 2005), 296. The reference to Jacques Lacan comes from *Écrits: A Selection*, trans. Alan Sheridan (New York: Norton, 1982), 86.

30. After summarizing the conditions of social death that marked the lives of his fellow Martinicans as part of working out his poetic thanatology of negritude, the narrator in Césaire's *Cahier d'un retour au pays natal* asks:

Qu'y puis-je?
Il faut bien commencer.
Commencer quoi?

What can I do?
Well, one has to start somewhere.
But start what?

The answer comes:

La seule chose au monde qu'il vaille la peine de commencer:
La Fin du monde parbleu.

The only thing in the world worth starting:
The End of the World, of course. (trans. mine)

See the bilingual edition of Aimé Césaire, *Notebook of a Return to My Native Land / Cahier d'un retour au pays natal* (Newcastle, UK: Bloodaxe, 1995), 98. Frantz Fanon restates this call for the end of the world in *Black Skin, White Masks* (New York: Grove Press, 2008), 191, and, I contend, elaborates this decolonial eschatology in more detail under the rubric of "violence" in the first chapter of *The Wretched of the Earth* (New York: Grove Press, 2004).

31. Barth, *Epistle to the Romans*, 496.

32. Ibid.

33. Ibid., 497, 498.

34. The argument presented in this chapter is further developed in my article "An Unlikely Convergence: W. E. B. Du Bois, Karl Barth, and the Problem of the Imperial God-Man," *CR: The New Centennial Review* (forthcoming).

CHAPTER 4

THERE ARE NO CLEAN SOULS

The Promise and Perils of Political Theology in

The Souls of Black Folk

JONATHON S. KAHN

There was a time, a recent time, when the idea of confronting W. E. B. Du Bois in a volume on race and political theology would have seemed absurd. Du Bois has long been characterized as lacking a serious religious dimension. The best twentieth-century scholarship on Du Bois—work by David Levering Lewis, Arnold Rampersad, Shamoon Zamir, and Adolph Reed—pronounced Du Bois and his writings as somewhere between unreligious and antireligious.[1] For most scholars, Du Bois stood as a twentieth-century ideal type for Weber's secularization narrative: As a child Du Bois came under the influence of religion, but as he matured into an adult, he put an end to his childish ways (as the scripture goes). There has been little room for the notion that Du Bois had something theological to offer; there has been little room for the notion that his theology affects his political vision; thus, there has been little room for thinking of Du Bois in terms of political theology.

Times have changed. Scholars of the early twenty-first century have begun radically reappraising the role and place of religious sensibilities, moods, rhetoric, and modalities in Du Bois's writings.[2] What has emerged is a Du Bois whose work is thoroughly inhabited by religious resources— a rich world of biblical rhetoric, religious virtues, invocations of Christ, and prayers. I've argued elsewhere that Du Bois's religious sensibilities were distinctly heterodox, deeply uncomfortable with religious institutions and their normative creedal commitments.[3] Du Bois's religious imagination was decidedly antimetaphysical, resisting at every turn questions about the afterlife, antecedent realities, or God's nature and power to effect change. As it was for Nietzsche, a certain type of God—imperious, authoritative, historically determinative—was dead for Du Bois. Du Bois's God lacked the power to intervene in history and actively shape it: "I do not believe that there is a personal conscious King of the world who will, upon fitting petition from me, change the course of world events to suit my needs or wishes."[4] For Du Bois, God was distant and opaque.[5]

Do not think, however, that because God for Du Bois is remote and hidden that Du Bois does not have a theology: "The argument for keeping God at a distance is itself a *theological* argument about where God resides, about the whole."[6] Do not also think that a hidden God has no political ramifications. Du Bois wrote about and used, to devastating political and moral effect, a historically ineffectual God. Du Bois persists with God-talk in order existentially and rhetorically to instill a proper sense of dependence and humility, and that, in turn, fires the appropriate type of moral and political activism and reform: "Remember with us tonight, O God, the homes that own us all. Make us true to the fathers and mothers of these children here—true to their hopes and ideals."[7] Paradoxically, God's very reclusiveness and obscurity direct Du Bois to the human communities that give our lives shape. Du Bois uses notions of Godly justice and sacrifice to begin to inspire fallible human efforts to create human modes of justice and moral sacrifice. In other words, honoring the theological reality of God's reclusiveness and obscurity is, for Du Bois, a primary political virtue.

The first goal of this essay, then, is to assert Du Bois as a political theologian, and to do this, I have to argue for a reformed notion of political theology, one that is distinct from theocratic political theology with its desires to give the nation over exclusively to God's anointed, whoever they may be. My attempt to do this gestures to George Shulman's distinction, in this volume's final essay, between antidemocratic forms of prophecy that cling to redemptive narratives and democratic prophetic voices that eschew redemption and instead urge us to see acknowledging finitude as a modern moral virtue.

The second goal is to give an account of the political theology of Du Bois's most renowned text, *The Souls of Black Folk*. My central claim is that *Souls* intervenes in the religio-political tradition of American exceptionalism. This dominant tradition of American political thought assumes that sui generis God favors the American experiment, that America is a place of unique religious destiny. Herman Melville captures this spirit exactly in claiming that "America is the Israel of our time; we bear the ark of liberties of the world."[8] Traditionally, scholars have enfolded or assimilated African American uses of jeremiadic religious rhetoric into this tradition.[9] African Americans, so this line of thinking goes, did not contest the religio-political myths about America as a new Jerusalem and a shining city on the hill; they simply wanted to be an equal part of it. Against this, I argue that the political theology of *Souls* dramatically resists the bald exceptionalism of white America by claiming that American exceptionalism is itself a form of white supremacy. In this way, the work that I see Du Bois doing in *Souls* leads directly to this volume's essay by J. Kameron Carter on Du Bois's internationalist critique in *Darkwater* of "the White Global Masculine, the problem of Imperial Man."

Finally, the third effort deals with the peculiar role that Jews play in *Souls*. As scholars of *Souls* know, the original 1903 edition contained eight references to Jews. All of them were derogatory, trafficking in classic European anti-Semitic stereotypes. Jews in *Souls* are "shrewd," "unscrupulous," and "enterprising" and reliant on "deception and flattery . . . cajoling and lying."[10] As scholars of *Souls* also know, Du Bois eliminated these derogatory references to Jews for the 1953 Fiftieth Anniversary Jubilee Edition. I am interested in these references not because I seek to indict Du Bois or *Souls* as anti-Semitic. Instead, I am interested in asking questions about the political theological work done by the presence or absence of Jews in the text. How do Du Bois's references to Jews affect the text's larger political theological project of rewriting divinely sanctioned American exceptionalism?

A Note on Political Theology

There is a secularist vein of liberalism—Richard Rorty and John Rawls are fair representatives[11]—that finds the very idea of political theology anathema. In this vein, theology and anything that smacks of the transcendent do not belong in democratic politics; politics and theology are structurally opposed. Properly understood, democratic politics, following Hannah Arendt, renounces the authority of absolutes and rests solely on the practice of human-made promises and agreement.[12] In this view, theology always recurs to transcendent anchors whose authority is unquestioned and unquestionable. Because democracy demands corrigible authority, theology is fundamentally incompatible with democracy. A syllogism underwrites this logic: Political theology is exclusively the way of theocrats, theocracy is inherently anti-democratic, and therefore political theology is against democratic practices.

This is a faulty syllogism. I will grant that all theocrats practice anti-democratic politics. Jeffrey Stout succinctly captures the necessary conflict between theocracy and democracy: "The ideal of a democratic republic holds that political power is to be shared by the entire citizenry and that no one is to be denied citizenship simply because of his or her religious beliefs or lack thereof. Theocracy holds that God's representatives on earth should rule everyone else. Democracy and theocracy are therefore at odds."[13] But if theocratic politics are not welcome within democracies, political theologians are. There is nothing incompatible in either holding theological commitments or using theological language and democratic practices. The list of Americans committed to democracy who held theological commitments or relied on theological language is near endless. Not all political theology or political theologians are theocratic.

This points to a further problem with the logic of secularist liberals: the assertion that all authorities in democratic life must be corrigible. Democracy does not demand this. The lesson of Tocqueville's *Democracy in America* is that citizens in a democracy can and will rely on any sort of authority they like. Tocqueville, in particular, found the ways in which Americans recurred to God to be essential to the success of the young American democracy. Tocqueville teaches that all democratic citizens should expect that (1) not all citizens will rely on the same sorts of authorities, (2) holding political office does not require believing in a certain sort of authority, (3) any citizen has the right to question the authorities used by other citizens, and (4) common "habits of the heart" among citizens are necessary for a democracy to work well.

Americans of all religious and political stripes like to gnash teeth over these habits, despair that they are eroding, and issue calls for statements of principle and belief.[14] But it is a mistake to think that "habits of the heart" are necessarily beliefs; they rarely are. They are practices—doings, which do not rely on fully articulated theoretical explanations. Talal Asad writes of religious belief: "It is a modern idea that a practitioner cannot know how to live religiously without being able to articulate that knowledge."[15] Something similar can also be said about the democratic citizen; she can know how to live democratically solely by engaging in democratic practices without needing to verbalize their nature abstractly. In other words, the corrigibility, which is to say the intelligibility, of authority is often not the issue within democratic life. The practices we engage in often are. Americans have long learned to live with neighbors whose beliefs they find false and untruthful yet with whom they find common grounds for principled political practice.

Shulman's *American Prophecy* powerfully argues that American prophets for racial equality—from Frederick Douglass to Henry David Thoreau to Martin Luther King Jr.—make a crucial distinction between *justifying* and *enacting* theological truth. Justification seeks to secure logical, theological proof—with the hope of convincing others of the theological truth itself. Enacting theological truth seeks social practices "without which a form of life is unimaginable and impossible."[16] The political theology of prophets for racial equality was "not epistemological in character . . . [did] not address 'knowing' God as a problem to be solved" but demanded "conflict about constitutive practices," practices that did not respect uncompromising notions of human equality or human dignity.[17] Think of the way King constantly sketched evocative visions of an America that treated the races equally; he wasn't trying to convince America to believe in God but was using his belief in God to shift the patterns, habits, and, yes, laws by which Americans lived. The language of God points not to God but to unjust social conditions. This emphasis on forms of life—on doings that build the sorts of communities and practices that we cannot do without—reframes matters from the apodictic to the social.

At its base, then, political theology is simply the use of religious sensibilities to inform political vision. As Mark Lilla writes, "When human beings have reflected on political questions they have appealed to God when answering them. Their thinking has taken the form of political theology."[18] Oliver O'Donovan's account of political theology refines matters further: "The name 'political theology' is generally given to proposals . . . which draw out an earthly political discourse from the political language of religious discourse."[19] O'Donovan helps close the captious gap between religion and politics; religious language is often already political. Most important, note what political theology is *not* in these accounts: It is not the attempt to bring the rule of the City of God on earth; it is not the attempt to make humans live according to God's laws. In this vein, O'Donovan emphasizes that "the proper goal of political theology is [not] to describe a set of political *institutions*; for political institutions are anyway too fluid to assume an ideal form."[20]

Seeing Du Bois as a political theologian, then, does work on two important fronts. In terms of political theory, Du Bois helps us better understand the way religion and democracy interact virtuously. And in terms of politics, Du Bois helps us argue against the new atheists' pernicious claims that all God-fearing folk are illiberal theocrats. At the same time, Du Bois (along with any number of other American prophets) stands as an example for those God-fearing religious folk who worry that the pluralistic demands of democracy are incompatible with holding religious commitments.

My crucial point is this: It is past time that democratically minded citizens claim "political theology" for themselves. To be sure, political theology is not innocuous. Amid their cant and vitriol, new atheists such as Christopher Hitchens and Sam Harris do raise legitimate fears about the connections between religion, violence, and viciously illiberal forms of politics. But there is nothing necessarily threatening to democratic life in political theology. Those of us interested in racial justice need to come to terms with what appears to amount to the historical necessity of political theologies in American life: "To face race in America is to be compelled toward prophecy."[21] How do political theologies instantiate the political project of protecting all citizens, of "remed[ying]" the American "systemic derangement about what (and who) we count as real"?[22] Du Bois's *The Souls of Black Folk* is a good place to search for answers.

The Souls of Black Folk *and*
Rewriting American Exceptionalism

Du Bois's *The Souls of Black Folk* was published in 1903, at a time that Michael Dawson describes as Du Bois's "radically egalitarian" period, in which a "severe critique of racism in American society" was coupled with "an impassioned appeal for America to live up to the best of its values."[23] Dawson is not wrong in his characterization. *Souls* is a text that in profound ways is committed to a form of political liberalism. Throughout, Du Bois champions liberal ideals of universal suffrage, freedom, self-determination, and equal opportunity and access. Indeed, nowhere does Du Bois imagine a separatist black nationalist politics.

At the same time, there is something potentially misleading in labeling *Souls* as unremittingly "liberal" and "egalitarian." As Nikhil Pal Singh argues, these terms are racially coded, their use implicitly invoking a complex set of assumptions about America and race. To call African American texts or public figures "liberal" implicitly commits them to a narrative of American triumph over racial injustice, "allow[ing] Americans not only to celebrate their progress into a more inclusive and tolerant people, but also tell[ing] themselves that this is who they always were."[24]

The problem is that this understanding of "liberal" and "egalitarian," particularly in relation to *Souls*, obscures the ways that these same liberal and egalitarian commitments can function to dramatically resist and contest mythic forms of American exceptionalism. Shulman's discussion of the "radical" Martin Luther King Jr. is a rare reading that does not insist that King had to abandon in toto his "liberal" aspirations in order to radically dissent from the myth of a redemptive America. Shulman makes clear that liberal notions such as democracy, opportunity, rights, and godliness figure centrally in King's radical rhetoric. The "radical" King held on to liberal ideals, even a national frame and a vision of American aspirations, in trying to expose an America that was from its start committed to racial exclusion and injustice. King was not trying to eliminate America. He was, however, trying to rewrite America: "as King puts black aspiration into the rhetoric of national promise, he 'blackens' this promise."[25] America would become America only when it was no longer committed to the myth of "America."

This frame of the radical King, who holds on to liberal idioms such as legal justice and democratic rights in the service of challenging American exceptionalism, is a very useful one for reading the political theology of *Souls*. In *Souls*, Du Bois uses a tremendously variegated language of spirituality, religion, and classical liberalism to craft an extremely radical project of rereading and rewriting America. Said slightly differently, *Souls* needs to be understood as a text committed to liberal reform—by this I mean reform of political, cultural, and legal structures committed to securing rights and opportunity. At the same time, through Du Bois's renderings of "the strange meaning of being black here in the dawning of the Twentieth Century," Du Bois exposes the limits of the liberal project: "The bright ideals of the past,—physical freedom, political power, the training of brains and the training of hands,—all these in turn have waxed and waned, until even the last grows dim and overcast. Are they all wrong,—all false? No, not that, but each alone was over-simple and incomplete."[26] *Souls* shows that the autonomous self-legislating self is neither possible nor desirable when it comes to dealing with the American color line. Resisting progressivism in the tradition of what Christopher Lasch has called New Radicalism, the essential and monumental effort of *Souls* is to render visible black political and cultural subjectivity.

The purpose of this effort is not to argue for legal procedure that is just; this, Du Bois assumes, is a given demand and not something he is going to abandon. No, the deeper purpose of *Souls* is Nietzschean, that is, deeply genealogical in nature: It is to change the larger historical narrative that America tells about itself, to show the way traditional values rest on obscured but all too real "violent forms of human action based on pervasive delusions."[27] Black Americans, *Souls* insists, must be made part of the American imaginary. The combination of the two—executing fair and just practices *and* lifting up black political subjectivity so that it can be accounted for in the national narrative—is required for dealing with the problem of the color line: "The power of the ballot we need in sheer self-defence,—else what shall save us from a second slavery? Freedom, too, the long-sought, we still seek,—the freedom of life and limb, the freedom to work and think, the freedom to love and aspire. Work, culture, liberty,—all these we need, not singly but together, not successively but together, each growing and aiding each, and all striving toward that vaster ideal that swims before the Negro people, the ideal of human brotherhood, gained through the unifying ideal of Race."[28]

The idea that *Souls* rephrases what it means for black and white Americans to be American is not original regarding readings of *Souls*. What is new, and beginning to become more broadly recognized, is that Du Bois affects this type of rewriting of the American narrative through religious modalities and means. *This is the political theology of Souls.* I am arguing that the primary way that Du Bois renders the black imaginary visible and then in-corporates it into the larger American imaginary is through religious inter-pretation. Religion—either through his focus on the history and practices of African American religion or his use of religious language—is the set of levers by which Du Bois practices his genealogical ways. How Du Bois talks about God is absolutely fundamental to his attack on the myth of a Godly America that extends liberal protections to all of its citizens. Du Bois's heady and almost percussive combination of religion, democracy, and liberal rights makes *Souls* a classic text of radical American liberalism.

In the wake of genealogical critique comes the opportunity for new narratives and new values. What are the new narrative and values of *Souls*? How does Du Bois do the work that I say he does? I make two claims. The first is that Du Bois uses religion to argue against white America's claim that God has sanctioned America's so-called liberal freedoms; in fact, Du Bois says, God is ready to curse America. The second is that Du Bois uses religion to assess the nature and contributions of black America to this country's history. By thinking through what Du Bois calls African Ameri-can spiritual contributions, he insists that black America embodies the true spirit of American democracy.

Both of these interventions—into the narrative that white America tells about itself and the narrative that black America tells about itself—are bat-tles against a deeply seated white supremacy that sees whites not simply as more human than blacks but as *divinely understood* as more human. This noxious notion represents, following Edward Blum's reading, a "white su-premacist theology," and it was pervasive at the turn of the century: "By 1900, white supremacist theology was firmly rooted in white American mainstream culture. Its arguments and ways of perceiving the world perme-ated scientific, missionary, and literary discourse in the United States." In one of the most important passages ever written about *Souls*, Blum locates the terrain of the text's political theology:

> [Du Bois] fashioned a new set of conceptual tools for champions of equality and social justice. Read in dialogue with the religious battle over the sacred status of whites and blacks, *Souls* stood as a spectacular intervention, an act of religious defiance and theological creation at the very same moment. Du Bois attacked white supremacists by reversing their spiritual and racialized assessment of the world. With *Souls* Du Bois tried to tear apart the confla-

tion of whiteness and godliness and, conversely, to connect blackness with
the divine. In Du Bois's hands, the story of Africans in America was one that
demonstrated that white society, not black society, was morally corrupt and
that people of color possessed souls that had much to teach humanity.[29]

This rewiring, in a sense, of the American account of divine favor is the
thrust of Du Bois's American genealogy. Through it he lays deeper claims
to the American republic. At the same time, to effect this rewiring, Du Bois
does not simply invert the values of white supremacist theology. That is, if in
Souls Du Bois connects blackness with the divine, he pointedly does not do
so by insisting that blacks are inherently divinely favored. African Americans
have, in a sense, earned their spiritual favor by their experiences and activities or, as Eddie Glaude might say, their "doings and sufferings."[30] Divine
favor is not sui generis. Nor it is it even *favor* exactly, at least in the sense that
divine sanction is somehow inherent. African Americans are exceptional,
but the account Du Bois gives of their humanity is not exceptionalist. This
is the crucial way in which Du Bois rewrites American exceptionalism.

For example, when Du Bois writes of the role that slave spirituals play
in America, he emphasizes the *contingency* of their spiritual excellence: "And
so by fateful chance the Negro folk-song—the rhythmic cry of the slave—
stands to-day not simply as the sole American music, but as the most beautiful expression of human experience born this side the seas."[31] And, in
his chapter on the African American religious thinker Alexander Crummell, Du Bois offers up a prayer of human catholicity: "The nineteenth was
the first century of human sympathy,—the age when half wonderingly we
began to descry in others that transfigured spark of divinity which we call
Myself; . . . when [Negroes] became throbbing souls whose warm pulsing
life touched us so nearly that we half gasped with surprise, crying, 'Thou
too! Hast Thou seen Sorrow and the dull waters of Hopelessness? Hast
Thou known Life?'" Du Bois does not use divinity here to aspire to metaphysical heights; there is no triumphalism in his voice. He contests white
supremacist theology with an account of the religious significance of suffering and despair. The virtues of this passage subvert the entire economy of
white American exceptionalism.

Finally, and most radically, in *Souls* Du Bois invokes divinity in an effort
to remake and rebuild larger American national claims. There is a crucial

passage that embodies this work, a passage that sublimely mixes the language of religion with the language of the nation:

> Your country? How came it yours? Before the Pilgrims landed we were here. Here we have brought our three gifts and mingled them with yours: a gift of story and song—soft, stirring melody in an ill-harmonized and unmelodious land; the gift of sweat and brawn to beat back the wilderness, conquer the soil, and lay the foundation of this vast economic empire two hundred years earlier than your weak hands could have done it; the third, a gift of the Spirit. Around us the history of the land has centred for thrice a hundred years; out of the nation's heart we have called all that was best to throttle and subdue all that was worst; fire and blood, prayer and sacrifice, have billowed over this people, and they have found peace only in the altars of the God of Right. Nor has our gift of the Spirit been merely passive. Actively we have woven ourselves with the very warp and woof of this nation,—we fought their battles, shared their sorrow, mingled our blood with theirs, and generation after generation have pleaded with a headstrong, careless people to despise not Justice, Mercy, and Truth, lest the nation be smitten with a curse. Our song, our toil, our cheer, and warning have been given to this nation in blood-brotherhood. Are not these gifts worth the giving? Is not this work and striving? Would America have been America without her Negro people?[32]

This passage is saturated with religious language and imagery: Prayer, spirit, altar, curse, and spirit all resonate theologically. At the same time, this passage is devoted to the project of nation: Du Bois's interest here is in the American identity and refashioning the nature of national experience. What is exceptional about this passage is the way Du Bois is able to combine the two—religion and the nation—to undermine white American exceptionalism. Improbably, he takes the critical constituent elements of the most noxious form of American political theology and produces a political theology of democratic hope and possibility. Religion, in this passage, is put in service not of divine triumph but a type of democratic pluralism. To be sure, it is a castigating pluralism: Du Bois offers brotherhood to white America on the condition that it recognize its own weaknesses and black America's strengths. God here is never a redemptive force; in fact, the divine is most present in the threat of a curse on the nation. Mostly, divinity is distant; what is proximal are human efforts to try to live up to a divine standard. The result is that never does Du Bois suggest that America is divinely approved or ratified. There is nothing in this that is exclusive or special to America; there is nothing in this that speaks to a special place that America occupies in the divine cosmos. For Du Bois, God's favor, if it is ever earned, will be utterly novel.

Shulman does not include a chapter on Du Bois, but Du Bois easily belongs to the tradition of American prophets he traces. Prophets function, Shulman writes, "by founding political community on covenants, which create a theater of appearance for action, a constitutional frame for contest, and a collective subject liable for its action."[33] In other words, prophets need defined communities to speak to. In turn, the prophetic action of *Souls* relies on a nationally framed covenantal community. Du Bois cannot do his work in *Souls*—the work of rewriting the national story for black and for white—without the nation, the American nation. What prophets like Du Bois show is that it is possible to produce a politics—a political theology—that is democratic and committed to local forms of identification, including national politics, without engaging in religiously nationalistic demagoguery. A Du Boisian political theology provides the possibility of an American nation that worships something other than itself.

Du Bois's Jewish Problem

From the moment of its publication, *Souls* stunned readers not simply with its lyricism and beauty but with a type of moral force. *Souls* was and is a text on the side of righteousness and justice, and to this day, readers cannot fail to be moved by the way the text remonstrates and then expands the American account of who counts as fully human.

It is thus notable that there are eight places in *Souls* where Du Bois makes specific reference to Jews, and all them are vilifying. In *Souls*, the Jew is represented as the "heir to the slave-baron." Du Bois depicts Jews as leaping into a power vacuum post-Reconstruction, capitalizing on social chaos. Jews seize land and "squeeze more blood from debt-cursed tenants" through mercenary ways.[34] Jews, as Du Bois portrays them, assume roles long held by whites. Is it too much to suggest that Du Bois's charges against Jews are that they have become a signifier of all that it means to be "white"?

In the decades after publication of *Souls*, philanthropist Jacob Schiff, Rabbi Steven Wise, and historian Morris U. Schappes all pointed out the offending passages to Du Bois.[35] At first, Du Bois "stoutly denied" the impression of anti-Semitism in his work,[36] and the ugly references to Jews remained until

Du Bois began to prepare a Fiftieth Anniversary Jubilee Edition for the Blue Heron Press. In a letter to Herbert Aptheker, Du Bois acknowledged that his references to Jews were "unjustly maligning a people in exactly the same way my folk were then and now falsely accused."[37] Du Bois first resolved to change these passages, and then, in a curious train of logic, he vacillated. Though "even unconscious repetition of current folklore such as the concept of Jews as more guilty of exploitation than others had helped the Hitlers of the world," and though "my first impulse was to eliminate all those references to Jews," Du Bois concluded: "But this I finally realized would be historically inaccurate. I have therefore with some regret let the passages stand as written believing that other references to Jews in this very book and my evident personal indebtedness to Jewish culture will absolve me from blame and unfairness."[38] Yet he reconsidered once again and finally eliminated all derogatory references to Jews for the 1953 edition. Interestingly, in the foreword to the Jubilee Edition, "Fifty Years Later," Du Bois speaks in only the most generic terms about the "less than half-dozen alterations in word or phrase and then not to change my thought as previously set down but to avoid any possible misunderstanding today of what I meant to say yesterday."[39] Indeed, in making no reference to the specific changes he made, Du Bois, it might be said, seeks to erase even the trace of anti-Semitism.

What are we to make of the original references to Jews in *Souls* and Du Bois's subsequent emendations? I find little value in contemplating them if they are used to make fundamental pronouncements on the anti-Semitism of *Souls* or of Du Bois. In our modern moment, claims of anti-Semitism are totalizing; they have the effect of elevating concerns about Jews above all others. In truth, the anti-Semitic passages in *Souls* are not only few but marginal to the main effort of the text to rewrite the narrative on African American contributions to American life. And, as Du Bois hoped, from all of the other evidence of his relationships to Jews—from his friendships, to expressions of sympathy with Jews under Nazi Germany, to his support of Jewish Palestine and the creation of the state of Israel—Du Bois has no need to defend himself against the charge of anti-Semitism.[40]

However, I find myself still interested in these passages, interested, that is, in asking further questions about how they might possibly relate to the whole. It is, I think, compelling to ask how or whether these references to

Jews affect what I see as efforts in *Souls* to intervene in a white Christian theology of American exceptionalism. In other words, is there a way in which the presence, and then absence, of Jews in the text affects what I see as the overriding political theology in *Souls*?

Scholarly questions about these passages have been rare. I have found only one full-length treatment of Du Bois's references to Jews, Michael Kramer's essay "W. E. B. Du Bois, American Nationalism, and the Jewish Question." In the main, scholars have been quick to dismiss Du Bois's maligning references to Jews as an all-too-human example of the way even the most stalwart defender of minorities was subject to the ethos of a larger anti-Semitic discourse. Typical are comments like these from Blum: "Even Du Bois, it appears in this case, in 1903 was a captive to his social and religious culture."[41] Nothing more follows.

This only begins to scratch the surface. What more explicitly is this social and religious culture to which Du Bois is in thrall? I suggest that Du Bois's anti-Semitic comments speak not of a culture of American anti-Semitism but of American nationalism. As I have emphasized previously, *Souls* is nothing if not a *national* text. When Du Bois uses his national notions to disrupt American exceptionalism, his nationalism is felicitous. In *Divine Discontent*, I go to further lengths to show the way that Du Bois uses national notions to imagine a cohesive, self-reliant black American political community; for these ends, Du Bois's nationalism also works propitiously. But nationalism, we need no reminding, is dangerously labile. What the Jewish passages in *Souls* should remind us of is that all nationalisms can turn vicious. Du Bois's noble efforts to disrupt white Christian American nationalism function in these moments as an exclusionary, nativistic nationalism.

What are the roots of this type of Du Boisian nationalism? Kramer insists on seeing these troubling passages in *Souls* as evidence that Du Bois's nationalism derives from the baneful tradition of Treitschkean German nationalism: "In *The Souls of Black Folk* is Treitschke's Jew—the quintessential figure of otherness, the scourge of nationalism, the telltale mark of Du Bois's intellectual roots in German philosophy."[42] I have my doubts about this. First, nowhere does Du Bois ever express any sympathy with Treitschke's politics, which were abominably racist. Lewis tells us explicitly that, while in Germany, Du Bois was dismayed by hearing Treitschke lecture.[43] Second, as Kramer acknowledges, to the degree that German notions of *Volk* and nation appear in Du Bois, they emerge in substantially altered forms that directly and deeply appeal to a tradition of American liberalism and egalitarianism. Du Bois's use of the idea of "folk" is deracinated from an oppressive Herderian metaphysics that endows *Volk* with characteristic essences that defy historical processes. Throughout *Souls* and throughout the vast length of his career, Du Bois consistently renounces the notion that black people represent in essence any one thing, any one set of pursuits or ideals.[44] This, of course, is not to deny that black people's experience, their doings and sufferings, have provided unifying pursuits and ideals. Black people do have gifts to give, and some of them are of the spirit, as Du Bois said. But Du Bois constructs his accounts of black ideals and gifts, the souls of black folk, on philosophically pragmatic grounds, not metaphysical ones. Du Bois builds his notions of race not from German but from an American philosophical tradition, that of American pragmatism.[45] If I am right about this, then it is equally plausible that Du Bois's odious anti-Semitic moments can be explained in terms that draw on particularly American national dynamics.

There is nothing more American, as Walter Benn Michaels has shown us, than American nativism: that passional push to withhold from certain races and certain ethnicities the ticket of American identity. White America withholds national confirmation from Jews, other white ethnic immigrants, and, of course, blacks. In return, Jews, white ethnics, and blacks struggle to figure out ways of claiming an American identity. Michael Rogin's *Blackface, White Noise* is a decisive account of how Jews laid claim to Americanness and became white by trafficking in racist constructs; Rogin argues that Hollywood minstrelsy—Jews "blacking up and then wiping off burnt cork"—served as "a rite of passage from immigrant to American."[46] Eric Goldstein argues that, at the turn of the century, "it was native-born whites, bent on preserving a stable and optimistic vision of their national culture, who had the greatest stake in seeing Jews take on the role of white Americans."[47] David Roediger and Matthew Frye Jacobson tell similar stories about the way working-class immigrants traded in racist categories to become white.[48]

Black Americans, it needs to be said, also sought the ticket of American identity. The dominant thread of nineteenth-century black American religious and political thought is devoted to claiming an original Americanness;

Du Bois's *Souls* is a crucial thread in this skein. It is the virtue of much African American thought that the wages for these claims for American identity—from David Walker, to Frederick Douglass, to Maria Stewart—were not rooted in exclusionary practices. By and large, African American accounts of black American identity were expansive. But we should not think that African American narratives of nationality were immune to America's nativist impulses, including anti-Semitism. No one is more honest on the nature of African American anti-Semitism than James Baldwin, who insists that "[Negroes] wear their anti-Semitism as a defiant proof of their citizenship."[49] Baldwin suggests that even though black Americans, to be sure, could not become white, they could rail against the attempts by Jews to, in effect, become white: "The most ironical thing about Negro anti-Semitism is that the Negro is really condemning the Jew for having become an American white man. . . . And if one blames the Jew for having become a white American, one may perfectly well, if one is black, be speaking out of nothing more than envy."[50] In other words, Baldwin invites us to see black anti-Semitism as an impossible attempt to possess the wages of whiteness.

It is possible to see the Jewish passages in *Souls* through this lens. As noted previously, Du Bois consistently depicts Jews post-Reconstruction as assuming the once-held economic roles of whites. In this way, Baldwin seems prescient: Du Bois traffics in anti-Semitic stereotypes as a way of protesting the manner in which Jews are, indeed, becoming white in late nineteenth- and early twentieth-century America. Kramer protests that "Jews in the South at the time were not, to any significant degree, landowners."[51] Yet to exclusively emphasize the historical inaccuracy of Du Bois's depiction of Jews is to ignore the larger cultural dynamics of the turn of the century as Jews increasingly are distinguished and seek to distinguish themselves from blacks. Philip Foner writes: "In the opening years of the twentieth century the image of Jews in black writings and speeches began to change. . . . Black Americans became increasingly disappointed and resentful that Jews, who themselves knew the meaning of persecution, of segregation, and the deprivation of elementary human rights, seemed to be indifferent to the mounting persecution of blacks."[52]

Thus, it is plausible to hear the Jewish passages in *Souls* as something like the following: "What kind of America allows Jews to possess more of the rights and more of the riches of America—in effect, to allow Jews to become white—when it doesn't allow its true native citizens, black Americans, the same sorts of rights and riches? America needs to understand that its Jews should not be allowed to become American at the expense of and before its black citizens." However understandable this sentiment may be, not only is it plainly nativist but I hear an inrushing of a pernicious form of political theology. This reading is poignantly and unfortunately reinforced by the nature of the changes that Du Bois makes for the Jubilee Edition of *Souls*. In six out of the eight places where Jews originally appeared, Du Bois substitutes "immigrant" or "foreigner." For example, where the 1903 version reads, "The Jew is the heir of the slave-baron in Dougherty," the 1953 version reads, "Immigrants are heirs of the slave-baron in Dougherty." "This plantation, owned now by a Russian Jew," is changed to "This plantation, owned now by an immigrant."[53] By substituting "immigrant" for "Jew," Du Bois only reinforces the nativist sentiment of these few passages. In an attempt to fix the anti-Semitism of *Souls*, Du Bois reinscribes not only what is plausibly the text's original nativist tics but the very sort of American theological exceptionalism he tries to disrupt.

Conclusion

What should we make of Du Bois's nativist references to Jews? What do the Jewish passages in *Souls* have to do with the text's political theological attempt to rewrite American exceptionalism? The passages do not amount to a great deal. They are tangential to the larger moves of the text. And the historical record on Du Bois regarding both anti-Semitism and immigrant-targeted nativism is overwhelmingly clear. Du Bois resoundingly denounced anti-Semitism and even black anti-Semitism: "The source of anti-Semitism for American Negroes . . . is simply slavish imitation of whites. . . . The forces in the world back of anti-Semitism are exactly the same facts that are back of color prejudice."[54] Lewis also tells us of Du Bois's protestations against unionist support of nativist immigration policies in the 1920s: "Du Bois had deplored the collusion of nativists and labor unionists. . . . He would have no truck with those Negro leaders who cynically applauded immigration restriction as a boon to black labor."[55] It is not apologetics to insist with the vast majority of Du Bois scholars that these small irruptions in *Souls* should be noted but understood as curiosities and anomalies.

But there is a better reading. The major key of Shulman's text is the recuperation of democratic possibility in American prophecy. I am, however, at this moment reminded of the minor key of Shulman's work: "Prophecy is the office that calls people to fateful 'decision' about what and who they count as real. . . . The Schmittian aura of 'decision' highlights the dangers in this prophetic practice of authority."[56] Prophetic politics, Shulman implies, have a tendency to run toward the *transcendent* and the *unconditional* and against the grain of the *conditional* and the *contingent*. What I think Shulman's book ultimately reveals is that the best of American democratic political theology engages these two poles dialectically, conducting a constant conversation between the two. Bonnie Honig has a similar conversation in this volume in her account of the tension between pedagogy and purge in Michael Walzer's reading of Exodus. Under the best of conditions, the transcendent subjects the conditional to criticism; in turn, the conditional subjects the transcendent to critical review. Under the worst of conditions, the transcendent arrogates total authority; and the conditional, so wrapped up in seeing multiple perspectives, is unable to discern right from wrong.

As a whole, Du Bois's *Souls* is a triumph of this dialectic. Du Bois frees America from the hold of the rampaging unconditional of white supremacy by focusing, first and foremost, on the concrete finitude of black American experience. But from these ordinary conditions, as Stanley Cavell might call them, Du Bois gives us a text that reaches for the unconditional in its rhetoric of souls and new religious ideals.

Yet in those few moments when Jews become more than who they conditionally are, *Souls* reminds us of how easily democratic political theology can fall victim to its transcendent moods. It lurks, for example, in Ralph Ellison's necessary but also proprietary affirmation of black America's use of the Exodus paradigm: "'Go Down Moses' is an absorption of certain Jewish religious traditions, and that's my possession; no one can take that away from me."[57] Democratic political theologians need to train their ears to hear and consider critically demands of authority and authenticity. Democratic political theology cannot do without these sorts of demands for the clarity and strength they provide. At the same time, democratic political theology works best when it uses these demands to initiate chastening conversations of self-criticism and self-review.

Souls is a triumph in that the text as a whole does just this. But, in these Jewish passages, Du Bois slightly betrays this very project. They should remind us of how difficult and how fragile democratic political theology is. That Du Bois was actually unable to correct his mistakes for the 1953 version—"immigrants" is no improvement over "Jews"—is a profound commentary on how sticky and resolute American national prejudices are. Americans would do well to see themselves as forever stuck in a dialectical relationship between the unconditional prophetic and the near sight of the contingent. And if any of us thinks that our politics are free of the transcendent, that our politics do not partake of the theological, we need to remind ourselves: There are no clean souls or *Souls*.

Notes

1. Not all scholars have toed this line. Manning Marable, Theophus Smith, Cynthia Schrager, and David Howard-Pitney all craft sympathetic accounts of Du Bois's relationship to religion. They are notable exceptions to the dominant interpretive tradition.

2. See Edward J. Blum's excellent text, *W. E. B. Du Bois, American Prophet* (Philadelphia: University of Pennsylvania Press, 2007), and the essays collected in *The Souls of W. E. B. Du Bois: New Essays and Reflections*, ed. Edward J. Blum and Jason R. Young (Macon, GA: Mercer University Press, 2009). Also see Brian L. Johnson, *W. E. B. Du Bois: Toward Agnosticism (1868–1934)* (New York: Rowman & Littlefield, 2008).

3. I make this argument in my *Divine Discontent: The Religious Imagination of W. E. B. Du Bois* (New York: Oxford University Press, 2009).

4. W. E. B. Du Bois, *The World of W. E. B. Du Bois: A Quotation Sourcebook* (Westport, CT: Greenwood, 1992), 169. Originally a letter "To Sydney Strong," May 4, 1929, W. E. B. Du Bois Papers, University of Massachusetts, Amherst.

5. In this sense, Du Bois's God resembles Joshua Mitchell's account of God in the early modern political thought of Rousseau, Luther, Hobbes, and Locke. See Joshua Mitchell, *Not by Reason Alone: Religion, History, and Identity in Early Modern Political Thought* (Chicago: University of Chicago Press, 1993).

6. Ibid., 131.

7. W. E. B. Du Bois, *Prayers for Dark People*, ed. Herbert Aptheker (Millwood, NY: Kraus-Thomson, 1982), 9.

8. Quoted in Eric J. Sundquist, *Strangers in the Land: Blacks, Jews, Post-Holocaust America* (Cambridge, MA: Belknap Press, 2005), 103.

9. See Sacvan Bercovitch, *The American Jeremiad* (Madison: University of Wisconsin Press, 1978); Howard-Pitney, *The Afro-American Jeremiad* (Philadelphia: Temple Univer-

sity Press, 1979); and Wilson Jeremiah Moses, *Black Messiahs and Uncle Toms* (University Park: Pennsylvania State University Press, 1982).

10. W. E. B. Du Bois, *The Souls of Black Folk*, ed. Henry Louis Gates Jr. and Terri Hume Oliver (New York: Norton, 1999), 108–109, 128. Hereafter cited as *Souls*.

11. See Richard Rorty, "Religion as a Conversation Stopper," *Common Knowledge* 3:1 (1994): 1–6, and "Religion in the Public Square: A Reconsideration," *Journal of Religious Ethics* 3:1 (2003): 141–149. See John Rawls's notion of "overlapping consensus" in *Political Liberalism* (New York: Columbia University Press, 1996). For a more recent example, see Stathis Gourgouris's exchange with Saba Mahmood, "Detranscendentalizing the Secular," and "Antisecularist Failures: A Counterresponse to Saba Mahmood," *Public Culture* 20:3 (2008): 437–445, 453–459. Gourgouris would disagree with my characterization of him as a secularist. But as I read his essay, he slips into the very secularist modes he claims to disown.

12. Arendt lays this out clearly in *On Revolution* (New York: Penguin, 2006), especially chaps. 4–5.

13. Jeffrey Stout, "2007 Presidential Address: The Folly of Secularism," *Journal of the American Academy of Religion* 76:3 (2008): 533.

14. See Robert Bellah, *The Broken Covenant: An American Civil Religion in Time of Trial* (New York: Seabury Press, 1975); Robert Putnam, *Bowling Alone: The Collapse and Revival of American Community* (New York: Simon & Schuster, 2000); Alasdair MacIntyre, *After Virtue: A Study in Moral Theory* (Notre Dame, IN: University of Notre Dame Press, 1981); and Nicholas Wolterstorff, *Justice: Rights and Wrongs* (Princeton, NJ: Princeton University Press, 2008).

15. Talal Asad, "The Construction of Religion as an Anthropological Category," in *Genealogies of Religion: Disciplines and Reasons of Power in Christianity and Islam* (Baltimore: Johns Hopkins University Press, 1993), 36.

16. George Shulman, *American Prophecy: Race and Redemption in American Political Culture* (Minneapolis: University of Minnesota Press, 2008), 29.

17. Ibid., 243, 241. Nikhil Pal Singh makes a similar argument in *Black Is a Country: Race and the Unfinished Struggle for Democracy* (Cambridge, MA: Harvard University Press, 2005).

18. Mark Lilla, *The Stillborn God: Religion, Politics, and the Modern West* (New York: Knopf, 2007), 3.

19. Oliver O'Donovan, *The Desire of Nations: Rediscovering the Roots of Political Theology* (Cambridge: Cambridge University Press, 1996), 2.

20. Oliver O'Donovan, "Political Theology, Tradition, and Modernity," in *The Cambridge Companion to Liberation Theology*, ed. Christopher Roland (Cambridge: Cambridge University Press, 2007), 277, emphasis in original.

21. Shulman, *American Prophecy*, xiii.

22. Ibid., xiv.

23. Michael C. Dawson, *Black Visions: The Roots of Contemporary African American Political Ideologies* (Chicago: University of Chicago Press, 2001), 15–16.

24. Singh, *Black Is a Country*, 4.

25. Shulman, *American Prophecy*, 116.

26. Du Bois, *Souls*, 5, 15.

27. Raymond Geuss, "Nietzsche and Genealogy," in *Nietzsche*, ed. John Richardson and Brian Leiter (Oxford: Oxford University Press, 2001), 326.

28. Du Bois, *Souls*, 15–16.

29. Blum, *W. E. B. Du Bois, American Prophet*, 63.

30. Glaude borrows this language from John Dewey and relies on it in both *Exodus! Religion, Race, and Nation in Early Nineteenth-Century Black America* (Chicago: University of Chicago Press, 2000), and *In a Shade of Blue: Pragmatism and the Politics of Black America* (Chicago: University of Chicago Press, 2007).

31. Du Bois, *Souls*, 155, 136.

32. Ibid., 162–163.

33. Ibid., 34.

34. Ibid., 83, 84.

35. See Herbert Aptheker, "From '*The Souls of Black Folk*: A Comparison of the 1903 and 1952 Editions,'" in *Strangers and Neighbors: Relations between Blacks and Jews in the United States*, ed. Maurianne Adams and John Bracy (Amherst: University of Massachusetts Press, 1999), 283–286; and Henry Louis Gates Jr. and Terri Hume Oliver, "Note on the Text," in *Souls*, xxxix–xli.

36. Quoted in Herbert Aptheker, *The Literary Legacy of W. E. B. Du Bois* (White Plains, NY: Kraus International Publications, 1989), 82. For Aptheker's full account of Du Bois's thinking about editing these passages, see 77–83.

37. W. E. B. Du Bois to Herbert Aptheker, February 27, 1953, in *The Correspondence of W. E. B. Du Bois*, ed. Herbert Aptheker (Amherst: University of Massachusetts Press, 1978), 3:343.

38. Aptheker, *Literary Legacy of W. E. B. Du Bois*, 82.

39. Gates and Oliver, *Souls*, xl. It should be noted that Du Bois made nine alterations to the text, not fewer than a half dozen.

40. Benjamin Sevitch's work stands as a persuasive and needed corrective against these mischaracterizations: "No black voice was heard more often, more eloquently, and for a longer period of time than W. E. B. Du Bois in his denunciation of anti-Semitism and his praise of Jewish people in general" ("W. E. B. Du Bois and Jews: A Lifetime of Opposing Anti-Semitism," *Journal of African American History* 87:3 [2002]: 323). Also see Sevitch, "W. E. B. Du Bois as America's Foremost Black Zionist," in Blum and Young, *The Souls of W. E. B. Du Bois*, 233–253. On Du Bois's sympathy with German Jews, see "Forum of Fact and Opinion," *Pittsburgh Courier*, February 21, 1931, and December 19, 1936, in *Newspaper Columns by W. E. B. Du Bois*, ed. Herbert Aptheker (White Plains, NY: Kraus-Thomson, 1986), 32–33, 149–150. On Zionism, see "As the Crow Flies: Zionism," *Amsterdam News*, May 11, 1940, in *Newspaper Columns*, 297–298.

41. Blum, *W. E. B. Du Bois, American Prophet*, 83. Henry Louis Gates Jr. suggests that the passages "reflected a larger anti-Semitic discourse, contrary to Du Bois's well-known . . . political positions." See Gates, "A Note to the Text," in *The Souls of Black Folk*, by W. E. B. Du Bois (New York: Bantam Books, 1989), xxviii. For a fuller account of scholarly dealings with these Jewish passages, see Michael P. Kramer, "W. E. B. Du Bois, American Nationalism, and the Jewish Question," in *Race and the Production*

of Modern American Nationalism, ed. Reynolds J. Scott-Childress (New York: Garland Publishing, 1999), 174–175.

42. Kramer, "W. E. B. Du Bois, American Nationalism, and the Jewish Question," 188.

43. David Levering Lewis, *W. E. B. Du Bois: Biography of a Race, 1863–1919* (New York: Holt, 1993), 136.

44. See Kahn, *Divine Discontent*, chaps. 1–3.

45. For a compelling account of Du Bois as a pragmatist, see Paul C. Taylor, "What's the Use of Calling Du Bois a Pragmatist?," *Metaphilosophy* 35:1–2 (January 2004): 99–114.

46. Michael Rogin, *Blackface, White Noise: Jewish Immigrants in the Hollywood Melting Pot* (Berkeley: University of California Press, 1998), 5.

47. Eric Goldstein, *The Price of Whiteness: Jews, Race, and American Identity* (Princeton, NJ: Princeton University Press, 2006), 5.

48. See David Roediger, *The Wages of Whiteness: Race and the Making of the American Working Class* (London: Verso, 1999); and Mathew Frye Jacobson, *Whiteness of a Different Color: European Immigrants and the Alchemy of Race* (Cambridge, MA: Harvard University Press, 1998).

49. James Baldwin, "The Harlem Ghetto," in *The Price of the Ticket: Collected Nonfiction 1948–1985* (New York: St. Martin's Press, 1985), 9.

50. James Baldwin, "Negroes Are Anti-Semitic Because They're Anti-White," *New York Times*, April 9, 1967, http://partners.nytimes.com/books/98/03/29/specials/baldwin-antisem.html?scp=4&sq=james%20baldwin&st=cse.

51. Kramer, "W. E. B. Du Bois, American Nationalism, and the Jewish Question," 173.

52. Philip S. Foner, "Black-Jewish Relations in the Opening Years of the Twentieth Century," in Adams and Bracey, *Strangers and Neighbors*, 238.

53. Gates and Oliver, "Note on the Text," in *Souls*, xli.

54. Du Bois, *Newspaper Columns*, 330. See also Du Bois's 1943 column in the *Amsterdam News* in which he says, "Whatever we Negroes have suffered in the world . . . cannot be compared to the long history of cruelty . . . which has been visited upon the Jewish people from days of Rome down through . . . the present policy of extermination under Hitler" (494). We should note that Du Bois's usage in 1943 of the word *extermination* was uncommon.

55. David Levering Lewis, *W. E. B. Du Bois: The Fight for Equality and the American Century, 1919–1963* (New York: Henry Holt, 2000), 90.

56. Shulman, *American Prophecy*, 30.

57. Quoted in Sundquist, *Strangers in the Land*, 96.

CHAPTER 5

THE RACE FOR THEOLOGY

Toward a Critical Political Theology of Freedom

COREY D. B. WALKER

Stuart Hall begins his germinal essay "What Is This 'Black' in Black Popular Culture?" with the following question: "What sort of moment is this in which to pose the question of black popular culture?"[1] It is this question that enables Hall to open a line of investigation into the cultural logics, economic relations, and political practices that (in)form contemporary racially and ethnically en(re)coded cultural productions. With the displacement of dominant models of European high culture, the consolidation of US global power and the concomitant redefinition and shifting of the focus of cultural production from Europe to America, and the political and intellectual decolonization of the third world, Hall understands the moment of the emergence of this question as critically linked to the changing flows in the geopolitical production of knowledge, power, and culture. Hall seeks to exploit the theoretical opening offered by this reconsideration for exploring the possibilities in creating "new spaces for contestations" that will present an "important opportunity for intervention in the popular cultural field" (466).

Needless to say, the terrain of culture is not a smooth and unambiguous one for Hall. Echoing Antonio Gramsci, Hall recognizes the centrality of the field of culture as a critical terrain in making a difference in political and ideological struggles. To be sure, such struggles are not without their contingencies and contradictions, as "cultural hegemony is never about pure victory or pure domination; it is never a zero-sum cultural game" (468). In staging a critical return to the field of popular culture in our contemporary moment, Hall seeks to engage the dialectic of culture—the ways in which new cultural forms and formations proliferate around the ambiguities of difference and marginalization in relation with a resurgence of new cultural flows that are resistant to the ideas, images, symbols, and politics of such a cultural politics of difference. Such a dialectic attenuates any naïve and nostalgic rendering of culture generally and of popular culture specifically. Indeed, Hall shows the arena of popular culture, bisected as it is by such dichotomies as "high and low; resistance [and] incorporation; authentic [and] inauthentic, experiential [and] formal; opposition [and] homogenization," to be always already shaped and formed by the mutual contamination of these dyads as well as by the workings of capital (470). But it is with the question of "the black" and the signifier "black" that Hall's essay gains exceptional critical traction.

Recognizing the critical and material differences that consolidate under the term "black," Hall's essay is animated by a central tension within the discourse of difference and popular culture. That is, to echo the criticism of Michelle Wallace, a serious questioning and interrogation of the global ascent of the postmodern as a moment in the (dis)continuity of the "now you see it, now you don't game that modernism once played with primitivism, to ask whether it is not once again achieved at the expense of the vast silencing about the West's fascination with the bodies of black men and women of other ethnicities" (467). The workings of (the) "black" cannot escape the ambiguities and multiplicities that obtain within this discursive matrix, nor can it guarantee a particular form or formation of politics relative to the veritable (im)possibility of an absolute categorization of the "black." To think the signifier "black" as well as the subject "the black" is to necessarily engage in a reflexive interrogation of the concepts, categories, and frameworks that (in)form these constructs along with the material, ideological, and historical (con)texts that animate *and* frustrate such theorizations.

Hall's essay is quite instructive for a critical understanding of the theoretical opportunities and limitations of thinking the historical and discursive dimensions of "the black," as well as how new configurations of thought can inform a theoretical and material politics. It is in this spirit that this essay begins by rehearsing Hall's project and extending it to the terrain of political theology in elaborating the conditions of possibility for an/other type of thinking appropriate for a *critical* political theology.[2] Such a political theology is able to *think* "the black" and the general economy of race without recourse to such theoretical short circuits as a race-relations paradigm or a naïve overcoming of race. Indeed, such a project speaks to nothing less than a desire for inaugurating a new project of thinking that gestures toward a new horizon for political theology—a political theology of freedom.

The important task of conceptualizing the critical coordinates for a political theology of freedom occurs in a moment bisected by the global mobilization of new and violent forms of nationalism and ethnocentrism, the ideologically assumed and militarily assured hegemony of capitalism, and the use of force to enforce the demands of a geopolitical configuration commensurate with the demands of perpetual war in the service of a provisional peace. Within this matrix, we necessarily find ourselves justly perplexed as to whether and how to fashion substantive forms of thought that not only demonstrate technical competence but also generate new possibilities for thinking and being otherwise. This task is made all the more difficult when these material formations are underwritten—to varying degrees—by appeals to the theological that work to authorize, secure, and guarantee the "rationality" of their logic and the "sufficiency" of their foundational basis. The invocation of these "theo-logics" highlights the precarious situation for thinking and being, particularly for those on the underside of modernity, as the boundaries of these new formations seek to limit modes of critical interrogation.

The intellectual ascendancy of the concept of political theology marks a new moment in the disenchantment of contemporary forms of thought in gaining critical purchase on the contemporary coordinates of our moment. In turn, the theoretical *enchantment* of political theology signals a deepening of the legitimation crisis that has gripped the political imagination in recent years. To be sure, the twin acts of the globalization of liberal democracy and the waning influence of Marxian-inspired forms of critical theory have facilitated the reemergence of political theology as a critical category for political analysis and an alternative framework for articulating new political subjectivities and emancipatory political projects. Despite the multitude of theoretical and political dreams fueled by various elaborations of political theology, these projects exhibit an acute tendency to evade any deep and sustained interrogation of one of the historic cognitive and political acts of modernity—race.[3] It is here where the freedom gestured to by the turn to political theology becomes but a dream deferred, for as Charles Long so ably argued, "The issue of race is raised within the structures of academic theology. The issue has not so much to do with the particular statements regarding race enunciated within a theology or by a particular theologian. The issue has more to do with the historical, religious, and philosophical structures of the intellectual task itself as this task implicates the meaning of race."[4] Thus, the (re)turn to political theology must stage a critical confrontation between contemporary elaborations of forms of theological thinking and a critical understanding of the function of race in developing the conditions of possibility for a style of thinking that not only has purchase in exposing the contradictions of the dominant intellectual protocols of critical thought and political practice, but also ruptures the spiritualized suture of democracy—in both its liberal and radical forms—and freedom. In so doing, we will be better positioned to formulate a conception of political theology attentive to the theoretical demands of race while elaborating the conditions of possibility for the inauguration of a new practice of freedom.

This essay undertakes a critical excavation of the manner in which those individuals signified as "black" authorize an/other type of thinking that is not limited to the racialized and racializing dictates that organize the racial logics of the project of modernity. Instead, the black countenances a new horizon for thinking with the bodies and logics of those subjects who were/are at the ends of the new beginning(s) of the modern world. To return to the black as a site of thinking fundamentally reconstructs the project of thought, in general, and theology, in particular. Thus, to think "black," we must confront the conditions of possibility of thinking as such while simultaneously articulating a strategy to meet the political and theoretical challenges inaugurated with the racialist protocols of Western reason.[5] In this engagement I will draw on the suggestive insights of Howard Thurman's 1947 Ingersoll Lecture, "The Negro Spiritual Speaks of Life and

Death," to provide the conditions of possibility for a critical political theology of freedom that does not flatten or render thinly transparent the (in)
finite range and (in)exhaustible depth of the black. Thurman thus inhabits the space of the imagination to facilitate the emergence of a mode of
thought that resists an epistemic imperialism, particularly the will to clarity
that so characterizes traditional political theological discourses. Thurman
thus enables us to think those disqualified knowledges and opaque dimensions of thought that open up new possibilities and practices of freedom.

IN REHEARSING A HISTORY of the influences on his intellectual development in his autobiography, *With Head and Heart*, Howard Thurman swiftly
recollects, in a single unadorned sentence, his introduction to the thought
of the South African writer Olive Schreiner: "My introduction to Olive
Schreiner came one evening when Shorty Collins read 'The Dream of the
Hunter.'"[6] This sentence comes at the end of Thurman's rich and detailed
description of a retreat he attended in September 1925 just prior to em-
barking on his final year of study at Rochester Theological Seminary. Thurman provides a comprehensive narrative of the occasion of the retreat, the
accommodations, the participants, and key speakers along with an itinerary
of the activities that participants engaged in when not attending to the
matters of the retreat. We learn that the retreat program "was informal and
unstructured," the facilities were rented in "an old hotel that had closed
for the winter," and the attendees "ate at a small restaurant operated during the summer months by two teachers of home economics at Teachers
College, Columbia University" (58). We also learn from Thurman that he
was "impressed by the fact that the theological students from Union, Yale,
Oberlin, and Rochester were raising essentially the same questions raised by
the undergraduates from Wellesley, Barnard, and Holyoke" (59). Thurman
also shares with us that "the afternoons were free for reading, hiking, and
other forms of recreation" and it was in these moments "when personal relationships deepened into friendships unbroken throughout the intervening
years" (59). It is after reading that "the evenings were memorable" because
"this was a time for sharing of treasures" that we come across—almost as an
afterthought—the sentence where Thurman reminds us of his introduction
to the thought of Olive Schreiner.

The economy of words with which Thurman explicitly communicates his "introduction to Olive Schreiner" belies the importance of this event in his life and thought.[7] Although he does not elaborate on why the World War I veteran, pacifist, and noted peace and justice activist George "Shorty" Collins chose to share this selection from Olive Schreiner, it is in the remarkably rich descriptive account of the *event* of the retreat that we can glimpse the signal contribution of this occasion to Thurman's thought.[8] Indeed, it is later in his autobiography that we learn of the critical importance of Thurman's "experience of encounter" not only with Shorty Collins and the Fellowship of Reconciliation—"I found a place to stand in my own spirit—a place so profoundly affirming that I was strengthened by a sense of immunity"—but, more important, with Olive Schreiner (265).[9] "As I listened to the reading of 'Dream of the Hunter,'" elaborates Thurman, "I knew that through its portals I was being led into a wonderland of the spirit and imagination" (225). Thurman then informs of the lasting trace of this encounter: "Since that time, I have secured a copy of any of her writings I could find in bookstores or libraries in this country, in England, and in her homeland of South Africa" (225).

Nearly half a century after his initial encounter with Olive Schreiner, Thurman edited and published a collection of her writings under the title *A Track to the Water's Edge: The Olive Schreiner Reader*. This reader gathers together those essential texts by Schreiner that invited Thurman into the expansive space of the imagination. "It was not until I read Olive Schreiner," writes Thurman in the introduction to the volume, "that I was able to establish sufficient psychological distance between me and the totality of such experiences to make the experience itself an object of thought" (226). "To make the experience itself an object of thought" was significant for Thurman in that it now "became possible for [him] to move from primary experience, to conceptualizing that experience, to a vision inclusive of all of life. The resulting creative synthesis was to [him] religious rather than metaphysical" (226). From the space of imagination—the creative nexus where Thurman was able to give expression to what he terms the unity of life, thought, and existence—Thurman is able to develop a practice of thinking hospitable to the demands of the depth of experience.

Perhaps it is not fortuitous that Thurman reconstructs the scene of this encounter as separate moments within his autobiography, since "the auto-biographical narrative, in selecting, ordering, and integrating the writer's lived experiences according to its own teleological demands, is beholden to certain imperatives of imaginative discourse."[10] While the demands of interpreting and presenting a narrative construal of his life certainly raise complex issues of structure, style, and meaning, Thurman's phenomenological rehearsal of this episode when repeated with a difference at a later moment in the text renders explicit the (in)finite trace of Schreiner's thought in general on his thinking and in particular the invitation to imagination that occasions Thurman's style of thinking that is "religious rather than metaphysical." The rehearsal takes on increased importance when we consider that it is Olive Schreiner's "The Hunter," an enigmatic tale of the quest of the Hunter who, with the shuttle of Imagination, pursues Truth. Only through a revolutionary patience and persistence with an openness to another knowledge beyond the mundane is the Hunter able to capture but a glimpse of Truth. Schreiner's allegory of the (mis)fortunes of "knowledge" (whereby the Hunter's quest is necessarily misrepresented by his fellows: "'What ails him?' said his comrades. 'He is mad,' said one. 'No, but he is worse,' said another; 'he would see that which none of us have seen, and make himself a wonder.' 'Come, let us forswear his company,' said all") provides the impetus for Thurman to plumb the depths of experience with a new thinking acutely attuned to the infinite particular.[11] Schreiner's 1876 statement, "This intellect is a good thing but it is not everything," aptly exposes an exemplary thinking that becomes critical for the Hunter—and for Thurman as well—in grasping a single feather of Truth.[12]

CERTAINLY THE NOTION of the imagination as a critical resource for thinking—and as a site for thinking political theology—has been a recurrent yet contested theme in the history of thought. Such an invitation, whether viewed with hesitation, such as "the seemingly irresolvable, albeit highly productive, contentiousness between Understanding and Imagination; or more exactly, between the intellectual synthesis of the categories of Understanding and the figurative synthesis of productive Imagination" in Immanuel Kant, or critically embraced as a preserve of possibility for the fate of thinking, as in Herbert Marcuse's view of imagination as "breaking the spell of the Establishment" and Nathan Scott's call for a "theology of imagination" that "renew[s] and reinvigorat[es] at the concrete level of sensibility and lifestyle . . . the imaginative style of a people," brings to the foreground the (im)possibilities of the imagination in extending and establishing new frameworks of knowledge.[13] Moreover, the imagination is highly suggestive of (and susceptible to) the desire to push thought into new (un)critical realms of speculation in order to render articulate the sensations and experiences of mind and body, space and time.

Such was the case with Thurman in his pivotal encounter with Schreiner. Religious knowing for Thurman, as it is in Schleiermacher—whom Thurman studied with George Cross, the author of the 1911 book *The Theology of Schleiermacher: A Condensed Presentation of His Chief Work "The Christian Faith"* that helped renew scholarly interest in the work of the famed theologian—quests "to break through the shackles of finitude in order to discover the universe that lies beyond humanity."[14] That is, for Thurman the impotence of modern thought to critically interrogate, or understand, the ever-expanding awareness of human thought, consciousness, and experience in general and religious experience in particular raised to a heightened level the limitations of thinking proper.

Of course, to raise the notion of the imagination, particularly with reference to the question of political theology, and link it to a practice of critical thinking conjures the specter of an unbridled and undisciplined irrationalism or, in more explicit terms, a vulgar emotionalism. Indeed, since Marx's (in)famous injunction regarding the criticism of religion as a necessary prerequisite for the proper function of criticism captured in his oft-quoted statements—"For Germany, the *criticism of religion* has been essentially completed, and the criticism of religion is the prerequisite of all criticism" and "The immediate task of philosophy, which is in the service of history, is to unmask human self-alienation in its secular form now that it has been unmasked in its sacred form"—we readily recognize that calls for the imagination as a critical resource must meet quite explicit and robust criteria for any proper and deliberate consideration for inclusion in the project of thought.[15] If not, the imagination as a site to host an inquiry into the plenitude of thinking new modes of political theology does not extend the terrain of thought in any significant way and almost by necessity arrests the development of any critical possibilities of freedom.

Thurman's receptivity to the possibilities of the imagination, forged within a moment of intense contest over the past and future prospects for thinking in a modern and scientific age, offers us an invitation to reassess the possibilities of the imagination as a site of thinking able to host the multitudinous questions that consolidate within what is colloquially termed the "return of religion" in our contemporary intellectual and political moment. It is the spectral pre(ab)sence of religion and its analogue, political theology, that challenges today's religious and theological studies scholars with the necessity to fashion a practice and to think anew our engagements with these very phenomena in our contemporary conjuncture. To this end, we have been inundated with a plethora of proposals advanced to meet this challenge in the academic study of religion ranging from projects advocating various (re)readings of orthodox religious categories, frameworks, and sources to dialogic engagements between religion and contemporary theory to epistemic and methodological interrogations of the disciplinary aims, goals, and foundations of the study of religion. But should we not learn to think *with* the specter? That is, should we once again revisit the empty tomb of religion to confront the critical question of what are the possibilities for a critical political theology? Can such a project emerge from another "corpus of sensibility"? It is here where Thurman's reception to the imagination and his welcoming of its potential in hosting an interrogation of his experiences as "an object of thought" presents the critical conditions of possibility for such a critical political theology of freedom.

TAKING UP Dean William Sperry's invitation extended to him in 1946, Howard Thurman delivered the annual Ingersoll Lecture on the Immortality of Man in Andover Chapel at Harvard University on April 14, 1947. For this lecture, he chose as his topic "The Negro Spiritual Speaks of Life and Death." Thurman began his investigation into the spirituals while serving a joint appointment as professor of philosophy and religion at Morehouse and Spelman colleges in the late 1920s. It was the occasion of taking charge of daily chapel service for the week of October 15–19, 1928, at Spelman when he formally "began a long quest into [his] own past as the deep resource for finding [his] way into wholeness in the present" (78).[16] Thurman's journey into this cultural form not only to wrest a message of personal validation and fulfillment but also to see "what they could tell . . . about life and death" required an intellectual imagination attuned to the questions of time, historicity, and meaning while not reducing the theoretical and experiential expressions of spirituals to a logic of the same (216). Thus, Thurman's task was to explicate the meaning(s) of life and death in the spirituals while simultaneously establishing "a beachhead of thought about the slave's religious creativity" (217). In so doing, Thurman exercises an (un)timely imagination that *thinks* the depth of mortality in order to disrupt the narrative of immortality.

Thurman's decentering of the logic of immortality followed an earlier effort by his former teacher, Rufus Jones, whose 1943 Ingersoll Lecture, "The Spell of Immortality," sought to enact a similar disruption. Thurman encountered Jones soon after being arrested by Jones's thought in *Finding the Trail of Life*. He spent several months in 1929 attending Jones's philosophy lectures and his special seminar on Meister Eckhart at Haverford College as a Fellow of the National Council on Religion in Higher Education (76). With Jones, Thurman "was invited but never urged to travel" the same intellectual path as his teacher while pursuing investigations into the life and thought of Madame Guyon and Saint Francis of Assisi and the exemplary ways in which "mystic discourse itself," as Michel de Certeau reminds us, "had to produce the condition of its functioning as language that could be spoken to others and to oneself" (76).[17] "Disillusioned over *arguments* for immortality," Jones's 1943 lecture presents "some experiences of persons through the ages . . . who in a peculiar degree have lived under a spell of immortality,"[18] and Jones articulates the conditions of possibility for presenting these (extra)ordinary experiences:

> We live and do our thinking, for the most part, too exclusively in the sphere and dominion of what Coleridge, and Kant before him called the "understanding"—*Verstand*. Its function is to organize, and categorize, that is to say, to handle logically, intelligently, the facts of the possible experience of a world that can be presented to sense, dealt with in terms of space-time and explained in a relation of cause and effect. But they both, and all the perennial thinkers, recognize in us higher capacities of Reason, Nous, Pneuma, Logos-Sophia, Vernunft—"Reason in its most exalted mood"—by which we

enter, partake with, and share in an Over-world of essential spiritual Reality. On this level the Above and the below meet, and we see rather than argue. We live our way into the Eternally Real rather than endeavor to prove and defend it by the way of categories, intended for lower-case matters. Of course this distinction must not be pushed to the extent of dualism. It only means that Reason operates on more than one story, more than one level, and that we are as truly rational beings when we have imaginative dominion over experience.[19]

The "imaginative dominion over experience" where Jones locates the possibility for understanding the meaning of the experiences for the historical subjects of his lecture must be radicalized in order to account for the experiences of those racialized others who exist within, outside, and beyond history and whose very pre(ab)sence constitutes a critique of the normality of time and meaning that coordinates the very constructions of (im)mortality. Thus, the path that is opened up by Jones's invitation is taken with a difference by Thurman in his lecture of 1947.

Thurman's Ingersoll Lecture interrogates the phenomena of the "songs of life and death," as he refers to the Negro spirituals, in order to glean "some of the insights to be found" in them.[20] Before plunging headlong into this discourse, Thurman recognizes that the spirituals require an/other kind of thinking, since "to be sure, the amazing rhythm and the peculiar, often weird 1-2-3-5-6-8- of the musical scale are always intriguing and challenging to the modern mind" (12). In other words, the *logic* of the spirituals does not translate in exact correspondence with the logic of the modern musical scale. But the logical gap is not one that can be sutured by proffering a new logical framework or the formalization of the logic of music proper; rather, what is needed is the inauguration of a thinking that is able to think the "illogical" fragments of thought and experience, time and space, history and memory, for as Thurman states, "the real significance of the songs, however, is revealed at a deeper level of experience, in the ebb and flow of the tides that feed the rivers of man's thinking and aspiring" (12). The logical frameworks and codes that have heretofore authorized, legitimated, and translated what is classified as the acceptable and translatable sounds of modern music must be rethought through a register that is able to make sense of these songs whose significance "is revealed at a deeper level of experience." Analogous to his former teacher's critique of what passes for the totality of thinking, Thurman's criticism of modern thought is not formulated on a dichotomous logic. Instead, he recognizes, akin to the idea advanced by Walter Benjamin in his programmatic essay "The Task of the Translator," that "the task of the translator consists in finding that intended effect upon the language into which he is translating which produces in it the echo of the original," that "an examination of the insights to be found here" does not quest for originality "in any personal or private sense" but instead must meet the challenge of the authentic in a very (in)authentic language and thought.[21] That is, in (re)reading the Negro spirituals for a critical understanding of conceptions of life and death—a theory of (im)mortality—the goal is not identity, for is it not (im)possible on the basis of a logic of identity to find the *necessary* correspondence with "the alchemy of . . . the world of nature, the stuff of experience, and the Bible, the sacred book of the Christians who had enslaved [them]?" (13). Rather, what is required is a critical epistemic openness to an event of disclosure of "the unique factor of the inspiring revelation . . . in that in the presence of their naked demand upon the primary sources of meanings, even without highly specialized tools or skills, the universe responded to them with overwhelming power" (13).

"How significant is death?" (15). With this question, Thurman excavates the history and experience of death in the life of the enslaved and thinks through its multiple meanings in confronting the condition of finitude and its work on/in the world. Thurman's archaeology of death confronts the very *facticity* of death that cannot be denied, repressed, or evaded. "Death was a fact," Thurman writes, "inescapable, persistent. For the slave, it was extremely compelling because of the cheapness with which his life was regarded. The slave was a tool, a thing, a utility, a commodity, but he was not a person. He was faced constantly with the imminent threat of death, of which the terrible overseer was the symbol, and the awareness that he (the slave) was only chattel property, the dramatization. . . . The situation itself stripped death of dignity, making it stark and nasty, like the difference between tragedy and melodrama" (13–14). Thurman reveals that the very ubiquity of death not only evacuates the exalted meaning of death as *the* absolute limit condition of humanity but, because of its ordinariness as a result of the middle passage to modernity, it must be rearticulated as the very *precondition* of the existence of the enslaved.[22] The existential datum of death then does not occasion the affective and reflective moment Nathan Scott describes in his discussion of Heidegger's ontology: "[T]he terrible dread that comes as we begin to reflect on the oblivion that ultimately awaits us, then, immediately—as we feel ourselves to be moving merely from 'thrownness' (*Geworfenheit*) to death—the world sinks into a profound kind of insignificance, and the only thing that remains is the primordial Noth-ingness."[23] Indeed, as the enslaved is nothing in the sense that the enslaved as chattel, as property, does not register within the theoretical framework of being proper, the very possibility of recognizing a meaning emerging from this being is foreclosed. Thus, with the (in)significance of death, Thurman's concern now confronts the *always already* question, "Is [death] the worst of all possible things that can happen to an individual?" (15).

The *facticity* of death serves as an invitation for Thurman to (re)think it as the limit condition par excellence for humanity. Death as the ultimate threat for moderns that authorizes the Heideggerian truth of "my being always totally vulnerable to the power of death" is confronted in the refrain of the spiritual "Oh Freedom!":

> Oh Freedom! Oh Freedom!
> Oh Freedom, I love thee!
> And before I'll be a slave,
> I'll be buried in my grave,
> And go home to my Lord and be free. (15)[24]

Since "the attitude toward death is profoundly influenced by the experience of life," the uncanny response of "Oh Freedom!" does not echo within a philosophical framework that *thinks* the absence of death, of considerations of death, of the categorical imperative of death. Rather, the pure presence of death—its everydayness—as the concrete existential datum for the enslaved must then disclose another logic that treats the very question of finitude not as that which is forgotten but the *fundamentum* of human existence. The disclosure of death as the existential analytic conditions an intelligibil-ity articulated within this spiritual that accepts and affirms the being of the enslaved prior to the condition of slavery in relation with the world. Thus, we come to understand that the response to the *always already* question of "Is it the worst of all possible things that can happen to an individual?" is

"Obvious indeed it is here that death is not regarded as life's worst offering." Thurman continues:

> There are some things in life that are worse than death. A man is not compelled to accept life without reference to the conditions upon which the offering is made. Here is something more than a mere counsel of suicide. It is a primary disclosure of an elemental affirmation having to do directly, not only with the ultimate dignity of the human spirit, but also with the ultimate basis of self-respect. We are face to face with a gross conception of the immortality of man. (15–16)

One is not "running toward death" since death is the inescapable fact of the very nothingness that is the *precondition* of the veiled being of the enslaved. Moreover, the certainty of death does not court the theater of the absurd and its logical response of suicide.[25] Rather, death's omnipresence is rendered as an affirmation of presence in plenitude.

Recognizing "the primary disclosure of an elemental affirmation" facilitates a truth with respect to immortality, since, as Heidegger reminds us, " 'There is' truth only in so far as Dasein is and as long as Dasein is. Entities are uncovered only *when* Dasein is, and only as long as Dasein *is*, are they disclosed."[26] This disclosure effects a decentering of what Rufus Jones termed "the spell of immortality" in his Ingersoll Lecture of 1943: that is, a conception of immortality that is out-there to be grasped as an entity or an object of knowledge independent of human existence. "A radical conception of the immortality of man is apparent," Thurman posits, "*because the human spirit has a final word over the effect of circumstances*" (16, emphasis added). Thurman's *immanent* notion of immortality is possible because of the conditions of intelligibility that have been disclosed through the enslaved's (pre)reflective disclosure of death. Thurman writes:

> The fact that death can be reduced to a manageable unit in any sense, whatsoever, reveals something that is profoundly significant concerning its character. The significant revelation is in the fact that death, as an event, is spatial, time compressed, if not actually time bound, and therefore partakes of the character of the episodic. Death not only affects man by involving him concretely in its fulfillment, but man seems to be aware that he is affected by death in the experience itself. There is, therefore, an element of detachment for the human spirit, even in so crucial an experience. Death is an experience *in* life and a man, under some circumstances, may be regarded as a spectator

of, as well as a participant *in*, the moment of his own death. The logic here is that man is both a space binder and a time binder. (17)

For Thurman, the Negro spirituals provide a critical disruption of an impoverished conception of death in which death is *the* limit condition. Rather, death discloses and introduces new meanings, conceptions, and formulations of the experiences of life as well as of space and time. Indeed, as Charles Long reminds us when reflecting on Thurman's "meditative critique," "one cannot hope that the structures of history that created the terror of temporality will be in continuity with a temporality of salvation. There must be another source for the overcoming of time."[27] Death as articulated in and through the spirituals serves as a ground for another temporality that exceeds the calculus and discipline of time. In so doing, the time of death thematizes an ontological time of life not as finite and mortal but as infinite and immortal.

"A reflective disclosure can critically introduce meanings, perspectives, interpretive and evaluative vocabularies, modes of perception, and action possibilities that stand in strikingly dissonant relations to already available meanings and familiar possibilities, to already existing ways of speaking, hearing, seeing, interpreting, and acting."[28] The Negro spirituals open a type of thinking that is not immediately available with the modernity of death. That is, death cleansed and mystified of the ordinary and the everyday—as Thurman submits, "We are all of us participants in the modern conspiracy to reduce immediate contact with death to zero"—thus isolated and removed from the time-space of human existence, it *must* then be thought as the condition of finitude that is forgotten. Such a conception of death is inauthentic for Thurman not only because "[t]his concept[ion] regards death merely as a private option, private because it involves the single individual as if he and he alone existed in all the universe" but also because "if death were not implicit in the fact of life in a time-space dimension, then in no true sense would there be any authentic options in human experience" (16). Against this understanding, Thurman reminds us, "This was not the situation with the creators of the Spirituals" (19). The fact of death that Thurman renders in a remarkably rich phenomenology of death opens up a significance that refocuses thought on a discarded and disturbing thinking—a thinking that is "not the 'other' of reason" but another thinking hosted within a capacious and critical imagination able to confront the plenitude of the presence of death. Thus, Thurman explains: "[T]he great idea about death itself is that it is not *the master of life*. It may be inevitable, yes; gruesome, perhaps; releasing, yes; but triumphant, NEVER. With such an affirmation ringing in their ears, it became possible for them, slaves though they were, to stand anything that life could bring against them" (24). "The radicality of Thurman's thought and technique," as Charles Long correctly assesses, "is in the manner in which he forces us to entertain another option regarding religion, historicity, and truth."[29]

Thurman's reading of death that registers "the note of the transcendence of death is never lacking" in the Negro spirituals incorporates and advances a proposal that recalibrates the coordinates of life to a perspective of *authentic* life that encompasses the experiences of anxiety, despair, disappointment, discouragement, frustration, and loneliness (24). To confront the contradictions and contingencies cannot be collapsed within the "double consciousness of DuBois [because that] places us within the dilemma of historical time [and thus] Thurman hopes to resituate the problematic within the structures of [the Spirituals] as the locus for a new rhythm of time"—and thus, of life.[30] Thurman's interrogation of the meaning(s) of life is formally opened by the questions, "Was life merely a 'veil of soul-making'? Was it merely a vast anteroom to the great beyond? Was it regarded as an end itself? Or was it a series of progressions, a pilgrimage, a meaningful sojourn?" (24). Thinking the preserve of possibility of the Negro spirituals in fashioning a response to these questions forces a critical confrontation with conceptions of life that evade the materiality of human existence. That is, the spirituals reveal the inescapability of "such experiences [that] are inherent in the process itself. Hence: *Let us cheer the weary traveler, Let us cheer the weary traveler, Along the heavenly way*" (25). However, the disappointments of life need not warrant a turn to nihilism, because life incorporates a conception of time that obviates recourse to an absolute meaninglessness that then overdetermines death. In other words, the conception of time that is bound up with Thurman's formulation of death disclosed in the logic of the spirituals prompts us to reformulate the conception of the time of life.

Thurman thus reads temporality not as a Sartrean *No Exit* circle with an end in the logic of suicide; rather, life is becoming, "a pilgrimage, a sojourn," whose proper backdrop "is beyond the vicissitudes of life with God!" (32). To be sure, Thurman's reading is not simply the consummation of life in a repetition of the God of traditional metaphysics or what Heidegger calls "onto-theo-logy." Rather, it is in relation to life as/and nothing that offers up precisely the infinite vastness of the excessive totality of life that forms the point of entry to the very question at hand. Thurman then elaborates a theory of time that underwrites such a conception of life, first by delineating the conditions of intelligibility of time as "a familiar theme of the human spirit":

> We are dealing with a striking theory of time. Time is measured in terms of events, actions, therefore intentions and desires. All experience, then, is made up of a series of more or less intense meaning—units that may fall in such rapid succession that the interval between is less than any quantitative value. Within the scope of an event-series all of human life is bound. Freedom can only mean, in this sense, the possibility of release from the tyranny of succeeding intervals of events. The totality of life, then, in its existential aspects, is thus completely exhausted in time. (32)

Such a conception of time renders life as that which is absolutely bound, and "death in such a view means complete cessation of any sense of interval and therefore of any sense of events. In short, here death means either finality or complete absorption from time-space awareness" (32). This conception leads by necessity to a vicious dualism between the finite and the infinite that forecloses any possibility of the immanence of transcendence that is the foundation of coming to an awareness of the meaning(s) of existence. Thus, Thurman astutely notes the ontological implications of such a rationality: "[W]hatever transpires beyond death, while it can be thought of only in terms of time-space intervals, is of another universe of discourse, another quality of being" (32).

Instead of the trap of "calculative thinking" that presupposes the summation of time in death, Thurman opens a thinking into "a question as to the relation between *before* and *after* in terms of death and life" (32–33).[31] The theory of time disclosed by the spirituals breaks a bounded conception of time that reduces the meaning of life and death. Thurman explains:

> There seems to be no real break between before and after. Any notion of the continuity of life that transcends the fact of death is significant because

of the advantage that is given to the meaning of life. . . . In light of man's conscious experience with life, death seems to be a moment for the release of potentials of which the individual is in some sense already aware. Life then becomes illustrative of a theory of time that is latitudinal or flowing. . . . Life always includes movement, process, inner activity and some form of irritation. Something more is implicit than what is apparent in any cycle or series of cycles that sustain all manifestations. . . . To think of life, then, as a pilgrimage means that not only is life characterized by an undertow of continuity but also that the individual has no alternative but to participate responsibly in that continuity. (33–34)

The basic presupposition of this conception of time is predicated on thinking life as living. By welcoming this thinking, Thurman becomes aware of an intelligibility disclosed in the spirituals that is committed to an inexhaustibility of the materiality of transcendence.

THURMAN'S CRITICAL EXAMINATION of the Negro spirituals reawakens the question of the meaning of life and death by jettisoning commitments to immortality that hold them as temporally and ontologically separate phenomena that only presage the more ponderous question of an *absolute* transcendent immortality. Immortality as such is inconceivable except outside history. For the enslaved, such a conception would render the omnipresence of death omnipotent with the corollary effect of evacuating human existence of all meaning. For Thurman the spirituals countenance a thinking that eschews an either/or logic, creating the space for an exemplary logic that grounds a critical observation that Thurman's teacher George Cross made in his 1922 classic *Creative Christianity*: "There can be no genuine knowledge of the universe in which we live our life, except on the presupposition of the immanency, permanency, and integrated unity of the forces and laws of the universe."[32] Thus, with Thurman's explication of the spirituals we "becom[e] more aware of our role in disclosing the world, we come to see that 'we are responding to something that is not us,' and so we come to see our relation to the world quite differently."[33]

Thurman's invitation to imagination "disrupt[s] the entrenched order and orderliness of a discursive terrain" of immortality that evacuates the meanings of the intimate relation of death to life.[34] In this instance, the Negro spirituals disturb the sedimented—and segregated—ways of thinking the question of immortality, thus inaugurating an exemplary thinking that reorders not only the coordinates of life and death but also the preserve of freedom. The occasion of the spirituals not only breaks the grip of onto-theology—"There was no elaborate scheme of separate office and function between God and Jesus and only a very rare reference to the Holy Spirit. . . . In short, God is active in history in a personal and primary manner" (38–39)—but also opens up a creative space of freedom not wedded to the traditional metaphysical distinctions of inner/outer, life/death, and mortality/immortality. "If time is regarded as having certain characteristics that are event transcending," Thurman surmises, "and the human spirit is not essentially time bound but a time binder, then the concept of personal survival of death follows automatically. For man is never completely involved in, nor absorbed by, experience. He is an experiencer with recollection and memory—so these songs insist. The logic of such a position is that man was not born *in* time, that he was not created by a time-space experience, but rather that man was born *into* time. Something of him enters all time-space relationships, even birth, completely and fully intact, and is not created by the time-space relationship" (*NS*, 52). In addition to rereading the spirituals as a relational reconceptualization of the key coordinates of time and being with respect to the notion of immortality, Thurman's proposal radically suggests the conditions of possibility for thinking immortality, the site par excellence, are the strange utterances of the excluded others of reason. However, the knowledge of such is revealed not in and through the coordinates of rationality proper but through the critical exercise of imagination.

"We may dismiss, then, the symbolism of these songs as touching life and death," Thurman warns, "if we understand the literal truth with which they have to do. The moment we accept the literal truth, we are once again faced with the urgency of a vehicular symbolism. The cycle is indeed vicious" (*NS*, 55). To (mis)read the spirituals through a logic of identity is to arrest the development of thinking that—as the history of modern thought demonstrates—takes the meaning of the spirituals as the *absolute* acknowledgment of a racialized Other instead of a disclosure of the very conditions of possibility of freedom.

Stuart Hall returns to the site of black popular culture in raising the question concerning the racial logic that governs the "black" in the formation of black popular culture as well as the conditions of possibility that inform the conjuncture in which the question is raised. Hall is thus able to suggest that the politics of the "black" may open up a space within the cultural terrain to contest dominant configurations of power within the field of popular culture. Almost half a century prior to Hall's critical intervention, Howard Thurman territorializes this question in the field of theology and inaugurates a practice of critically reading the black within the cultural formation of the Negro spiritual. Thurman does not just encode the logic of the black within the domain of culture but rather *thinks* the black in opening up another space for the project of thought itself. In so doing, Thurman provides us with an untimely thinking of the imagination and "stands," as Charles Long reminds us, "among a small but growing group of Post-Colonial thinkers who struggle to provide a proper orientation for that world that might be coming."[35] By thinking with Thurman, we may be able to develop a critical political theology whose horizon is a "world that might be coming."

Notes

1. Stuart Hall, "What Is This 'Black' in Black Popular Culture?," in *Stuart Hall: Critical Dialogues in Cultural Studies*, ed. David Morley and Kuan-Hsing Chen (London: Routledge, 1996), 465; hereafter cited parenthetically in the text.

2. Recently, David Theo Goldberg engaged Hall's thought to rethink what he terms "a peculiar sort of political theology" with specific reference to the history and afterlife of apartheid in South Africa. See Goldberg, "A Political Theology of Race: Articulating Racial Southafricanization," *Cultural Studies* 23:4 (2009): 513–37. Interestingly, while noting Hall's lack of engagement with religion, Goldberg fails to take notice of Hall's highly instructive essay of the mid-1980s and his exchange on politics and religion with Saba Mahmood in the mid-1990s. See Stuart Hall, "Religious Ideologies and Social Movements in Jamaica," in *Religion and Ideology: A Reader*, ed. Robert Bocock and Kenneth Thompson (Manchester, UK: Manchester University Press, 1985), 269–96; and Hall, "Response to Saba Mahmood," *Cultural Studies* 10:1 (1996): 12–15.

3. In the preface to the recently published volume *Political Theologies: Public Religions in a Post-secular World* (New York: Fordham University Press, 2006), Hent de Vries and Lawrence Sullivan write, "When the collaborative effort was first discussed, in 1997–98, political theology was a term seldom heard in the wider academic debate, beyond historical references to the writings of Ernst Kantorowicz, Carl Schmitt, and 'theologies of liberation'" (xi). When one thinks that significant strands of "theologies of liberation" directly and consistently engaged the issue of race in elaborating various political theologies, the revival of the concept absent race should occasion considerable critical and reflexive interrogation.

4. Charles H. Long, *Significations: Signs, Symbols, and Images in the Interpretation of Religion* (Aurora, CO: The Davies Group, 1995), 203.

5. For an astute engagement with this problematic, albeit to a different end, see J. Kameron Carter, "Between W. E. B. Du Bois and Karl Barth: The Problem of Modern Political Theology," in this volume.

6. Howard Thurman, *With Head and Heart: The Autobiography of Howard Thurman* (New York: Harcourt Brace, 1979), 59; hereafter cited parenthetically in the text.

7. For an extended study of the relationship between Thurman and Schreiner, see Mozella G. Mitchell, "Howard Thurman and Olive Schreiner: Post-modern Marriage Post-mortem," *Journal of Religious Thought* 38:1 (1981): 62–73.

8. See Paul Dekar, "The 'Good War' and Baptists Who Refused to Fight It," *Peace and Change* 32:3 (2007): 186–202.

9. See Alton B. Pollard III, "Howard Thurman and the Experience of Encounter: A Phenomenological View," *Journal of Religious Thought* 46:2 (1989–90): 28–41.

10. Louis A. Renza, "The Veto of the Imagination: A Theory of Autobiography," *New Literary History* 9:1 (1977): 2. See also Luther E. Smith, "Intimate Mystery: Howard Thurman's Search for Ultimate Meaning," *Ultimate Reality and Meaning: Interdisciplinary Studies in the Philosophy of Understanding* 11 (1988): 85–101.

11. Olive Schreiner, "The Hunter," in *Dreams* (Boston: Roberts Brothers, 1892), 25–50.

12. As quoted in Mark Sanders, "Towards a Genealogy of Intellectual Life: Olive Schreiner's *The Story of an African Farm*," *Novel* 34:1 (2000): 77.

13. Ronald A. T. Judy, *(Dis)Forming the American Canon: African-Arabic Slave Narratives and the Vernacular* (Minneapolis: University of Minnesota Press, 1993), 124; Charlie Reitz, *Art, Alienation, and the Humanities: A Critical Engagement with Herbert Marcuse* (Albany: State University of New York Press, 2000), 118; Linda-Marie Delloff, "Nathan Scott, the Arts and Religious Journalism," in *Morphologies of Faith: Essays in Religion and Culture in Honor of Nathan A. Scott, Jr.*, ed. Mary Gerhart and Anthony C. Yu (Atlanta: Scholars Press, 1990), 169. For a recent treatment of Kant and the imagination, see Jane Kneller, *Kant and the Power of Imagination* (Cambridge: Cambridge University Press, 2007).

14. Christine Helmer, "Mysticism and Metaphysics: Schleiermacher and a Historical-Theological Trajectory," *Journal of Religion* 83:4 (2003): 529.

15. Karl Marx, "Contribution to a Critique of Hegel's *Philosophy of Right*," in *The Marx-Engels Reader*, ed. Robert C. Tucker, 2nd ed. (New York: W. W. Norton, 1978), 16–25.

16. As early as 1925, Thurman began to revisit the theological import of the spirituals in an announced speech on "Negro Spirituals" at First Baptist Church, Lockport, New York, on November 15, 1925. See Howard Washington Thurman, *The Papers of Howard Washington Thurman*, vol. 1, *My People Need Me, June 1918–March 1936*, ed. Walter Earl Fluker (Columbia: University of South Carolina Press, 2009).

17. Michel de Certeau, *The Mystic Fable*, vol. 1, *The Sixteenth and Seventeenth Centuries*, trans. Michael B. Smith (Chicago: University of Chicago Press, 1992), 164. See also Marie-Florine Bruneau, *Women Mystics Confront the Modern World: Marie De L'Incarnation (1599–1672) and Madame Guyon (1648–1717)* (Albany: State University of New York Press, 1998).

18. Rufus Jones, "The Spell of Immortality," *Official Register of Harvard University: Harvard Divinity School Bulletin* 41:21 (1944): 9.

19. Ibid.

20. Howard Thurman, "The Negro Spiritual Speaks of Life and Death," in *"Deep River" and "The Negro Spiritual Speaks of Life and Death"* (Richmond, IN: Friends United Press, 1975), 13; hereafter cited parenthetically in the text as *NS*.

21. Walter Benjamin, "The Task of the Translator," in *Illuminations*, trans. Harry Zohn (New York: Schocken Books, 1968), 76.

22. The idea of a "middle passage to modernity" seeks to complicate the revisionist narrative of modernity offered by Louis Dupré, *The Passage to Modernity: An Essay on the Hermeneutics of Nature and Culture* (New Haven, CT: Yale University Press, 1995).

23. Nathan A. Scott Jr., *The Poetics of Belief: Studies in Coleridge, Arnold, Pater, Santayana, Stevens, and Heidegger* (Chapel Hill: University of North Carolina Press, 1985), 149.

24. Piotr Hoffman, "Death, Time, and History: Division II of *Being and Time*," in *The Cambridge Companion to Heidegger*, ed. Charles B. Guignon, 2nd ed. (Cambridge: Cambridge University Press, 1993), 225.

25. In his Dudleian Lecture of the same date as Thurman's Ingersoll Lecture, the Jesuit scholar, racial justice activist, and editor of the periodical *America*, Reverend John LaFarge, S.J., in closing his lecture, rejects Sartre's "immanentism" in his famed 1943 play *No Exit*, which seeks to repeal what he terms "the challenge of militant naturalism" of the time. See Reverend John LaFarge, S.J., "Two World Concepts," *The Harvard Divinity School Bulletin* 13 (1948): 27–41.

26. Martin Heidegger as cited in Nikolas Kompridis, *Critique and Disclosure: Critical Theory between Past and Future* (Cambridge, MA: MIT Press, 2006), 34.

27. Charles H. Long, "Howard Thurman and the Meaning of Religion in America," in *The Human Search: Howard Thurman and the Quest for Freedom, Proceedings of the Second Annual Thurman Convocation*, ed. Mozella G. Mitchell (New York: Peter Lang, 1990), 141.

28. Kompridis, *Critique and Disclosure*, 35.

29. Long, "Howard Thurman and the Meaning of Religion in America," 142.

30. Ibid., 141.

31. Martin Heidegger as cited in Scott, *The Poetics of Belief*, 153.

32. George Cross, *Creative Christianity: A Study of the Genius of the Christian Faith* (New York: Macmillan, 1922), 24.

33. Kompridis, *Critique and Disclosure*, 38.

34. Joseph A. Buttigieg, "Introduction: Criticism without Borders," in *Criticism without Borders: Directions and Crosscurrents in Postmodern Critical Theory*, ed. Joseph A. Buttigieg (Notre Dame, IN: University of Notre Dame Press, 1987), 4.

35. Long, "Howard Thurman and the Meaning of Religion in America," 142.

CHAPTER 6

THE ENEMY'S TWO BODIES
(POLITICAL THEOLOGY TOO)

GIL ANIDJAR

"The body is with the king, but the king is not with the body. The king is a thing—."[1] Hamlet's cryptic statement, which has baffled centuries of readers, only began to make sense in the light of medieval political theology.[2] At the center of this doctrine, famously explained by Ernst Kantorowicz, there lies, therefore, a body. More precisely, two bodies lie there—the king's two bodies, along with the possibility of their violent separation.[3] Political theology, the doctrine of a complex relationship—one might say, the community—of sacred and social, divine and human, and of religion and politics, comes together and falls apart under the figure of those two bodies that are one, the two bodies in one king, the two bodies as one thing: "The king is a thing."

The striking story of this coming together and falling apart is the narrative, the tragic narrative, of *Richard II*, a narrative in which, Kantorowicz writes, Richard "'undoes his kingship' and releases his body politic into thin air" (35). "Bit by bit," Kantorowicz continues, Richard "deprives his body politic of the symbols of its dignity and exposes his poor body natural to the eyes of the spectators" (36). Political theology, the theory of the king's two bodies, comes together insofar as the king's body politic, "god-like or angellike" (27), remains attached to the king's body natural. Shakespeare's play, at

the same time that it provides Kantorowicz with a privileged example of political theology, a privileged example of the unity of the theologico-political,
also constitutes a staging of the undoing of this unity, "that most unpleasant
idea of a violent separation of the King's Two Bodies" (41).

"Political Shakespeare" here, however, primarily refers to a notion of community where unity and association—the figure that Kantorowicz emphasizes is the "symbol" (17)—provide the focal point of the narrative,[4] a unity
of the "body natural" with "the body politic," a unity of the sovereign with
the transcendent source of his authority, a unity of the community with its
sovereign, and finally, a unity of the secular with the spiritual. In what follows,
I pursue the work that has been done on political theology in Shakespeare
and ask about the coming together and falling apart of another community,
that of Arab and Jew. To be textually more precise, I ask about the community and "fellowship" (as Marlowe's Barabas suggests to Ithamore) of those
two Venetian bodies who, not quite *of* the community, are nonetheless "situated in a potentially threatening position very near the 'inside' of authority
and power." These two Venetian strangers and Venetian enemies are, then, the
Moor and the Jew.[5]

> Why this is something! Make account of me
> As of thy fellow; we are villains both:
> Both circumcisèd, we hate Christians both.
> Be true and secret, thou shalt want no gold.[6]

There is to this day no comparative study, no extended association by
way of literary analysis of the two plays once best known as *The Merchant
of Venice* and *The Moor of Venice*, an absence that has failed to be noticed
even by the very few who do engage the comparison.[7] This state of affairs
could hardly be considered arbitrary, for the divide between the two plays
can be justified, affirmed, and confirmed by way of varied and convincing
terms. Such terms extend from comedy versus tragedy, religion versus race,
theology versus politics, and all the way to law versus love, ancient versus
modern, Jew versus Moor, and more. In the context of political theology, moreover, it is striking that *The Merchant of Venice* presents us with
multiple examples of successfully negotiated friendships and love affairs,
whereas *The Moor of Venice* is filled with betrayal and the falling apart of
social relations: "all the bonds that link humanity and make living together

possible have been dissolved by Iago" writes Allan Bloom,[8] and the same may be said concerning audience response. As Stephen Greenblatt points out, the tragedy of *Othello* "heightens audience anxiety" and thus performs the painful state of dissociation, the harsh separation between the stage and an audience who is unable "to intervene and stop the murderous chain of lies and misunderstandings." In contrast, a "sardonic detachment" is impossible to maintain in the case of *The Merchant of Venice*, where "the audience's pleasure depends upon a sympathetic engagement with the characters' situation."[9] It should not be entirely surprising, therefore, that *The Moor of Venice* is predominantly considered a nonpolitical play. Stanley Cavell, for example, claims that there is no longer "any argument . . . with the description [that], compared with the cases of Shakespeare's other tragedies . . . this one [*Othello*] is not political but domestic."[10]

In a different perspective, one will find confirmation of the divide between the two plays in that *The Moor of Venice* is located within the sphere of politics, even if, as Tom Cohen points out in an illuminating essay, the Moor has a negative connection to political power, even if "the Moor never represented a sovereign subject to begin with."[11] It is, thus, "more insistently time-bound, concerned with the here and now rather than with eternal verities," whereas *The Merchant of Venice* clearly stages a struggle over metaphysical truths.[12] Laurence Danson confirms this line of thought by arguing that a "concern with the idea of kingship" may be relevant for a number of Shakespeare's plays, "but it is virtually irrelevant to a consideration of *Othello*. And similarly with this matter of Christian doctrine: In *The Merchant of Venice* the relationship of justice to mercy, and the theological vocabulary the theme entails, is strikingly prominent."[13]

It would thus be futile to argue that the division of the two plays, the very absence of any extended comparative study, is "wrong." Indeed, what one could call the incomparability, even the incommensurability, of the two plays is, to my mind, crucial. For if, as has been argued, the association and dissociation of theology and politics are at work within each of the two plays,[14] the narrative that is produced by their separation, its staging in two thoroughly distinct plays, becomes highly relevant. And if it is indeed the case that each play stages in its own fashion a certain political theology, then the distance between the two plays, each of which ostensibly sounds one of the two notions—politics and theology—as its "major" note, this separation of theology from politics, comes to the fore as worthy of being read.

Prefiguring the image of Hobbes's Leviathan and testifying to the development of a notion of corporation and incorporation, of the body as a model of community, the theory of the two bodies that articulates itself in *Richard II* found one of its sources in the transfer of Paul's theology to political thought. In Ephesians 5 (Pseudo-)Paul was thus thought to have already provided the ground for a political theology: "For the husband is the head of the wife just as Christ is the head of the Church, the body of which he is the savior."[15]

The hermeneutic transfer of this verse from the church to the state, to the political sphere "proper" in the hands of medieval jurists, produced a new definition of "the relations between Prince and state" on the basis of a powerful analogy that led, for example, to basing the staging of coronations on the model of marriage ceremonies. In this way, the classical spirit-body distinction was refigured, by way of the husband-wife analogy, into a theologico-political notion. Hence, if it was said that "the man is the head of the wife and the wife the body of the man," a jurist could infer that "after the same fashion, the Prince is the head of the realm, and the realm the body of the Prince."[16] Love and matrimony thus provide the analogical basis for thinking the body politic that is "at one and the same time a plural entity consisting of all . . . subjects and a single entity, the King."[17] This "bodily thought" considers that rather than institute the opposition of body to spirit, the body politic is at once the relationship between the sovereign and the community and the community itself.

Elaborating on Kantorowicz's research, Albert Rolls can therefore suggest that the relationship of Desdemona to Othello ("she shunned / The wealthy, curled darlings of our nations" [*O*, 1.2.67–68]) constitutes an important moment toward an understanding of Shakespeare's political theology. Like other Moors in Shakespeare, such as Aaron and Morocco, Othello can no doubt claim a political and military status: "I fetch my life and being / From men of royal siege" (1.2.21–22). "My parts, my title, and my perfect soul / Shall manifest me rightly" (1.2.31–32), a status that, as Iago points out, the state itself is temporarily eager to approve ("the state . . . cannot with safety cast him" [1.1.145–147]). This politico-military configuration explicitly includes Desdemona (even if perhaps inappropriately, or not seriously), whom both Othello and Iago figure as a "fair warrior" (2.1.180) or as "the general" (2.3.310).

A well-recognized storyteller and rhetorician, if also a troubled reader, Othello ultimately "writes" a story that proves to be a matter of state, worthy of being reported to the state ("and to the state / This heavy act with heavy heart relate" [5.2.368–369]). Othello is thus undoubtedly a statesman bound to the community and the city of Venice, yet his statesmanship can be questioned if the foremost and exemplary member of this community is "abused, stolen from me and corrupted / By spells and medicines bought of mountebanks," as Brabantio charges (1.3.61–62), rather than bound to him by love as would fit the head and the body.[18] Othello himself associates Desdemona with Venice and may even be suggesting that he is married to the city itself when he tells Desdemona: "I took you for that cunning whore of Venice / That married with Othello" (4.2.91–92).[19] Arguing for the political meaning of the "character of the relationship between Desdemona and Othello,"[20] Allan Bloom pursues Brabantio's questioning and relates this strange unity, "the strange love that united Othello and Desdemona," to Othello's failed statesmanship (38). Bloom concludes by rhetorically performing the analogical gesture that transfers love to politics and, more precisely, love to bad politics: "What was supposed to be love now turns into a tyranny" (56).

AT THIS MOMENT in the history of the theologico-political, there is little doubt that association (or love) strikes the dominant and preferred, if at times also tragic, note. It constitutes the political imperative and normative ideal that governs the community, as well as the relation of theology to politics. To revisit the question of Shakespeare's political theology is therefore to pursue the bodies of two lovers, two bodies as—and in relation to—the body politic, insofar as they are linked. But it is also to pursue the relation— of love and enmity, of association and dissociation, of coming together and falling apart—that operates between them in Shakespeare's writing. It is to pursue a community in its making and unmaking.[21]

The term "political theology" is itself the site of a dissociation, one that occurs in Kantorowicz's own book. There is no doubt that Kantorowicz was well aware of the complex history of this notion, a history that goes back at least to Varro, whom Augustine quoted in *The City of God*.[22] Yet Kantorowicz abstains from referring to this history and to the fact that the phrase "political theology" was revived, in the 1920s, by the German legal theorist Carl Schmitt. Like Kantorowicz, who by the 1950s had developed a different, more discreet political agenda, Schmitt was engaged in questioning the descriptive and prescriptive value of the notion of secularization. He lamented, warned against, and questioned the attempt to conceive of political existence detached from theology. Hence, Schmitt's famous statement: "All significant concepts of the modern theory of the state are secularized theological concepts not only because of their historical development— in which they were transferred from theology to the theory of the state, whereby, for example, the omnipotent God became the omnipotent law-giver—but also because of their systematic structure, the recognition of which is necessary for a sociological consideration of these concepts."[23]

In Schmitt's reading, the political ("the modern theory of the state") is constituted upon the separation of theology from politics ("secularization"), yet this separation is not a strict and hermetic rupture. Rather, the separation itself becomes the site of a "transfer," of a structural translation of theology into politics. The latter thus preserves theology (even if insufficiently, according to Schmitt) as a constitutive moment "within" it. Both medieval *and* modern political doctrines must therefore be understood as moments of the theologico-political. Both, in other words, could be described as "political theologies." In Kantorowicz's account, medieval political theology hinges on the king's two bodies, that is, on the relation between the king and the body politic. Constitutive of this complex political relation is love, as we saw around the relationship of Othello and Desdemona. More important perhaps, and as Schmitt also emphasized, law and jurisprudence provide the privileged space of political thought, the privileged space for the transfer of theological concepts to political ones. Law and love thus constitute a grid according to which one can engage in a reflection on the history of political theology, a grid in which these two terms—"law" and "love"—appear as founding concepts. The more compelling readings of *The Merchant of Venice* as a reflection on theologico-political issues put the two terms at the center of their argument.

Yet to privilege law and love would run the risk of ignoring enmity, and more specifically the dissociative dimension with which we began. It would run the risk of ignoring the narrative of a "violent separation of the King's Two Bodies" such as it occurs in *Richard II* and elsewhere. Schmitt's discreet followers (Kantorowicz and Straussians like Bloom) may have placed more emphasis on love and friendship, but in so doing they occluded more than their relationship to Schmitt. They also ignored that Schmitt had underscored the importance of friendship, as well as that of enmity and hostility. Seeking, in fact, to determine what the "special distinction" is "which can serve as a simple criterion of the political and of what it consists," Schmitt offers a radical addition to the distinctions made "in the realm of morality" (good and evil) or in the aesthetic realm (beautiful and ugly). As to the political sphere, Schmitt writes, "The specific political distinction to which political actions and motives can be reduced is that between friend and enemy."[24] Schmitt goes on to emphasize that this distinction "denotes the utmost degree of intensity of a union *or* separation, of an association *or* dissociation."[25]

Another chapter in Shakespeare's political theology would therefore have to ask about the dissociation, about the "undoing" of the unity of the king's two bodies and "that most unpleasant idea of a violent separation" of theological from political under the figure of the enemy. It would have to ask about the place of the enemy in political theology.[26] Hence, whether or not Schmitt is correct in asserting that the political entity exists as such only insofar as the decision is made regarding the friend–enemy distinction, the perspective that he thereby offers for a history of political theology and of political history is undeniable, for it underscores the minor note of Shakespeare's political theology, the dissonant note of dissociation and enmity. Following Schmitt, therefore, and his claim that the failure to decide on the friend–enemy distinction is the destruction of the political entity, there remains the question of the theological history of that distinction, the theological history of the concept of enemy. It is this staging of political theology considered from the perspective of the friend–enemy distinction that Shakespeare places under renewed scrutiny. It is a staging that demonstrates that the apparently marginal division, the perhaps only emerging dissociation of theology from politics, is located in a larger trajectory that hinges upon the concept of enemy. Shakespeare maps out this theologico-political trajectory and the crucial moment in which it comes together and apart as the history of political theology.

LET ME RESTATE THE OBVIOUS. Shylock is a theological enemy. He is "the Jew Shylock," the "mere enemy" (*MV*, 3.2.260), that is to say, the *absolute* enemy, who hates and is hated on the explicit basis of his religion. And if he does lend the money, as Antonio calls on him to do, it is not "as to thy friends" but rather "as to thine enemy" (1.3.129–131). Othello, on the other hand, "horribly stuffed with epithets of war" (*O*, 1.1.13), bears all the marks of a political and military enemy. Othello, whom Iago—that is, "I hate the Moor" Iago—and others call "the general" (2.3.310), is employed against the "general enemy Ottoman" ("Valiant Othello, we must straight employ you / against the general enemy Ottoman" [1.3.49–50]). Othello fights the Turk, and as the final scene suggests, he himself may very well be the "malignant and turbanned Turk" (5.2.351). As John Gillies writes, "His symbolic association with the Turks is a critical commonplace."[27] Othello is a Moor, and "the Moors were popularly considered barbarous, heathens naturally at war with Christians and Europeans."[28] And though he himself wonders, "Are we turned Turks?" (2.3.166), his conversion and, more generally, his religious status remain mysterious. As Julia Lupton puts it, "The play never decisively determines whether he has converted from a pagan religion or from Islam."[29]

Given the dimness of a "religion question" in the play, any claim that it has anything to do with the theological must be prepared to do argumentative battle. Indeed, were one to argue, as Lupton does, that "in *Othello* religious difference is more powerfully felt . . . than racial difference," one would still have to account for the apparent exhaustion of that power in the history of Shakespearean criticism.[30] Similarly, were one to emphasize that "ranking somatic, religious or national differences *vis-à-vis* each other is to continue to think of them as discrete categories," and indeed that such separation is mistaken, as James Shapiro and Ania Loomba do, one would still have to account for the way the two plays—and they are two very distinct plays that cannot be collapsed into each other—stage and sediment that separation between the Jew and the Moor.[31]

If we return to the matter of the body (or, shall we say, to the matter of race), we will notice that in spite of Shylock's concern with carnality and with flesh and "fair flesh," his own flesh seems to have failed to inscribe itself onto his progeny. Shylock's flesh "turned," and there is "more difference," therefore—the difference, one might say, introduced by the word *more*—between Shylock's flesh and Jessica's, "more difference between thy flesh and hers than between jet and ivory" (*MV*, 3.1.36–37). Between Shylock's "jet" and "fair Jessica's" ivory, we witness the turns of Samuel Marochitanus, "a blackamoor turned white," a Jew-turned-Christian and therefore white.[32] In Shylock's case, at any rate, the body of the Jew who, making both "breed as fast," "cannot tell" whether "gold and silver" are as "ewes and rams" (1.3.92–93), fails to ensure his own carnality, the reproduction of his own flesh.[33] As such, Shylock could be said to constitute a peculiar body, one that is also devoid of body, devoid of flesh. In his famous monologue, Shylock needs in fact to insist that he does have a body, eyes, hands, organs, and more: "Hath not a Jew eyes? Hath not a Jew hands, organs, dimensions, senses, affections, passions?" (3.1.55–57). Standing for the letter of the law, for a reading "according to the flesh," Shylock seems to lack a reliable and convincing body—"I never felt it till now" (3.1.81–82); he stands for the embodiment of the law and justice while lacking both. "Is that the law?" he finally asks. The theological enemy is also the failure to master the flesh. Shylock simply doesn't cut it.

In this, Shylock also fails to stand up to the comparison with Othello. Indeed, whereas Shylock consistently fails to exercise and even to understand the law—whereas he fails, as Martin Yaffe recently wrote, even to be a good Jew ("far from being a paragon representative of [Jewish law], he is knowingly inconsistent with regard to it"), and whereas Shylock even fails to bring down the power of "Jewish" revenge, Othello never fails.[34] "His problem," Stanley Cavell convincingly writes, "is over success, not failure."[35] Both the play as a whole and the character of Othello powerfully recall, as Allan Bloom recognizes, "the God of the Old Testament who commands love and promises revenge unto the third and fourth generation for those who are not obedient."[36] Othello, like the Old Testament God—"He's that he is" (*O*, 4.1.270), against Iago's "I am not what I am" (1.1.64)—is indeed jealous. He is "the jealous husband" who "acts out on the human scene a god's role; he is . . . a leader who can command and punish wherever he goes. He insists on honor and wreaks bloody vengeance on those who disobey."[37] Othello—"fire and brimstone!" (4.1.233) and "Justice to break her sword!" (5.2.17)—is thus not only "a judge"; he is also "a decent general doing justice on the basis of acts done" and rightfully regards himself as "the dispenser of justice": "Good, good, the justice of it pleases; very good" (4.1.206–207).[38]

Yet, with the staging of this "Semitic" justice (as Julia Lupton strangely suggests), one could already notice that the very incommensurability between Shylock and Othello is beginning to feel counterintuitive.[39] It is not as if Othello could, with any more certainty, be located on the site of the successful body or that of the powerful flesh.[40] It is not as if he could, with any more certainty, be located on the side of the political (or the racial) rather than on the side of the theological. In spite of the absence of comparative studies of the two plays, in spite of this unremarked if not unremarkable absence, it would be difficult to dismiss the obviousness of the link between them, a link that is at once so strong that it hardly merits lingering, and so weak, so minor, as to go virtually unnoticed in its obviousness. Lupton summarizes this obviousness and writes that "*Othello*, one of Shakespeare's middle tragedies, has often been taken as a rewriting of *The Merchant of Venice*:[41] both are set in the mercantile city-state of Venice, both employ clearly marked 'others,' and both use the theme of conspicuous exogamy to heighten the conventional comedic situation of young lovers blocked by an old father."[42] Allan Bloom concurs and asserts that "Othello and Shylock are the figures who are the most foreign to the context in which they move and to the audience for which they were intended."[43] Bloom strengthens the link between the plays when he states that "*Othello* is about a man who tried to assimilate and failed," whereas "in *The Merchant of Venice*, we see the soul of a man who refused to assimilate."[44] Finally, Leslie Fiedler humorously suggests that, in the writing of the two plays, it is "almost as if Shakespeare had said to himself: *Let's try that Venetian fable again, but this time let's turn everything upside down.*"[45]

In the light of the claim that, regarding discussions of the Jew Shylock, "the distinction between theology and race" has now been "eliminated," it remains therefore striking that most discussions of either one of the two plays rarely even mention the other.[46] It is as if the author of *The Merchant of Venice* had never even written *The Moor of Venice*, and vice versa. Even in the works I have mentioned, the divide between the two plays remains so consistent as to become invisible in its peculiarity. Indeed, if, as James Shapiro argues on the basis of Shylock's distinct hue ("jet") and his association with Tubal and Chus (*MV*, 3.2.285), "*The Merchant of Venice* provides another instance of the identification of Jews with blackness,"[47] and if, as Shapiro also has it, "the conventional critical view that what sets Shylock apart is his religion has deflected attention away from the more complex ways in which Shakespeare situates Jews within a larger, confused network of national and racial otherness,"[48] then the very persistence of the divide between the two plays along the very lines of "religious" versus "national and racial otherness," along the very lines of theological versus political, in Shapiro's own work as well as in others, should become conspicuous. It has not.

I cannot conclude without pointing out that as Shakespeare writes and as the separation between the two Venetian enemies is reinscribed and sedimented, what comes undone with it is the unity of the theologico-political. What was previously considered a complex (if difficult) unity, the coming apart of which represented catastrophe or senselessness itself ("The body is with the king, but the king is not with the body. The king is a thing—"), this unity of theology and politics has come apart in such a way as to become invisible even to those who argue against it. But this coming apart occurs in a particular staging, the staging of a separation that logically, historically, and rhetorically precedes the separation of theology from politics, of religion from race.

Beginning with the title, Shakespeare marked the distance between the two dimensions of the body politic, the two dimensions of the polis of Venice, and he did so under the figure of two enemies: the theological enemy and the political enemy, the merchant of Venice and the Moor of Venice.[49] The arbitrariness of the decision that separates between Moor and Jew, and historically between Muslim and Jew, between Arab and Jew, however, could not have failed to appear in Shakespeare's own text. Indeed, it is striking that having "convinced" generations upon generations of readers that the two plays, indeed, the two bodies, had nothing in common—though we all know that "nothing" in Shakespeare hardly amounts to nothing (and in fact when Hamlet says "The king is a thing—," Guildenstern interrupts with "A thing, my lord?" And Hamlet replies "Of nothing")—it is

Shakespeare himself who made manifest that much as the community is constituted by the unity of theology and politics, so there is a community, unimaginable and dissociative as it is, of two bodies, the Jew's and the Moor's, or, as Othello himself suggested in a famous variant, of the Moor's and the Judean's (*O*, 5.2.345), that invisibly sustains the link between two plays that ostensibly address two distinct kinds of "erring" and "extravagant" strangers, two distinct kinds of enemies.

"This passage has not been explained":[50] A jealous husband comes on the stage and catches his wife in a compromising position with a man he knows to have long been a friend. At this point in *The Merchant of Venice*, Lorenzo ("I shall grow jealous of you shortly, Lancelot, if you thus get my wife into corners" [*MV*, 3.4.26–27]) walks in on Lancelot and Jessica. Then, upon Jessica's report, he hears Lancelot's criticisms regarding his engagement to "the Jew's daughter." Noting that there are two distinct moments to Lancelot's diatribe, "Fair Jessica" reports to Lorenzo with great accuracy what Lancelot told her first: "He tells me flatly there's no mercy for me in heaven because I am a Jew's daughter." She then goes on to the second point made by Lancelot: "and he says you are no good member of the commonwealth, for in converting Jews to Christians, you raise the price of pork" (3.5.29–33). To this accusation, Lorenzo responds by telling Lancelot that he, Lancelot, does, in fact, the "same." Doing so, Lorenzo illustrates ever so fleetingly the comparability of Jew with Moor, of Shylock with Othello: "I shall answer that better to the commonwealth than you can the getting up of the Negro's belly. The Moor is with child by you, Lancelot!" (3.5.34–36).

Unreadable as it has remained, Lorenzo's associating Jew with Moor upon the figure of a pregnant body, which may or may not be saved according to the spirit (revisiting what results when "mercy seasons justice," Shakespeare would have provided, this time, Othello's answer: "I that am cruel am yet merciful" [5.2.86]), thus appears to produce and dismiss at the same time the unimaginable community of Jew and Arab, of theological and political enemy. The dual body of the enemy occurs at the moment when its salvation, as enemy body, will make it disappear. The two bodies are therefore associated at the very moment when their dissociation—the dissociation of theological from political—is asserted and denied. This is political theology at its best, but it is also political theology at its end. With it, Shakespeare traces the history of the concept of enemy. More important, perhaps, Shakespeare announces the modern separation of theology from politics, of anti-Semitism from Islamophobia, at the same time that he demonstrates that at the historical root of the theologico-political, one does find two bodies, the body of the Jew and the body of the Moor, the Jew and the Arab. If the history of reading *The Merchant of Venice* and *The Moor of Venice* is any indication, the association and dissociation of these two bodies hardly stands to reason, but then again, it is "much that the Moor should be more than reason" (3.5.40).

Notes

An earlier version of this chapter appeared in Gil Anidjar, *The Jew, the Arab: A History of the Enemy*. Copyright © 2003 by the Board of Trustees of the Leland Stanford Jr. University. All rights reserved. Used with the permission of Stanford University Press, www.sup.org.

  1. William Shakespeare, *Hamlet*, ed. G. R. Hibbard (Oxford: Oxford University Press, 1987), 4.2.

  2. The "making sense" I am referring to was offered by Jerah Johnson, "The Concept of the 'King's Two Bodies' in *Hamlet*," *Shakespeare Quarterly* 18:4 (1967): 430–434.

  3. Ernst Kantorowicz's *The King's Two Bodies: A Study in Medieval Political Theology* (Princeton, NJ: Princeton University Press, 1997) has been called "perhaps the most important work in the history of medieval political thought" (Peter Riesenberg, quoted in William Chester Jordan's "Preface" to Kantorowicz's book, ix). After a short introductory chapter on "the problem," Kantorowicz turns to Shakespeare and thus locates the dramatist at the very crux of a history of political theology. Further citations will be made parenthetically in the text.

  4. "Political Shakespeare" and its derivations ("Shakespeare's Politics" or "Political Criticism of Shakespeare") is a common title in Shakespeare scholarship, but it is one that often enough indicates less an interest in political theory than in issues that have since been "politicized." To use Shaul Bassi's description, "political Shakespeare" has thus meant an emphasis on "the micropolitics of class, gender, and race" rather than the "macropolitics of kings and cardinals" (Shaul Bassi, "Mixed Marriages, Mixed Philosophies and Mixed Criticisms: *Othello* and *Nigredo*," unpublished paper, 2001). By way of the two bodies, I address both of these dimensions, cultural and philosophical.

  5. I will refer to the following editions of Shakespeare's plays. *The Merchant of Venice*, ed. Jay L. Halio (Oxford: Oxford University Press, 1993), hereafter abbreviated *MV*; and *Othello*, ed. E. A. J. Honigmann (London: The Arden Shakespeare, 1997), hereafter abbreviated *O*.

  6. Christopher Marlowe, *The Jew of Malta*, ed. N. W. Bawcutt (Manchester, UK: Manchester University Press, 1978), 2.3.215–218.

  7. "It is worth remarking that in the dramatist's own lifetime the play seems to

have been universally known not as *Othello* but as *The Moor of Venice*" (Barbara Everett, "'Spanish' Othello: The Making of Shakespeare's Moor," in *Shakespeare and Race*, ed. Catherine M. S. Alexander and Stanley Wells [Cambridge: Cambridge University Press, 2000], 65). The situation has hardly changed since I published the present essay in *The Jew, the Arab* in 2003. Othello might be briefly mentioned in a pointedly titled study of *The Merchant* (Janet Adelman, *Blood Relations: Christian and Jew in* The Merchant of Venice [Chicago: University of Chicago Press, 2008], for instance), or Shylock in a study of *Othello* (Emily Bartels, *Speaking of the Moor: From 'Alcazar' to 'Othello'* [Philadelphia: University of Pennsylvania Press, 2009]); commonalities might be underscored in parallel readings of the plays (as in Julia Reinhard Lupton, *Citizen-Saints: Shakespeare and Political Theology* [Chicago: University of Chicago Press, 2005]); and better yet, the comparison might be at once banalized and denied, and strangely redeployed (most recently in Stephen—"Shylock-refuses-to-be-a-suicide-bomber"—Greenblatt, *Shakespeare's Freedom* [Chicago: University of Chicago Press, 2010]). One can finally survey the bibliography on Shakespeare and political theology and never discuss Shylock or Othello (Jennifer R. Rust, "Political Theology and Shakespeare Studies," *Literature Compass* 6:1 [2009]: 175–190). Scholarship is no mere incident here but is a symptomatic element of problems that, already at work in Shakespeare, affected his world and continue to govern ours.

8. Allan Bloom, *Shakespeare's Politics* (Chicago: University of Chicago Press, 1986), 64.

9. Stephen Greenblatt, *Shakespearean Negotiations: The Circulation of Social Energy in Renaissance England* (Berkeley: University of California Press, 1988), 134.

10. Stanley Cavell, *Disowning Knowledge in Six Plays of Shakespeare* (Cambridge: Cambridge University Press, 1987), 129.

11. Tom Cohen, "*Othello*, Bakhtin and the Death(s) of Dialogue," in Cohen, *Anti-Mimesis from Plato to Hitchcock* (Cambridge: Cambridge University Press, 1994), 42.

12. Honigmann, "Introduction," in *Othello*, 107.

13. Lawrence Danson, *The Harmonies of the Merchant of Venice* (New Haven, CT: Yale University Press, 1978), 16.

14. I am thinking here of Julia Lupton, whose reading of Othello's theological significance also reinscribes the importance of the struggle of Christendom with Islam in *Othello* (Lupton, *Citizen-Saints*, 103–124).

15. Ephesians 5:23 (New International Version).

16. Kantorowicz, *The King's Two Bodies*, 216.

17. Albert Rolls, *The Theory of the King's Two Bodies in the Age of Shakespeare* (Lewiston, NY: Edwin Mellen Press, 2000), 73.

18. The question of how to read Othello's assertion of "discord" becomes here highly relevant ("And this, and this the greatest discords be—*They kiss*" [2.1.196]) and underscores the theologico-political dimension crucial to an understanding of the relationship between Othello and Desdemona.

19. The syntax and the ambiguous genitive leave productively undecided whether Othello would here be admitting to being married to "Venice the whore" or to Desdemona, "the whore of Venice." The city's morality (and its embodiment in the female population) had after all already provided Iago with a crucial element in his deceit of

Othello: "I know our country disposition well— / In Venice they do let God see the pranks / They dare not show their husbands" (3.3.204–206). Otherwise put, the city did have a "reputation for sexual licentiousness" (Honigmann, "Introduction," in *Othello*, 11).

20. Bloom, *Shakespeare's Politics*, 36. Further citations will be made parenthetically in the text.

21. Although I take a different and somewhat critical perspective, it should already be clear that my argument is not only indebted to but closely parallels Lupton's "*Othello* Circumcised" (in *Citizen-Saints*). Lupton importantly emphasizes, for example, the importance of Paul and of a discourse of law and justice. These are, in fact, the basis for her reconsideration of *Othello* in the context of theological categories. In relation to the political meaning of the matrimonial relation, Lupton crucially points out that "whereas studies of race in the play tend to emphasize the movement of paganization, feminist critics have noted Othello's increasing association with justice, usually taken as the masculinist tenets of Judeo-Christian patriarchy. My point is somewhat different: Othello, not unlike Shylock, 'stands for justice,' an allegorizing tendency that separates the Semitic strands out of the Judeo-Christian synthesis even while grotesquely reinforcing the authority of the husband. Although Othello's increasing alliance with the law is indeed 'patriarchal,' I would insist on the Abrahamic (Judeo-Islamic) connotations of the concept" (Lupton, *Citizen-Saints*, 117–118).

22. Augustine, *The City of God*, trans. Henry Bettenson (London: Penguin Books, 1984), VI, 5. There is some debate about the origins of the phrase and its pertinent genealogy in regard to Schmitt's work. In his introduction to Kantorowicz's book, William Chester Jordan does not trace the history of the phrase, but he states almost at the outset that the phrase "political theology" was "associated with the German and Nazi-leaning jurist Carl Schmitt" (Jordan, in Kantorowicz, *The King's Two Bodies*, x).

23. Carl Schmitt, *Political Theology: Four Chapters on the Concept of Sovereignty*, trans. George Schwab (Cambridge, MA: MIT Press, 1985), 36.

24. Carl Schmitt, *The Concept of the Political*, trans. George Schwab (Chicago: University of Chicago Press, 1996), 26.

25. Ibid., 26; emphasis added.

26. This crucial question was implicitly raised by Jacob Taubes, whose formidable work signals the momentous place of the "enemy" already in Romans 11:28 (against Carl Schmitt's assertion that the New Testament does not deploy a political notion of the enemy). It is worth noting that although the importance of the friend-enemy distinction does not yet explicitly figure in Schmitt's *Political Theology*, Schmitt himself does conclude his main critique of liberalism with the charge that liberalism "wants to dissolve metaphysical truth in a discussion." With such discussions and with endless negotiations, Schmitt continues, liberalism defers "the decisive bloody battle" and, more gravely, "permit[s] the decision to be suspended" (Schmitt, *Political Theology*, 63). The decision is postponed along with the "decisive" bloody battle, but with it the question of enmity begins to emerge within *Political Theology* itself. It will take a few more years for Schmitt to place the enemy at the center of his political theory in *The Concept of the Political*. Insofar as he was continuing to reflect on sovereignty and putting the emphasis on a sovereign decision, however, Schmitt may not have felt the need to make explicit

that the sovereign decision had been translated into a decision over the enemy, which becomes sovereign with that decision (Schmitt, *Concept of the Political*, 38–39). At any rate, Schmitt did not make explicit the connection between political theology and the concept of the enemy.

27. John Gillies, *Shakespeare and the Geography of Difference* (Cambridge: Cambridge University Press, 1994), 32.

28. Bloom, *Shakespeare's Politics*, 42.

29. Lupton, *Citizen-Saints*, 105; see also Honigmann's comment that "we cannot prove Othello to be a Christian convert" (Honigmann, "Introduction," in *Othello*, 23) and Emily Bartels's assertion that "Othello's religious past is unclear" (Emily C. Bartels, "Making More of the Moor: Aaron, Othello, and Renaissance Refashionings of Race," *Shakespeare Quarterly* 41:4 [1990]: 436).

30. Lupton, *Citizen-Saints*, 106.

31. Ania Loomba, "'Delicious Traffick': Racial and Religious Difference on Early Modern Stages," in Alexander and Wells, *Shakespeare and Race*, 206. See also James Shapiro, "Race, Nation, or Alien?," in Shapiro, *Shakespeare and the Jews* (New York: Columbia University Press, 1996); and Michael Neill, "'Mulattos,' 'Blacks,' and 'Indian Moors': *Othello* and Early Modern Constructions of Human Difference," *Shakespeare Quarterly* 49:4 (1998): 361–374.

32. The "turns" of Samuel Marochitanus, the "blessed Jew of Morocco," already tell the story of "a blackamoor turned white," of a Jew-turned-Muslim but also turned-Christian. There is, as of yet, no study of "his" book, a heavily edited translation of which appeared in English in the seventeenth century under the title *The Blessed Jew of Marocco: or, A Blackmoor Made White. Being a Demonstration of the True Messias out of the Law and Prophets, by Rabbi Samuel, a Jew Turned Christian* (York, UK: T. Broad, 1648); for more on "race" as it applied to Jews and Moors, see, for example, James R. Andreas Sr., "The Curse of Cush: Othello's Judaic Ancestry," in *Othello: New Critical Essays*, ed. Philip C. Kolin (New York: Routledge, 2002), 169–187.

33. As will become clearer, the distinction between Shylock and Othello, between Jew and Moor, is already breaking down. As Julia Lupton puts it, "Even Iago's infamous image of bestial cross-coupling, 'an old black ram / Is tupping your white ewe' (1.1.90–91), echoes *Merchant*'s most egregious pun, that between 'ewes' and "'Iewes'" (Lupton, "*Othello* Circumcised," 77). Shylock's excessive love of gold, moreover, was already announced by Morocco's failure to stay away from it, or, as Barbara Lewalski writes, "This defeat and lessoning of Morocco . . . foreshadows the defeat and conversion of Shylock, for he represents in somewhat different guise these same antichristian values of worldliness and self-righteousness" (Barbara K. Lewalski, "Biblical Allusion and Allegory in 'The Merchant of Venice,'" *Shakespeare Quarterly* 13:3 [1962]: 337). For an illuminating comparison of Shylock and Morocco, which credits Shakespeare with "the juxtaposition of Moor and Jew" so as to "rewrite the categories of exclusion," see Alan Rosen, "The Rhetoric of Exclusion: Jew, Moor, and the Boundaries of Discourse in *The Merchant of Venice*," in *Race, Ethnicity, and Power in the Renaissance*, ed. Joyce Green MacDonald (Cranbury, NJ: Fairleigh Dickinson University Press, 1997).

34. Martin Yaffe, *Shylock and the Jewish Question* (Baltimore: Johns Hopkins University Press, 1997), 61.

35. Cavell, *Disowning Knowledge*, 10.

36. Bloom, *Shakespeare's Politics*, 53.

37. Ibid.

38. Ibid., 54, 55.

39. Lupton, *Citizen-Saints*, 118. The use of the word *Semitic* is obviously what is strange to me (would one speak of "Aryan injustice"?). For more on the matter, see my *Semites: Race, Religion, Literature* (Stanford, CA: Stanford University Press, 2008).

40. See, for example, Cavell's interpretation of *Othello*, which situates Othello as "other" to and as "separate" from Desdemona's "flesh and blood" (Cavell, *Disowning Knowledge*, 138). Bloom goes so far as to call Othello "curiously insubstantial" (Bloom, *Shakespeare's Politics*, 58).

41. The "often" is, of course, quite unwarranted as the two plays are, again, barely ever discussed together, except to point out that they both take place in Venice. It is significant that Lupton, who in an earlier version of her essay had left the "often" hanging without reference, reported having no other study to mention than that of Leslie Fiedler, *The Stranger in Shakespeare* (New York: Stein and Day, 1972) (personal communication; the reference to Fiedler was added in Lupton, *Citizen-Saints*). Note, however, that Jean-Pierre Petit wrote what is perhaps the most striking exception to the lack of comparison of the two plays. In four short pages, he juxtaposes Othello and Shylock, discussing one after the other. Incidentally, he also minimizes the importance of "race" and sees in the two plays primarily stories of conversion (J.-P. Petit, "Deux étrangers shakespeariens," in *Regards européens sur le monde anglo-américain: Hommage à Maurice-Paul Gautier* [Paris: Presses de l'université de Paris-Sorbonne, 1992], 127–130).

42. Lupton, *Citizen-Saints*, 105.

43. Bloom, *Shakespeare's Politics*, 14.

44. Ibid., 21.

45. Fiedler, *The Stranger*, 141; emphasis in original.

46. Mary J. Metzger, "'Now by My Hood, a Gentle and No Jew': Jessica, *The Merchant of Venice*, and the Discourse of Early Modern English Identity," *PMLA* 113:1 (1998): 52; see also Loomba, "'Delicious Traffick,'" 203–224. The argument here is one I elaborated in *Semites*, that "religion" and "race" are less distinct (historically as well) than they are co-constitutive. What should be obvious throughout is that the division between Shylock and Othello already functions as an iteration of the distinction of religion from race or, in a more contemporary idiom, of Islamophobia from anti-Semitism.

47. Shapiro, *Shakespeare and the Jews*, 172. Notably, Shapiro himself never even discusses *Othello*.

48. Ibid., 173.

49. That the merchant may not be Shylock has been argued often enough, if only on the basis of Portia's own famous query: "Which is the merchant here, and which the Jew?" (*MV*, 4.1.171). But this uncertainty does not diminish the distance between the two strangers and between the two plays. Such distance, in fact, mutually determines the two plays—and the two enemy bodies. See David Simpson's illuminating discus-

sion, "'Which is the merchant here? And which the Jew?': Friends and Enemies in Walter Scott's Crusader Novels," *Studies in Romanticism* 47:4 (Winter 2008): 437–452.

50. "This passage has not been explained; it might be an outcrop of a lost source, or a topical allusion. Perhaps it was introduced simply for the sake of the elaborate pun of Moor/more" (J. R. Brown, quoted in Eldred Jones, *Othello's Countrymen: The African in English Renaissance Drama* [London: Oxford University Press, 1965], 71).

CHAPTER 7

THE DOUBLE MARK OF
THE MALE MUSLIM

Eracing Othello

DANIEL BOYARIN

"The Jew, the Arab constitute the condition of religion and politics."[1] This
is an essay about the inscription of difference on the body, thus an emblem of the social production of "race." The mark divides two modern
races, the Semitic and the Aryan, but before the Aryan and Semite, divided
identically—so I will suggest, if not quite argue—between the Christian in
Christendom and those circumcised others within, the ones who must be
expelled. I argue that *Othello*, in particular Othello's penis, marks the site
of the knotting and unraveling of a complex that is intimately bound up
with what I would call a political theology of race. One wonders if Othello
(like Daniel Deronda) ever looked at his penis. It is notorious that Deronda
never "looked down":[2]

> The text's insistent reference leads relentlessly to the referent—to *la chose*, in
> fact: the hero's penis, which must have been circumcised, given what we are
> told of his story. . . . Deronda must have known, but he did not: otherwise,
> of course, there could be no story. The plot can function only if *la chose*,
> Deronda's circumcised penis, is disregarded; yet the novel's realism and refer-
> entiality function precisely to draw attention to it.[3]

I offer this only to set off the much less studied question of *Othello*'s penis.
Othello's penis seems just as much a mystery (to him) as Deronda's is to

him, for if a child raised for two years among orthodox Jews was surely circumcised, so at least as surely was a Muslim man grown to adulthood among Muslims.

Julia Lupton has written: "Looking east, toward Arabia and Turkey, and to the northern parts of Africa, Othello would become a Muslim-turned-Christian, . . . inheritor of a monotheistic civilization already marked by frequent contacts with Christian Europe and hence more likely to go renegade."[4] On my reading, this is precisely where we are bound to look, for that is what a Moor is and where a Moor comes from. I would only slightly refocus the point by remarking that it is not only that the Moor is the inheritor of such a monotheistic civilization in contact with Christian Europe but that Moors had been ruling much of "Christian" Europe for *eight* centuries, eight hundred years—not only in Spain—and the anxiety about the Christianness of Christian Europe itself is at stake in Othello's penis, a circumcised penis penetrating to the very center of Europe:[5] that "old black ram" tupping/topping, conquering, defeating your white you.[6] Desdemona's vagina is, in a powerful sense, a displacement of the male Christian's (Brabantio's) anus, with being sodomized, of course, the *historically* classic sign of political/military defeat for a man.[7]

It is by now notorious that modern *Othello* criticism and performance practice both are driven by a profound and tenacious feeling that the play is about "race," race as we experience it.[8] Reading for race in the modern sense is as anachronistic—perhaps—as a hypothetical claim that the play is about homosexuality, since the latter hadn't been invented yet.[9] The compelling, and more correct in my view, generalization about this text of Shakespeare's is that in it we encounter a system of differences that are neither racial nor religious, neither sexuality generated nor quite gendered, but all of these aggregated, laid on one another in ways that make nonsense of (or rather demonstrate the recent construction of) our own social and critical litanies. Oddly, Othello's alleged "thick lips" and dark skin seem less significant a marker of his indelible identity than his hidden penis. I offer the notion that the figure of Othello's ambiguously circumcised penis is as important a—or even a more important—signifier of his "race" than the color of his skin.[10] Lynda E. Boose, who has been thinking in similar directions, has asked: "Was skin color the most defining feature for constructing

Otherness in sixteenth-century England?"[11] Julia Lupton has put the point even more finely that "in *Othello* religious difference is more powerfully felt than racial difference."[12] This is still to partly miss the point, however, that "race and religion" are simply not discrete categories in the play: "race" is a religious difference; "religion," a racial one. The play is, in part, about the refusal of these categories to become or stay discrete, about the impossibility of a Christian Moor, as impossible it seems as a Christian Jew. In this brief essay I suggest that the ambivalent—but not, I think, ambiguous—fleshly sign of Othello's circumcision and *Othello* itself provide an exemplary early instance of the queering of the very identity markers that form our contemporary mantras of race, gender, or religion; or better put, by letting the categories of the play form themselves before our reading eyes, we open our eyes to the constructedness of our most naturalized of differences, the differences between differences.

The first times we meet Othello's "race," it is his blackness (and notoriously his "thick lips") that are in evidence:

IAGO
'Zounds, sir, you're robb'd; for shame, put on your gown;
Your heart is burst, you have lost half your soul;
Even now, now, very now, an old black ram
Is tupping your white ewe. Arise, arise;
Awake the snorting citizens with the bell,
Or else the devil will make a grandsire of you:
Arise, I say. (1.1.92–98)

"Race," of course, very much in its modern sense seemingly could not be clearer here, and miscegenation, the monstrous image of the rampant black penis entering the lily-white female body (as well as the specter of a grandchild with horns and black skin) is raised with all its fascinating, arousing horror.

When it is linked with another related image, we can see, however, that Shakespeare is not simply playing, at any rate, the nineteenth- and twentieth-century race card:

IAGO
'Zounds, sir, you are one of those that will not
serve God, if the devil bid you. Because we come to

do you service and you think we are ruffians, you'll
have your daughter covered with a Barbary horse;
you'll have your nephews neigh to you; you'll have
coursers for cousins and gennets for germans. (1.1.118–124)

Othello and his sex have thus been figured as bestial in two ways within
the space of a few lines. But the African here is clearly not the (pagan) sub-
Saharan black African but the Muslim Moor of North Africa. This identification is, I think, quite decisive for the play. Shakespeare and, indeed, Iago
are not confused as to the placing of a Moor. He is from Barbary, North
African [the word *Moor* refers, at least originally, to Mauretania], a Barbary
stallion. There is another pun hidden here as well that supports this reading:
The coursers have hidden within them "corsairs," as well, Barbary pirates.
For Iago, his Barbary, Muslim "nature" figures Othello as bestial other, despite whatever "baptism" he has been known to have undergone. And lest
there be any doubt of Shakespeare's discrimination with respect to Moors,
it is important to remember that at the court of Elizabeth, there was a
Moorish ambassador, the ambassador of Morocco, clearly portrayed in contemporary art as a Barbary warrior and not a sub-Saharan "black" (in our
racialized terminologics).[13]

The very images of the Moor's bestial sexuality mobilized by the Christian Iago need some fleshing out. If for the rampant male sexuality of the
ram we have to go to Greece and satyrs (cum devils), for the horses we
need go no further than Ezekiel 23:20: "There she lusted after her lovers,
whose genitals were like those of donkeys and whose emission was like that
of horses." We need to pay some attention to the differential force of these
images, let them play out their different logics of miscegenation. In the first,
Desdemona is herself bestialized through her bestial intercourse. (As Cassio
says: "Reputation, reputation, reputation! O, I have lost / my reputation! I
have lost the immortal part of / myself, and what remains is bestial. My reputation, / Iago, my reputation!" (266–269). If, in the first, Othello is rami-
fied, she is rendered sheepish as well. Her fantasized monstrous child, spawn
of the devil, is so not because his father is a sheep, his mother a human but
because they are sheep of different colors—seemingly, then, a raced image.
The horses, however, are an entirely different kettle of fish. Here it is only
Othello who is rendered a stallion; Desdemona remains a human woman.

It is equine nephews, cousins, germans, Barbary corsairs whom Brabantio will acquire through this marriage, not even a mule for a grandchild. This (ungrammatical) detail suggests strongly that we look to the biblical allusion to delve more deeply into Shakespeare's design here.

The context of Ezekiel 23 will provide, in fact, a rich and important clue for the reading of *Othello*, for the entire chapter is a graphic, vivid, horrifying depiction of miscegenation as bestiality with such appalling outcome that the passage in the play becomes a *mise en abyme* and thus hermeneutic key. The chapter tells a parable of two sisters, Aholah and Aholibah, who both went whoring after foreign lovers (one is, as we are told, Samaria; and the other, Jerusalem). Their lovers, in both cases, were profoundly attractive young military men: "She doted upon the Assyrians her neighbours, captains and rulers clothed most gorgeously, horsemen riding upon horses, all of them desirable young men" (23:12). It is of these young men that it is said that their penises are like the penises of asses and their ejaculations like those of horses. And the consequences are predictable (at least for Ezekiel): "Therefore, O Aholibah, thus saith the Lord GOD; Behold, I will raise up thy lovers against thee, from whom thy mind is alienated, and I will bring them against thee on every side" (23:22). While Shakespeare certainly does not allow the punitive moralizing tone of the biblical passage to creep into his text, this intertextual reading does open up a significant moment in the play, a reading of Desdemona as tragic heroine in her own right. It is her desire, her very falling in love, it would seem, with the religious and racial other who so attracts with his stories of derring-do that dooms her to her tragic fate. No more a punishment than the downfalls of any other tragic heroes and with equal (if not greater) admiration of and deep sympathy for the tragic hero whose flaw causes his downfall, Desdemona's loving not wisely but too well also is the author of her destruction, for, as in the biblical text, it is the very male partner in an "improper" love who becomes the enemy who destroys the female lover. She loves the Barbary horse, whose penis is a horse's. But he is a Barbary horse, not just any horse, and hence a circumcised one. The figure thus works within the Shakespearean text very closely, mutatis mutandis (as already noted), to the biblical co-text, for there, sex is a figure for religious infidelity, and so here too. The Othellan figure of Desdemona's desire for the other is thus a representation of the nearly sexual attractiveness of Islam as well.[14]

Moors are Muslims; Muslims are circumcised and yet, Othello famously ends his life with the following speech:

OTHELLO
Soft you; a word or two before you go.
I have done the state some service, and they know't.
No more of that. I pray you, in your letters,
When you shall these unlucky deeds relate,
Speak of me as I am; nothing extenuate,
Nor set down aught in malice: then must you speak
Of one that loved not wisely but too well;
Of one not easily jealous, but being wrought
Perplex'd in the extreme; of one whose hand,
Like the base Indian/Iudean [Quarto/Folio],[15] threw a pearl away
Richer than all his tribe; of one whose subdued eyes,
Albeit unused to the melting mood,
Drop tears as fast as the Arabian trees
Their medicinal gum. Set you down this;
And say besides, that in Aleppo once,
Where a malignant and a turban'd Turk
Beat a Venetian and traduced the state,
I took by the throat the circumcised dog,
And smote him, thus.

Stabs himself. (5.2.389–406)

Leaving aside the loving wisely (or not), loving too well (or not), I would begin by focusing on the last line but one: "I took by the throat the circumcised dog," which posits circumcision as the very sign and emblem of a "malignant and a turban'd Turk." In denying his own circumcision, as it were, Othello's project here is constructing himself as a Christian, Venetian patriot—"muscular Christian"—one of "us," not one of the (feminized and bestialized) others, and hence, it would seem a fit sexual partner for Desdemona. Othello's own penis then becomes a site unseen of ambiguity with regard to the components of an identity (sexualized) of both the European "white" self and the components of its own constructed otherings.

The passage itself is in its own right a conflicted, almost logically tortured one (and I don't think this is mimesis of Othello's own internal state of unrest). Othello explicitly demands that the author of his biography, the historian of the sad events, narrate only that which relates to his unhappy sexual history, his relation with Desdemona and its tragic end, and explicitly not mention the service he has done the state, especially not in order to "extenuate" him. But then, at the very end of the speech, he insists that the narrator of the events must indeed make mention of the events in Aleppo, when in defending Venice's honor against the Muslim Turk, he stabbed him as he stabs himself now. The contradiction says (as the Hebrew expression has it), Interpret me!

Let's take Othello at his word: The reason that Othello wants his Aleppan exploit spoken of is not to extenuate his circumstances but only to make us understand that he dies a Christian, a proper Venetian—he is not a circumcised pagan murderer but a Christian who killed his wife for honor (an irony in the present moment in which "honor killing" has become one of the very instruments with which to vilify a demonized Islam). He is asserting his status as Christian and non-Turk, as European. Julia Lupton gets it right: "Shakespeare does not use Christianity to rise above color-based racism so much as his play renders visible the blindspot of *ethnos* that mortgages the inclusive vision of Christian humanism, a blindspot marked above all by the unerasable yet nongenetic scar of circumcision in Shakespeare's Venetian plays."[16] But at the very same time, Othello is not justifying himself as the good Christian but killing himself as the "dog" that he knows himself to be. The "circumcision" remains an unerasable scar on the Christian white surface of Christendom. In the end, having himself never quite unturned Turk (for the prepuce does not grow back), the circumcised Turk that is Othello must be killed again.

There is, of course, that other specter of a circumcised penis haunting Europe always, unerasably, an indelible stain on Christendom. The original circumcised dogs are the Jews, called indeed "the circumcision," according to Paul: "Beware of dogs; beware of evil-doers; beware of the circumcision" (Philippians 3:2). With this allusion, Shakespeare reveals the deep haunting of Europe by a dual figure, the Jew-Muslim, far far from the Jew-Christian versus Muslim binary with which our theological politics works even today. Gil Anidjar has written: "Without diminishing the accuracy of these accounts or the injustice involved in making Palestinians pay for the guilt of Europe vis-à-vis the Jews, one must nonetheless consider that these accounts entirely take for granted distinct states of enmity (between Jews and Arabs, between Europe and the Arabs, between Europe and the Jews, compounded in this last case by some eternally irreparable guilt) while ignoring the possibility of hidden links and associations between these pairings."[17] Or, as Jonathan Boyarin has recently put it in an account sharply relevant for the project in this essay, "If we identify processes of double consciousness at work in the cultural politics of difference in late medieval Europe, we should be most cautious in identifying them too closely with the *Reconquista*, the Inquisition, and the liminal status of *conversos* remaining in Spain—not least because, after 1492, the situation of *Moriscos* was structurally analogous to that of the *conversos* themselves."[18] On my reading, Shakespeare, at any rate, did not ignore this possibility at all, locating it firmly, as it were, at the site of the open secret of the hidden circumcision. Eliminating "the circumcision" from Christendom is at the heart of *The Moor of Venice* (as it is of *The Merchant of Venice*), and the two form a virtual unity on this reading.[19]

In an essay in two voices (but largely written by Jonathan Boyarin), "Self-Exposure as Theory: The Double Mark of the Male Jew," my brother and I sought to articulate a self-informed, critical account of our own identities as part of the circumcision.[20] We wrote then, "We understand ourselves as more profoundly born to, native to, an anamnestic generational tradition than to any national state or territory. The mark on our bodies, it seems to us, works harder than our birth certificates. Partly for that reason, we have chosen to affirm this mark in its detachable double, the headcovering that signals us as observant Jews."[21] One might say that Othello's doffing of his turban (Turkish yarmulke)—that very turban so prominently on the head of the Moorish ambassador referenced earlier—enacts precisely the hiding of the mark that the Boyarin brothers, exhibitionists that we are, sought/ seek to expose. Othello himself, it would seem, is represented as "travelling along a marginal trajectory providing a connecting thread among an ever-widening field of articulated differences," but, as Jonathan Boyarin happily wrote in the sequel to this sentence, "in order for such a marginal trajectory to be traversable, it must be moored in the past."[22]

What, then, of the Moor's own penis? As Jonathan Boyarin wrote nearly two decades ago, "Consideration for a moment of the fact that for a long time Europe's Others consisted of Jews, Turks, 'Saracens,' and 'Moors'—all circumcised, of course—yields the surprising implication that uncircumcision becomes ultimately the diacritic of Christianness, while absorption of Paul's affect as in the passage [from Philippians] just quoted renders circumcision a highly charged negative sign of un-Christianness."[23] By this token, Othello must always remain un-Christian at best, still "of the circumcision."

To the best of my memory, there is only one place in the play where Othello is even remarked at all as Christian convert, when Iago says:

IAGO
For 'tis most easy
The inclining Desdemona to subdue
In any honest suit: she's framed as fruitful
As the free elements. And then for her
To win the Moor—were't to renounce his baptism,
All seals and symbols of redeemed sin,
His soul is so enfetter'd to her love,
That she may make, unmake, do what she list,
Even as her appetite shall play the god
With his weak function. (2.3.335–350)

So Othello has been baptized but would renounce his own baptism for the sake of Desdemona, because his soul is so enfettered to her love. The changeability of the Moor in his will (desire, 1.3.336) signals also his changeability with respect to Desdemona but also, and even more important perhaps, with respect to religion. She could win him (over) even to having him renounce his baptism. But, once again, another reading lies hard by the surface of the text, for at least in one very plausible take on the syntax, it is *Desdemona* who, in her desire for Othello, will renounce *his* baptism. After all, why should he have to renounce his baptism for her? One would think the opposite. This second reading takes account of her desire for him, not only his desire for her, so curiously elided by the critics and interpreters. "Even as her appetite shall play the god," interpreted in the Arden (and everywhere else it seems) as his appetite for her, not hers for him. If we renounce this appetite suppressant, however, then it seems that it is her desire that will lead her to do anything to win him, even "were't to renounce his baptism." For her to win the Moor, she will renounce *his* baptism, that baptism that is in question because of his circumcision. If the deep text implies that Othello's baptism is itself in question, because of the indelible mark on his penis—as I read the play here: the mark that baptism itself was to supersede as sign and symbol—then Desdemona to win the Moor would have to renounce his baptism and take that circumcised, hence unbaptized, organ into her body. In the confusion of the syntax is hidden the knife that circumcised Othello.

There is more than a hint, already in the beginning of the play, that his conversion, his Christianity, is very much in question among the Venetian signory:

BRABANTIO
How! the duke in council!
In this time of the night! Bring him away:
Mine's not an idle cause: the duke himself,
Or any of my brothers of the state,
Cannot but feel this wrong as 'twere their own;
For if such actions may have passage free,
Bond-slaves and pagans shall our statesmen be. (1.2.110–115)

Here, at any rate, it seems clear that Othello is not a "Christian." If his action in kidnapping or magicking Desdemona were to go unpunished by the duke or the state's council, then Venice would be in danger of being ruled by "bond-slaves" (Othello) and "pagans" (Othello). This passage calls up a biblical allusion to Proverbs 3: "Under three things the earth trembles; under four it cannot bear up: a slave when he becomes king, and a fool when he is filled with food; an unloved woman when she gets a husband, and a maidservant when she displaces her mistress" (21–23). Othello is the slave who would be king. Othello is both bonds-man and "pagan," hence not Christian in Brabantio's eyes, for all his conversion. "Pagan" here is not in contradistinction to Muslim but signifies Muslim; the mark of Cain is not Othello's blackness but the hidden/not hidden evidence of his not-quite Christianity. There is no evidence that I know of to the contrary and, at least in the *Merchant of Venice*, good reason to understand Shakespeare's pagan as any non-Christian: "Adieu! tears exhibit my tongue. Most beautiful pagan, / most sweet Jew! if a Christian did not play / the knave and get thee, I am much deceived. But, / adieu: these foolish drops do something drown my / manly spirit: adieu" (2.3.10–14). If a sweet Jew be a beautiful pagan, then it would seem almost a fortiori that a Muslim is a pagan, too, for Shakespeare. This general view is supported by multiple medieval representations of Muslims as idolaters. If further proof were needed, let James I's famous poem on the battle of Lepanto in which the Venetians after their battle with the Turk, thanking God for having "redeemd" them "from cruel Pagans thrall," be my witness.[24] *Willing*, then (in his changeable will), perhaps to renounce all signs and seals of his redeemed sin for the sake of Desdemona, he cannot, however, renounce (but only denounce) the signs and seals of his sin; they are inscribed on his penis.

There is a deep anxiety abroad in the play about the ability of the Turk to turn Christian and back to Turk as he wills, to hide, as it were, his true (or always false) identity. As a preacher only slightly later than Shakespeare argued: "Many, and as I am informed, many hundreds, are Musselmans in Turkie, and Christians at home; doffing their religion as they do their clothes, and keeping a conscience for every harbor they shall put in. And those Apostates and circumcised Renegadoes . . ."[25]

If such anxieties attend the Christian converted and reconverted back from Islam, a fortiori the Muslim convert, too. Turbans can be doffed and donned, but foreskins not so easily. Boose writes, "Clothes, or rather cultural signifiers, make the man and cultural and theological alignments—unlike biological ones—can always be changed."[26] This claim, right as far as it goes, in setting up a binary opposition between "clothes" that can always be changed, and then glossing them as "cultural signifiers," and "biological ones," quite misses the point of the constructed and indelible mark on the body, that is, bodily but not biological, indelible but still a cultural signifier.[27] There is, thus, a theological alignment, a theological orientation of the flesh, that cannot be changed.[28] Shakespeare himself, I think, sends us a powerful clue here in the emblematic name Iago. A direct association with Sant/Iago, dubbed Matamoros, the Moorkiller, is to me irresistible, inscribing these two in a drama in which the Christian it is who kills, as he is fated to, the Muslim, indelibly marked in his penis as such, who plausibly, so plausibly enters Europe in the guise of a convert to Christianity.[29] The Christian Othello must kill the circumcised Turk that he is; there is no other way for him to demonstrate (and effectuate) an "ethnic" cleansing of Europe. Not surprising then, that the Muslim Moor seeks, even—or rather precisely—at the very end, to erase the ineradicable mark (at least discursively) by cursing and stabbing the circumcised Turk. But he cannot. Indeed, far from turning away from his "pagan" past, he himself "turns Turk," as he himself has warned (in yet another *mise en abyme*):

> Why, how now, ho! from whence ariseth this?
> Are we turn'd Turks, and to ourselves do that
> Which heaven hath forbid the Ottomites?
> For Christian shame, put by this barbarous brawl:
> He that stirs next to carve for his own rage
> Holds his soul light. (2.3.169–178)

Othello does indeed turn Turk and turns on the Turk that he has turned, stabs himself to death, and the politico-religious *tragedia è finita*. Othello is his own worst enemy, as we are given to say with far less literal force than here, split between the turban that can be removed and the mark on his penis that cannot; hence, he *must* die (it has very little to do, on this reading, with a domestic drama).[30] "Before you can try to eliminate an enemy, you must first identify that enemy. The definition of the political self and the political other has varied throughout history. The history of that variation is the history of political identities, be they religious, national, racial or otherwise."[31] What *Othello* teaches us, at one of the moments of the very founding of an enmity, is how corrosively ambiguous are not only the boundaries of category in the sense of who's in and who's out, but the very distinction of category itself, "be they religious, national, racial or otherwise," all overdetermined and imbricated with each other. The politics of race are thus at their very foundation moments inextricably a theological politics, a political theology. The tragedy of *Othello* may be ended, but the tragedy, the plot of a fantasmatic indelible enmity of the Muslim, a plot of which it signifies one beginning, is a tragedy seemingly without end.

Notes

An earlier and shorter version of this chapter was published as Daniel Boyarin, "Othello's Penis: Or, Islam in the Closet," in *Shakesqueer*, ed. Madhavi Menon, 254–262. Copyright © 2011, Duke University Press. All rights reserved. Reprinted by permission of the publisher. I wish to thank Janet Adelman (her memory for a blessing), Jonathan Boyarin, Julia Reinhard Lupton, and Madhavi Menon for their generous comments on an earlier version of this essay. None of them ought take any responsibility, however, for its flaws other than aiding and abetting after the fact.

1. Gil Anidjar, *The Jew, the Arab: A History of the Enemy* (Stanford, CA: Stanford University Press, 2003), xii.

2. Steven Marcus, "Human Nature, Social Orders, and Nineteenth-Century Systems of Explanation: Starting In with George Eliot," *Salmagundi* 28 (1975): 41.

3. Cynthia Chase, *Decomposing Figures: Rhetorical Readings in the Romantic Tradition* (Baltimore: Johns Hopkins University Press, 1986), 169.

4. Julia Reinhard Lupton, "*Othello* Circumcised: Shakespeare and the Pauline Discourse of Nations," *Representations* 57 (Winter 1997): 74.

5. Cf. Daniel J. Vitkus, "Turning Turk in *Othello*: The Conversion and Damnation of the Moor," *Shakespeare Quarterly* 48:2 (1997): 146, who doesn't quite get or make the point of the sexualization of this anxiety.

6. For the "ewe/you" pun, see Janet Adelman, "Iago's Alter Ego: Race as Projection in Othello," *Shakespeare Quarterly* 48:2 (1997): 129, who does not bring out, however, the political anxiety of this topping of you by the Moor.

7. For Iago's anal fantasy, see Adelman, "Iago's Alter Ego," 129. For the politics of anal abuse, see Michael L. Satlow, "'They Abused Him Like a Woman': Homoeroticism, Gender Blurring, and the Rabbis in Late Antiquity," *Journal of the History of Sexuality* 5:1 (1994): 1–25.

8. Note how it has become virtually de rigueur for the part to be played by African or African American actors, an admirable corrective to long-standing racist practices, but surely a sign of the closing down of possible readings/meanings of the text.

9. "The delusion of race as contemporary Anglo-American culture understands it was an order that was quite probably just on the horizon by the end of the sixteenth century." Lynda E. Boose, "'The Getting of a Lawful Race': Racial Discourse in Early Modern England and the Unrepresentable Black Woman," in *Women, 'Race,' and Writing in the Early Modern Period*, ed. Margo Hendricks and Patricia Parker (London: Routledge, 1994), 37.

10. For a very different approach to Othello's circumcision, see Lupton, "*Othello* Circumcised," who considers Othello's Islam an ambiguous proposition, a reading with which I implicitly disagree in my argument.

11. Boose, "'The Getting of a Lawful Race,'" 35.

12. Lupton, "*Othello* Circumcised," 74. Cf. Anidjar, *The Jew, the Arab*, 214, whose disagreement is quite differently couched.

13. This painting, depicting a clearly "white," or only slightly dark, Moor, clearly a North African Muslim, can be found in the Birmingham Museum. Copies of it apparently were circulated quite widely in Elizabethan England, strongly enhancing the case that it is of such an image that Shakespeare and his audience would have thought when thinking about the Moor of Venice.

14. Vitkus, "Turning Turk in *Othello*," 145–146.

15. See Lupton, "*Othello* Circumcised," 88n25, for bibliography on the textual question. It should be noted in this context that this particular variation of readings was endemic in medieval and early modern texts. See Jonathan Boyarin, *The Unconverted Self: Jews, Indians, and the Identity of Christian Europe* (Chicago: University of Chicago Press, 2009), 39, and literature cited in 39n9. This book—published as the current essay was being completed—and especially, chapter 2, "Muslims," is entirely germane to the project of this essay.

16. Lupton, "*Othello* Circumcised," 74–75.

17. Anidjar, *The Jew, the Arab*, xvii.

18. Jonathan Boyarin, *The Unconverted Self*, 34.

19. As in the reading of Anidjar as well, with whose thesis I am in complete agreement. In a sense, this particular analysis of *Othello*, or better put, of particular passages of the play, can be read as entirely the provision of strong textual support for Anidjar's work. Anidjar's own reading of *Othello* could have done with some thickening agent, which starch I hope to be adding here. On this last point—but not referring to Shakespeare—see Jonathan Boyarin, *The Unconverted Self*, 47–51, the section tellingly entitled "Muslims as Jews."

20. The theoretical parts were mostly written by Jonathan; the rabbinic materials in the second half of the essay and the thoughts about Paul (and Othello, a very early inchoate version of the present argument) were mine. I say this to indicate here that I am reading the words of an-other brother, not merely narcissistically returning to my own.

21. Jonathan Boyarin, *Thinking in Jewish* (Chicago: University of Chicago Press, 1996), 35.

22. Ibid., 37.

23. Ibid., 41. Anticipating the argument of the present essay, we continued this sentence: "Othello's cry just before his suicide that thus had he done to a circumcised Turkish dog—an allusion to Paul that educated Christian audiences could not miss—makes this claim palpable."

24. Cited in Vitkus, "Turning Turk in *Othello*," 150. For Muslims explicitly marked as pagans, see 163n67. See also Jeremy Cohen, *Living Letters of the Law: Ideas of the Jew in Medieval Christianity* (Berkeley: University of California Press, 1999), 174. Cohen remarks that this was an "age in which pagan usually meant Muslim" (179).

25. Henry Byam, from a sermon preached March 16, 1627, cited in Vitkus, "Turning Turk in *Othello*," 152.

26. Boose, "'The Getting of a Lawful Race,'" 37.

27. Cf. race as "always written on and produced by and through the body," Jeffrey J. Cohen, *Medieval Identity Machines* (Minneapolis: University of Minnesota Press, 2003), 193.

28. Boose herself makes a related claim ("'The Getting of a Lawful Race,'" 40). I am thus not arguing against her but with her and amplifying certain points. Boose's own main arguments lie elsewhere.

29. I do not, then, have any truck with readings that take Iago as a Jewish figure in any way, shape, or form; I think that such readings make nonsense of the religious interplay of the text at large (but, of course, I could be wrong!).

30. *Pace* Stanley Cavell, *Disowning Knowledge in Six Plays of Shakespeare* (Cambridge: Cambridge University Press, 1987), 129. See also discussion in Anidjar, *The Jew, the Arab*, 103.

31. Mahmood Mamdani, *When Victims Become Killers: Colonialism, Nativism, and the Genocide in Rwanda* (Princeton, NJ: Princeton University Press, 2001), 9. See also Stephen Greenblatt, *Renaissance Self-Fashioning: From More to Shakespeare* (Chicago: University of Chicago Press, 1980), 9.

CHAPTER 8

BETWEEN SACRED AND SECULAR?

Michael Walzer's Exodus Story

BONNIE HONIG

Friction

Before leaving Germany for Palestine in 1923, Gerhardt Scholem visited Franz Rosenzweig and the two men had an argument. Rosenzweig argued against Zionism and in favor of diasporic life. Scholem was used to such arguments, having grown up defending Zionism against his father, but this time the opposition came not from the German nationalist perspective of the elder Scholem, already thoroughly rejected by the son. Instead, Rosenzweig argued his case on specifically Jewish grounds. The men's argument was surprisingly heated. Perhaps what upset Scholem was the unexpected, indeed, uncanny reappearance of his secular German father in the guise of a Jewish luminary, Rosenzweig.

Scholem was also unsettled by the condition in which he found Rosenzweig at the time of their meeting. He had not known it, but Rosenzweig was already severely handicapped by the amyotrophic lateral sclerosis that would in a few short years take his life just shy of his forty-second birthday.[1] Rosenzweig could not speak. He communicated with his visitors the same way he wrote his letters, essays, and translations. In the early stages of the disease, he used a kind of typewriting machine, and later he communicated with the help of his wife. He would point to letters on a board, or his wife would recite them for him. She would guess at and then voice the words he spelled out laboriously.

It must have been surprising to Scholem to reprise his filial rebellion with a man seemingly so different from his real-life father. Where Scholem senior was embodied, powerful, practical, Rosenzweig was diseased, weak, bookish (but also practical). Where the wife of Scholem senior, Scholem's mother, subverted the paternal law by sneaking forbidden Hebrew lessons to her defiant son like candy and giving him a portrait of his beloved Zionist leader, Theodore Herzl, as a Christmas present, the wife of Rosenzweig only enabled and supported her crippled husband, offering him first the machine and then the words by way of which to communicate his disapproval to Scholem, the prodigal son. No wonder, then, that the quarrel between the two men became heated. It must have been all too uncannily familiar to Scholem, who had to face it this time, however, without the maternal subversion he had relied on in his first, formative confrontations with paternal power.

Scholem left for Palestine soon after this meeting.[2] When just a few years later, he was asked to write something on the occasion of Rosenzweig's fortieth birthday, Scholem had come to regret the argument. Perhaps he had heard what Rosenzweig thought about it: Rosenzweig said that Scholem had become distant because he projected his own guilt for the episode onto Rosenzweig. If so, it was just one in a series of projections, as I have suggested here.

When Scholem wrote the birthday present for Rosenzweig, whose illness was by then widely known, Scholem wrote not about the promise of Zionism but about its betrayal. Perhaps he was extending an olive branch to Rosenzweig, who had been critical of Zionism on Judaic grounds. Now Scholem himself was worried that Zionism's secularization of Hebrew betrayed the sacred character of the language. This new secularized language was useful; it was pressed into service on behalf of technical transmission. But, being useful, it could no longer open its bearers to revelation. (My mundane use in this paragraph of the term "olive branch" is an instance of how a once live, revelatory metaphor can be deadened.)

It was not, however, simply the loss of access to revelation that bothered Scholem, as it would have troubled Rosenzweig. The problem for Scholem was that modernized Hebrew performed the repression of the revelatory without awareness and *without guilt*, thus leaving its speakers unprepared for the return of the repressed. The detheologization of Hebrew enables it to work as one language among others, but this requires the repression of the sacred, which is never entirely successful. The sacred names of the Hebrew language resist, Golemlike, the Zionist project of secularization. Speakers of secular Hebrew in the streets of Jerusalem in Mandatory Palestine find themselves surprised again and again to be speaking a language out of which erupt, lavalike, significations from another world. Presumably the speakers of this new language were also sometimes surprised to find themselves trapped in heated arguments they never set out to have.

Scholem describes the experience of speaking the new Hebrew in Jerusalem: "We sometimes shudder, when out of the thoughtless conversation, a word from the religious sphere terrifies us, just there where it was perhaps intended to comfort. Hebrew is pregnant with catastrophes . . . the language turns against its speakers . . . these are . . . stigmatizing moments in which the daring lack of measure of our undertaking reveals itself to us."[3] This turning against, Scholem describes as "the uprising of a sacred language."[4]

Scholem casts the secularization of the sacred language as a kind of becoming (m)other—a process of maternalization. The problem, he all but says, is that Hebrew is now a *mother* tongue. No longer acquired by study, devotion, and merit, modern Hebrew is learned and spoken thoughtlessly by a generation born into it and for whom it is the only tongue.[5] It is not insignificant then that Scholem articulates his fears by way of metaphors of pregnancy and personifies them by thinking of the children who will suffer when sacred Hebrew rises up one day in revenge.[6] Indeed, such metaphors may be overdetermined. It may well be that when Scholem in his essay for Rosenzweig laments the betrayals of the new mother tongue, modern Hebrew, he is working out, acting out, his relationship to the betraying mother of his last scene with Rosenzweig, Rosenzweig's wife.

We could also see Scholem's gift to Rosenzweig as an admission that he was right—not to oppose Zionism (a position Rosenzweig came to attenuate, in any case) but to see that Zionism would betray itself. Still, it is an odd gift, perhaps even a poisoned one. Of all the things to offer a man of words who suffers from an illness that deprives him of speech, Scholem offers Rosenzweig a meditation on language and its power. But there is implied solace here too, for the essay meditates on the betrayals of spoken language, in particular that coarsened through daily use.

In "The Eyes of Language: The Abyss and the Volcano," Jacques Derrida comments on Scholem's letter. Focusing on his line "If and when the language turns against its speakers," Derrida says that this is not just an account of the surprise encounter with sacredness in the secular but also or more fundamentally (to use Scholem's term to illustrate Derrida's idea) the *catastrophe* of language, as such: its refusal to mean only what we want or intend. This refusal, the catastrophe that is language, is tied by Scholem to the perduring sacredness of Hebrew, but those familiar with deconstruction will see that the issue here involves certain traits of language as such: as linguistic creatures we fall into a repertoire that exceeds any human capacity to control it, a repertoire that takes up its human users and presses them against their intentions into new and fraught situations or into nonsense, even as it also enables them to make sense.[7]

But Derrida also exhibits empathy for the particular contingent situation in which Scholem undergoes this (poststructural) experience. Perhaps it struck a chord or was reminiscent of some aspect of life in Algeria in the same decade in which Scholem wrote, and the next, and the next. Derrida says:

> One should not throw oneself too quickly into sophisticated interpretations of this letter, [not too quickly; this is the pause, the reflection that prevents such quickness] not, in any case, before having reconstructed the daily, concrete, pathetic landscape, but also the paradigmatic scene of this Berliner intellectual from the diaspora, living two cultures, familiar as are so many others, with sacred nonspoken texts reserved for study and liturgy, and who all at once hears, in the Palestine of the 1920's, these sacred names in the street, on the bus, at the corner store, in the newspapers that every day publish lists of new words to be inscribed in the code of secular Hebrew. One must imagine the desire and the terror in the face of this outpouring, this prodigious, unbridled prodigality that flooded everyday life with sacred names, language giving itself out, like a miraculous manna, but also like profanatory *jouissance*, in the face of which a sort of religious concupiscence recoils in fright.[8]

Manna and *jouissance* are the precisely right terms to use here, for the power both miraculous and profane at work is the product of the unnatural trans-formation of the language of the father into a mother tongue, out of which pour, in a boundary-defiant way, all sorts of meanings and meaninglessness.[9]

The issue here for Derrida is the nature of language as such, whereas for Scholem, of course, what is at stake is the Exodus story, whose ful-fillment is what Scholem seeks to help actualize with his immigration: the promise of the Promised Land. The Exodus story, however, just like language as such, carries with it many political and theological possibili-ties, all implicated in an ethnic and racial politics of exceptionalism and sacredness.

Michael Walzer knows this, and sixty years after the Scholem-Rosen-zweig contretemps about diaspora and Zionism, Walzer enters the fray of Exodus reception history to mobilize the story in a biblical realist way on behalf of a social democratic politics. He takes his cue from a "black preacher" who in 1960 gave what Walzer describes as "the most extraor-dinary sermon" he had ever heard. "There on his pulpit, the preacher, whose name I have long forgotten, acted out the 'going out' from Egypt and expounded its contemporary analogues: he cringed under the lash, challenged the pharaoh, hesitated fearfully at the sea, accepted the cov-enant and the law at the foot of the mountain."[10] The Exodus story widely circulates among those who struggle against oppression, and the fact that the story itself has an ending—the people arrive in the Promised Land—does not mean the story is inappropriate for those whose struggles seem never ending. Quite the contrary, says Walzer: the preacher knew "that the Exodus did not happen once and for all, that liberation [from slavery] is no guarantee of liberty. . . . In fact, the return to Egypt is part of the story, though it exists in the text only as a possibility: that's why the story can be retold so often" (5).[11]

I turn now to assess Walzer's own retelling of the story. I will close with some brief thoughts about how the story's template offers a useful way to think about James Baldwin's critical dissent from an American exception-alism that Walzer elsewhere supports.[12] Both Walzer and Baldwin want to decenter the Promised Land. Both in effect privilege the desert experience as the appropriate scene of political life, rejecting what both cast as the utopianism of the Promised Land on behalf of what Walzer calls realism and what I elsewhere have called, on Baldwin's behalf, a gothic view of political life.[13]

Biblical Realism: Between Sacred and Secular, Pedagogy and Purge

Walzer's *Exodus and Revolution* aims to do precisely what Scholem faulted the early Zionists for doing: to actualize the sacred as secular.[14] If the Zionists saw in ancient Hebrew the possibility of a new mother tongue for a returning diasporic Jewry, Walzer seeks in the Exodus story a repertoire for a new, postexilic politics.[15] What draws Walzer to Exodus is the possibility of finding at the very source of apocalyptic or messianic politics a more this-worldly alternative. Walzer says he wants to read Exodus as a human story, as "a realistic account, in which miracles play a part but which is not itself wholly miraculous" (9). "I don't mean to disparage the sacred," he explains, "only to explore the secular" (x). Within the "sacred history of Exodus" we can discern a "vivid and realistic secular history" (x). One might even hazard that for Walzer, as for biblical realists generally, the sacred text is, to invert Scholem's claim, pregnant with the secular.[16]

Walzer approaches the Exodus story through hundreds of years of reception history, much of it apocalyptic or Leninist. If Leninists turn to this story with some frequency, they do so, Walzer conjectures, because people who advocate political purging need to seek out authoritative justifications for their views. For Leninists, the violent suppressions of dissent in the desert provide such justification. Exodus history was also "the source for messianic politics." On this, Walzer cites several seventeenth-century and other sources, such as John Canne, an English Fifth Monarchyman. One wrote in 1657, "In the Lord's bringing Israel out of Egypt was shadowed out the deliverance of his church and people from all tyranny and oppression in the last days" (146). But, Walzer argues, if we read the Exodus story "without its shadows," we find that "the Exodus [also] provides the chief *alternative* to messianism" (146; emphasis added), a rival secular alternative (as indeed, Walzer notes, it was for Benjamin Franklin).

The problem with political messianism is that it leaves "no room for argument. Then politics is absolute, enemies satanic, compromise impossible." Walzer concedes that "Exodus politics slides sometimes toward absolutism,"[17] but, he insists, the text offers other options as well. It is subject to endless argument and various interpretations, and, for those working in its tradition, "there is no ultimate struggle, but a long series of decisions, backslidings, and reforms. . . . Absolutism is effectively barred," Walzer adds, "by the character of the people, frightened, stubborn, contentious, and at the same time, members of the covenant. The people can't be killed (not all of them anyway) or cast aside or miraculously transformed. They must be led, chastised, defended, argued with, educated—activities that undercut and defeat any simple designation of 'enemies'" (147–48).

Key here is that the people themselves force absolutism into a less absolute posture. They resist the irresistible and argue with a god they know is all powerful.[18] Thus, they press on Walzer a certain paradox. The absolutism that he wants to excise on behalf of a realist politics in fact serves as the ground of the Israelites' entry *into* politics, its birth point or crucible, in fact. It is precisely in contentious response to their commanding God, who brooks no disagreement, that the ornery Israelites emerge, in Walzer's account, as a self-governing people. Arguing with the inarguable, the people force realism on their leaders and on later readers: "The pace of the march must be set with their feelings in mind, because their rebellions must be dealt with, leaders chosen from their midst and the law expounded in their hearing. They can't easily be divided into friends and enemies," even though their leaders and their God do sometimes orient them in such absolutist directions. So Walzer finds the people's "stiff-neckedness is somehow admirable" (148): when they argue with the inarguable, the Israelites explode idealist ambitions.

Focusing on the people's agency and recalcitrance, Walzer develops a new reading of Exodus, a rival secular reading that might serve as a welcome alternative to both the violence-centered secular readings (Leninist) and the (theological) ones more centered on the chosenness of the people. He acknowledges the presence of violence and chosenness in the story—the purges are there; the exceptionalism is there—but he refuses to allow them to dominate the story or play their usual roles in it. He insists on the importance of not just purge but also pedagogy to the formation of the Israelites into a free people. And he sees their chosenness not as a divinely given sign of superiority but as an expression of their sense of political promise and purpose, necessary to effect their release from slavery.

For realists, Walzer argues, the lesson of the Exodus story is about "the meaning and possibility of politics and about its proper form," and the form is stunningly simple:

—first, that wherever you live, it is probably Egypt;
—second, that there is a better place, a world more attractive, a promised land;
—and third, that "the way to the land is through the wilderness."[19] There is no way to get from here to there except by joining together and marching. (149)

Walzer innovates by focusing on what he calls, in familiar progressive terms, the march, not the destination, on the recalcitrance, not the chosenness.[20] "The Israelites do not, as is sometimes said, go wandering in the wilderness; the Exodus is a journey forward—not only in time and space. It is a march toward a goal [but not a land per se], a moral progress, a transformation" (12). The point is made as well in *Exodus!* by Eddie Glaude in the context of nineteenth-century African American narrations of their experiences as "biblical drama": for them, the "crucial struggle, then, was and is not in quests for land or in efforts to eradicate demonized enemies. Rather, the struggle lies in the effort to create a free people and to live up to the moral principles that signify the best way of living" (162).

For Walzer, once the land is moved out of the picture, the adventurousness of the march becomes even clearer. Walzer charts, unflinchingly, the violence through which whole segments of the Israelite people are destroyed in the desert. Korach and his followers are swallowed up by a ground that opens suddenly and horrifically to bury them alive before the eyes of the crowd. Just before this and perhaps not unrelated, a man who broke the Sabbath is ordered by Moses or God to be stoned by the community, which obliges. There follows the commandment to all male Israelites to wear the tzitzit, the fringe that will remind men of their responsibilities henceforth. Later, a plague wipes out a significant portion of the people. These, Walzer says, deliberately invoking Lenin, are the purges, and they are not usually recorded with such clarity by readers of Exodus.

But Walzer's text also domesticates the violence. He says that the violence may have been necessary to the formative desert experience—"at some point I suppose the counter revolution must be defeated if Egyptian bondage is ever to be left behind" (69). His "I suppose" marks his realist acceptance of the violence and subtly positions those who criticize it as parties to an idealism that he has already affiliated with the very violence they might seek to reject. To be a realist is to accept the inevitability of violence. To decry violence in politics is to fall sway to an idealism that invariably absolutizes politics and ushers in more rather than fewer harms. In sum, rather than cancel and preserve the purges, transforming them as Hegel might, Walzer preserves so he can cancel them. Once they are mentioned and acknowledged, the purges can be set aside.

Elsewhere, with the term "sadly," the text marks the unavoidable violence as lamentable. Noting that after the incident with the golden calf, Moses moved the tabernacle outside the Israelites' camp (Exodus 33:7), Walzer says the common rabbinic explanation for this is that God and Moses could no longer dwell among such an impure people. But Walzer suggests a different explanation: "One might say, *more sadly*, that neither God nor Moses could dwell among a people whose brothers, companions and neighbors they (one or the other of them anyway) had ordered killed" (66). This is Walzer's own "Leninist" reading of the Exodus story, and he develops it at some length. But he also seeks to dispose of it: The violence may be necessary, but it could never be sufficient—"the counter-revolution has deep roots; it cannot be defeated by force alone. Indeed God and the Levites could easily kill all the people who yearn for the fleshpots (or the idols) of Egypt. But then the Levites would arrive in the promised land virtually alone, and that would not be a fulfilment of the promise" of chosenness and the land (69).

Thus, Walzer splits the journey and the destination, and also pedagogy and purge.[21] "If there is a Leninist reading, there is also . . . a social democratic reading—which stresses the indirection of the march and the role of Moses as the pedagogue of the people and their defender before god" (66). So which reading has more merit? "Was it the purging or the teaching that made the decisive difference?" Walzer asks. "The text can be read either way," he says (69).

Elsewhere, in good realist fashion, Walzer resists such easy choices: he braids together the carnal and the spiritual (against the Christian view; he speaks insightfully of the "high theory of milk and honey" and grants that it is clear that the "Levites have a material interest in holiness" [104]).[22] But when confronted with purge and pedagogy, Walzer insists we must choose. The biblical text does not force the choice, however. It tells of incidents of purging and of education; it does not split pedagogy and purge. Indeed, it may equally well suggest that the purges themselves are pedagogical, not just lamentable sideshows but, as we would say in the United States now, *teachable moments*.

Rather than treat the purges as discrete events—some dissenters or transgressors die, and the people go on—we may reflect upon the likelihood that when the people go on, they do so with images of violence burned into their minds: that of, say, the image of Korach and his followers dropping into a crevasse in the desert, disappearing into the earth's open wound. In the case of the Sabbath-breaker who is stoned right before Korach appears and whose fate may be the proximate cause of Korach's rebellion, the people march on, knowing they all have this man's blood on their hands. Still, they march on together.

In treating these analytically as two distinct and separate strands of the desert experience, Walzer gives the impression that the violence and the pedagogy are two separate things, that the violence is for the really recalcitrant (the counterrevolutionaries), those who cannot give up those Egyptian fleshpots, but the reasonable majority require only pedagogy, not purge. A deeper realism might press on us the possibility that pedagogy involves purge or violence. Why not? It is likely that when Israelite men feel the fringe of the tzitzit, they recall not just the Lord their God but also the man they stoned for violating the Sabbath and the stones they threw. When the Israelites were asked if they would accept the covenant, again and again (since they stray repeatedly; that is the Bible's realism), might they not have thought of the brothers and neighbors who died, because they in effect hazarded a no to the very same question? (The possibility is captured in the biblical instruction *v'shenantem l'vane'cha*, which means you will teach them [the laws] to your children through their teeth—with pain: key here is the fact that the word for teaching has the same root [as it were] as the word for teeth.)[23] If, as Walzer says, "the memory of Egypt is a crucial feature of the new national consciousness" (109), then why should we not think that so too are the memories of the murders, natural disasters, and plagues visited upon the people in the desert?

Clearly, Walzer's goal is to leave apocalyptic politics behind in the desert, along with the purged bodies of those lost by the wayside of the march. He finds in Exodus support for his aim of replacing the apocalyptic dream of new beginnings with an acceptance of the ongoing struggles of piecemeal politics.[24] But, as Derrida argues elsewhere, the apocalyptic violence of both Egypt and the desert march are burned into the unconscious of the people; the trauma survives the desert generation and haunts the free-born generation that enters the land. If Walzer worries the question of which—pedagogy or purge—is the more necessary to recraft a slave people into a people capable of freedom (evidence for which, he says, is they are ready to fight rather than flee their own battles at the end of their journey), Derrida notes that neither will succeed: the trace of violence remains in the people who will never be free of it. Hence, pedagogy/purge will recur.

And sure enough, we see their trace in Scholem's account of the revenge of language, in his guilty displacement perhaps of the very thing it trumps: the Arabs in Palestine. In his letter to Rosenzweig, Scholem says that the real threat to Zionism comes not from the Arabs, about whom there is much talk, but rather from the much talk, about which little is said. In the new actualized secular Hebrew, daily life is lived above an abyss to which all are blind, Scholem says. Positioning himself with the desert generation of the Exodus that transitions from slavery to freedom, he says: "If we—the generation of *transition*—resuscitate the language of the ancient book so that it can reveal itself anew to [our children], must not the religious violence of this language one day break out against those who speak it?"[25] Scholem continues: "We or those who come after us [the children], must we not fall to the bottom of this abyss?" (Here the abyss stands for divine violence. By the end of the letter, the abyss or at least the void stands for empty secularism-nihilism.)[26] Who else but poor Korach and his followers are in play when Scholem adds, "And no one knows whether the sacrifice of individuals who will be annihilated in this abyss will be sufficient to close it"?[27] Those who remain will find out if more purges are to come after Korach is gone. But the people can also act. The decision remains theirs, Scholem says: when people speak secularly a language that solicits divinity "a thousandfold into our life, God will not stay silent," and the people will be confronted with a "decisive sign of the only available choice: to submit or go under."[28]

One merit of Walzer's reading, it seems to me, is its resistance to such absolutisms. He also insists that the people must decide, but the context for such decisions is not the either-or of Scholem's eternally recurring choice, to submit or go under, but rather the never-ending march. The only promise the land will keep, Walzer says, is that of the perpetuity of the march.[29] This is the legacy of the stiff-necked people Walzer admires. This stiff-necked people do not only march, however. As Walzer knows, they also fight. They do not only suffer; they also commit violence together, and even when they submit, they also argue, so they live out and reenact the purge and pedagogy by which they were and are shaped. The two are inextricably intertwined.

So, why use a sacred text at all if the aim is a realist politics? One of Walzer's avowed reasons is to take away from its Leninist and apocalyptic users the authority they gain from the selfsame text. Another good reason has to do with the continued fecundity of the text, still much cited by progressives, for progressive politics. Yet another reason, however, less avowed, may surely be that Walzer's secular Exodus politics is energized in ways it does not fully avow by this magical, enchanted, sacred text, though this violates his realism or alters it—it is now surely at least a magical realism.

Touched, enchanted by the chosenness it also wants to set aside, Walzer's Israelites quarrel, die, march, doubt, love, struggle, and emerge into a kind of political maturity. But their external enemies are not also heroes. Here the text may bear the traces of that which it wants to set aside, and in this regard the story is different from, say, Homer's, where we might find that Hector and Achilles pull equally on our sympathies because (as Simone Weil and Hannah Arendt both point out) Homer presents them to us impartially.[30]

It was the presence of an external enemy pivotal to the story and yet not represented sympathetically in it that seems to have (at least in part) motivated Edward Said to write a scathing review of *Exodus and Revolution*. Said criticized Walzer for failing to note the presence in the Promised Land of the seven Canaanite nations who were destroyed and whose land the Israelites took by force at the end of their march.[31] Walzer's response was irritated, surely because already in *Exodus and Revolution* and without Said's prodding, Walzer had acknowledged his neglect of the Canaanites: "If the movement from Egypt to Canaan is taken as a metaphor for a transforming politics, then attention is focused on internal rather than external wars, on the purges of the recalcitrant Israelites rather than on the destruction of the Canaanite nations. And so I have focused my own attention in this book." Moreover, for Walzer the appeal of the Exodus story is precisely that it is not the property of the Israelites. It appeals to many radicals and progressives, regardless of their land or cause, because of its "linearity," its "idea of a promised end." Many have found and will continue to find inspiration in the "purposiveness of the Israelite march" (142).

This contretemps of the mid-1980s made an impression on many partly because it broke all the rules of academic exchange. It was too heated, too raw, impolite. Why? The obvious explanations—political correctness or academic sensitivity—are not adequate to account for it. What is? Recall that Walzer's intention (stated repeatedly in his text) is to secularize the Exodus story. Said is a secularist as well. But when he responds to Walzer's effort as if Walzer's text still traffics in the chosenness it rejects, Said is charging that the "thorn of the sacred" (to borrow Scholem's figure from his letter to Rosenzweig) remains. Walzer is surprised and dismayed by this. Like the people described by Scholem in 1920s Jerusalem, Walzer thinks he has left the sacred behind only to find himself enveloped in or captured or assaulted by it—trapped in the trappings of chosenness and divinity that reassert themselves, over and above—against!—his intentions; hence his irritation. When Said insisted that the chosenness persisted, this introduced the question—for Walzer, for us—of what would count as evidence that a secularization has succeeded or failed? Would it be the absence of objections like Said's?

The uprising of the sacred, entirely unexpected between two secularists, is similar to what Scholem worried about in his letter to Rosenzweig. Of course, the uprising of the sacred may have been at the core of that earlier argument between Scholem and Rosenzweig as well. After all, Rosenzweig surprised Scholem by giving him unexpectedly sacred (rather than familiar German nationalist) reasons for not moving to Palestine. It may be that in the earlier heated exchange, the sacred erupted unexpectedly as well. This may have overdetermined Scholem's sensitivity to its eruptions later, in the streets of Jerusalem, and may have led him to write about it to Rosenzweig years later.

In both of these heated arguments, the sacred and the secular coexist and surprise each other in various ways. Might the same be true for the other things Walzer tries to distinguish, for example, pedagogy and purge? To explore more deeply the mutual implication of pedagogy and purge, I turn now to a biblical practice that seems familiar to secularists but also harbors sacred signification: the census.

Count, Forward and Back

"If the dream of Zionism is numbers and borders and if we can't exist without them, then Zionism will fail," says Scholem (quoted in *Exodus and Revolution*, 141), who means to object to a purely this-worldly Zionism such as that advanced by Walzer. But Scholem underestimates the power of the count. In Numbers 26, God calls for the people to be counted. The count of the Israelites is presented as a prelude to the Israelites' entry into the Promised Land. But the count does not only look forward; it also looks back. It is called for, as we are told in Numbers, "after the plague" (Numbers 25:19). What plague?

The plague is the latest in a series of natural and health disasters that are God's wrathful responses in the desert to the Israelites' unruliness.[32] The plague ends when Pinchas kills an Israelite man and a Moabite woman, Zimri and Kozbi, for their "flagrant immorality."[33] Pinchas's violent act is only quietly decried, if at all, in the Bible. Worse yet, we are told that for his deed Pinchas is awarded the high priesthood for himself and his line. Rashi tries to find the sense in this. He suggests that the reward offered to Pinchas is not simply a reward. The priesthood will teach Pinchas to cool his temper and provide him with the discipline he clearly lacks. The commentary in *Etz Hayim* notes that the letter *yud* in Pinchas's name appears smaller than the other letters, suggesting the divinity in Pinchas (symbolized by the *yud*) is diminished by his act; in verse 12 the *vav* in God's offer to Pinchas of a *brit shalom* is written with a break in the letter's stem, suggesting a critique of zealotry and absolutism: "the sort of peace one achieves by destroying one's opponent will inevitably be a flawed, incomplete peace."[34]

The Hassidic commentator Mordechai Yosef Leiner, also known as the Isbitzer, introduces a more radical possibility: Zimri and Kozbi are cosmic soul mates, and their joining together across lines of enmity is part of a mystical process of *tikkun olam*, world healing or correction, which the Isbitzer says can take many forms, including that of a masculine and feminine erotic union. Pinchas missed this because he was so focused on the rules forbidding the union that he could not see beyond them. Usually we think the greatest human temptation is to transgress the rules. But the Isbitzer suggests there is another temptation as well: to take the rules too seriously, to get stuck on them. This makes us miss the realm of deeper meaning that moral or religious rules seek to sensitize us to but also occlude from our view.

This reading is attractive for its unlikely magnanimity, but it is surely worth noting that in this story not just the eros of Kozbi and Zimri is motivated by extrajuridical passions; so too is the zealous violence of Pinchas, which the Isbitzer means with these observations to condemn. Eros and thanatos here mirror each other just as God's wrath and his desire for the people he has chosen are two sides of the same coin. When the Isbitzer opposes the *tikkun olam* of eros to the destructive passion of Pinchas's murders, the Isbitzer calls to mind Walzer's juxtaposition of pedagogy and purge—which also rules out in advance the possibility of eros's violence, the possibility that God's wrath and purge are part of his loving desire for his people and not an exception to it or a suspension of it. Indeed, we might say that a sacred reading of the text suggests that what God can combine in his manifold manyness must be divided in the human world, personified by two separate characters in the Bible, Pinchas and his other. Thus, this reading invites us to look further for what may be a more perfect *tikkun olam* because when we approach the Other, whether through eros or violence, we are always already in a prior partition of the sensible[35] whose division of the human into Same and Other is expressed in one or more of these two ways: the desire for or the rage against the Other.[36]

With this in mind, we can analyze the census. For it is after the plague, after Pinchas's violent act of moral outrage, that God calls for the count. Rashi says the census count is like what the shepherd does after his flock is attacked: he counts his flock, lovingly, to see how many are left. God's love is more complicated, though, than that of Rashi's shepherd, since it is God himself who harmed his flock. Perhaps God is counting, as we are told to do these days, to calm his temper. In any case, here, to stand up and be counted means in part, surely, to be thankful one is still alive. It means still more, however, for the count looks forward as well as back. Only men of age to bear arms are to be counted. Based on their numbers, each tribe will be given a piece of land in the Promised Land. Since women, children, and old men are not counted, it seems the aim is not merely to provide space as needed but to sign men up for service and to recognize tribal contributions to the collective fighting force that will take the land.

But recognition's rationality is interrupted or supplemented by chance. The count—rational and distributive—is not the only mechanism of land assignment. The count assigns to each group a "share," but which specific piece of land each will get as its share will be decided by lot, a second principle of distribution that seems to introduce contingency into the system. "Each [group] is to be assigned its share according to its enrolment" (54). And "each portion shall be assigned by lot" (56). Combining these two incommensurable principles of distribution—the count and the lot—the procedure lets tribes know that their assigned share is theirs as a matter of both recognition and lottery, rationality and luck, deservingness and chance.[37]

It is surely significant that the count, which gratefully reconstitutes the remnant of the nation, enacts the rational distribution of the land, and seeks justly to reward the people according to their contribution in gaining it, is contaminated from the very beginning by the lottery's contingency. We could leave matters here, in the terrain between the count and the lot, the rules and their suspension, the rational and the contingent, but we would then fail to take away the true lesson of this apparent *contamination*: The marking of contingency by way of the lottery marks the deeper contingency of rationality itself, the nonnecessity of this particular partition of the sensible, a partitioning that could have been and may yet be otherwise.

To open ourselves to this possibility means insisting on the role of desire in all this—a point brought out by Judith Butler in a reading of Foucault when she notes that rational self-reflection is not a natural part of rationality but rather "arrive[s] as an incitement, a form of seduction, an imposition or demand from outside to which one yields."[38] It may also be true of rationality itself that it is elicited in response to an incitement, that it is an *expression* of the very thing it will soon oppose: desire.

The biblical melding of lottery and count, its treatment of distribution as part lottery, part count, might be not mere contamination but rather itself a *tikkun olam* designed to indicate to us the place(lessness) of desire. Amid the rationality of our countings, the lot comes in to mark the unruly, boundary-violating, mannalike *jouissance* that falls out of the sky, gives no account of itself, or refuses to do so because to give an account of oneself is always already to (have) enter(ed) into rationality and to abide by its partition of the sensible. A similar point is also made by John Rawls, whose rationalism is well known among political theorists but whose fidelity to desire is less noted. It becomes evident, however, in Rawls's text *A Theory of Justice* when we approach that text with the help of Jacques Rancière.

Exposure

For Jacques Rancière, exposure to random contingency is fundamental to democracy:

> The demos is not the glorious, imaginary body that is heir to the sacrificed royal body. It's not the body of the people. It's the abstract assemblage of "ordinary people," who have no individual title to govern. It is the pure addition of "chance" that comes to revoke all ideas of legitimate domination, all notions of personal "virtue" destining a special category of people to govern.[39]

The pure addition of "chance" nods to contingency. Without it, the "people" may come to replace without significant difference the king, the rightful ruler, the deserving hero. But there would be no revolution in this. Democracy needs to take its chances with contingency. *With* the nod to contingency, democracy wins. It can only do so when the demos, as such, is undeserving, more specifically, when the demos breaks the tables of value whereby deservingness has hitherto been ladled out.[40] John Rawls's *A Theory of Justice* is arguably also animated by a desire for radical equality. We find evidence of this in Rawls's critique of desert. No symbolic or political order, regardless of how it grounds its distributions, can ground legitimately any departure from absolute equality by way of appeal to desert or deservingness. Any appeal to natural talent or any other basis for unequal distributions necessarily turns out to be grounded in nothing other than contingency. If some are smarter than others, the reason is that the former are contingent winners in what we would now call the genetic lottery or that contingently they happened to have been raised in households that value intelligence over, say, athleticism, or earnest commitment over cool underachievement.

Any trait-based or even effort-based argument that renders unequal distributions deserved falls irretrievably into a spiral of contingency.

Although many have claimed that this argument is a mark of Rawls's neo-Kantian noumenalism in which phenomenal contingency does not matter "from a moral point of view," it could be said that Rawls's critique of desert is significant for another, rather different, reason. In the critique of desert as a basis for distribution, Rawls's own desire, a desire for absolute equality, finds expression. Rawls's reputation is for rationalism, but his rationalism, I would argue, is always already contaminated by desire. His legitimated distributive principles at their core hinge on contingency; his manna is possessed of and by *jouissance*. Indeed, Rawls, who was born and raised in Maryland, once told me in a dinner conversation that his motivation in writing *A Theory of Justice* was to reject the racism of the South. The topic is never mentioned in the book, and the desire for equality is also almost immediately betrayed in the effort to give it some institutional or symbolic expression—to make it accord to a rule. This is no more and no less than Jacques Lacan's account of desire should lead us to expect. But that betrayal should not make us blind to what we can see here, from a Lacanian perspective: Rawls's critique of desert—in which *no one* is more or less valuable or singular or meritorious than anyone else—*is* a moment of *democratic* desire.

Todd May intuits Rawls's desire for equality but finds it wanting in contrast with Rancière's. Rawls, May argues, offers a "passive equality," one on which the distributions of political order are based. But Rancière theorizes an "active equality" in which equality is an activity, something that is taken, enacted, performed, not accepted or received passively.[41] May's distinction between active and passive equality captures something important to democratic politics: it matters how distributions are made or taken, not just whether they are in the end equal or justifiably unequal in outcomes. But May's distinction also occludes something: the moment of democratic desire that Rawls's early project of justice voices when it rejects any and all arguments for intrinsic or earned inequality. Rancière's radical egalitarianism is in Rawls, perhaps even ready to erupt. If Rawls ends up advocating a scheme in which departures from absolute equality are permissible when justified according to certain criteria that he theorizes, the reason is,

I would argue, that his democratic desire is ultimately buried alive within what Rancière would call the police order of Rawlsian liberal thought.

Something analogous is evident in the Exodus story. As Walzer notes, God makes two promises to the people. "I will bring you in to a land flowing with milk and honey," and "Ye shall be unto me a kingdom of priests and a holy nation" (101). Crucially, the first promise swears to bring about a passive equality by abolishing scarcity. The second promise swears to bring about the Israelites' radical and active equality: they will be a nation of prophets, not divided into leaders and led, not partitioned, but radically equal. After the incident with the golden calf, this second promise is deferred, ultimately to messianic times. The people will now be led by the Levites, a development that Walzer calls a "defeat for revolutionary aspiration" (109). And popular prophecy will sometimes be tolerated (as with Eldad and Medad [110]) but sometimes not (as with Korach, who, Walzer says with great empathy, "had experienced the great moment of deliverance and the enthusiasm of the original covenanting not as a promise of what might be in the far future but as an immediate reality" [111]). It is perhaps significant that the promise of radical prophetic equality was the *second* promise of the covenant (the first represents a more passive equality—milk and honey) and that in this it parallels the lot, which was the *second* procedure of distribution used in Numbers, in the company of the count, the *first* principle of land distribution.

Can we find an instance of this radical equality—deferred and yet perhaps foretasted—as well in the Exodus story? Walzer notes that one rabbinic commentary suggests "that the kingdom [of equality, of popular prophecy] actually existed briefly, between the covenant and the calf. During that time every Israelite (or perhaps only every first born Israelite) had the privileges of a priest" (11). Walzer does not quite credit this commentary. The possibility is too magical for his realism. Still, he is taken with it. And it may inspire him when he develops his other option: the march. The march exposes the people to each other and to nature, to rationality and contingency. In it, they are both nurtured and unsettled by manna and *jouissance*. The land will bring with it the responsibility for distributions. The march, by contrast, while not anarchic, is more anarchic. And like all anarchies, it works itself out in agonistic struggle with the impulses of rule and desire, pedagogy and purge. It may draw its energies from the in-between radical equality imagined by the rabbis or from a postmessianic beyond, such as that imagined by Derrida: "This desire and promise [for the other, for the unreadable] let all my spectres loose. A desire without a horizon, for that is its luck, its condition. And a promise that no longer expects what it waits for. There where striving for what is given to come, I finally know how not to have to distinguish any longer between desire and terror [or between pedagogy and purge]."[42]

The key, however, is that to be truly postmessianic, we must do more than simply untether the march from the land, as Walzer tries to do, because the march is still informed by the land that was its constitutive destination. The desert is between what Walzer still calls a here and a there: "There is no way to get from here to there except by joining together and marching" (149). This is what allows Walzer to see the violence in the desert as acceptable. It is a means to an end. Here the sacred survives in the so-called secular. A more radical secularization sees, instead, that life in the desert as such has to be embraced, not as march but as an always already arrived-at destination from which there is no reprieve or redemption.

This is the task taken up not by the black preacher whom Walzer witnessed in 1960 but by James Baldwin. Baldwin argues against black nationalists and separatists that the shared past and shared fate of black and white Americans must be embraced. There is no escaping the need of each to deal with the other. Of course, this call is issued by a writer who leaves the United States to live in France and whose own short story, "Exodus," tells of a young African American woman's decision to escape to the North and leave behind both her sinning, irresponsible brother and her God-fearing, ex-slave mother.[43] Still, Baldwin insists that any move forward in the United States can happen only on land that hosts the blood of both races, that there is no escaping the violence of the past, which must be accepted—it cannot be denied—but which can never be scripted as "acceptable."

Thus, Baldwin invites us to recast the Exodus story more radically still, to the point where we have what Derrida calls "a desert without a desert crossing." To dispense in this way with the Promised Land entirely, as Walzer never does, as Rosenzweig never does, is, as Derrida says, to risk "what today . . . one so often calls unreadability."[44] But to read the unreadable is not impossible. The Isbitzer did it, or tried to; he took that to be the task of *tikkun olam*. It is after all the task of deconstruction. And perhaps also of political theology.

Notes

I am grateful for comments, criticisms, and good conversation to Vincent Lloyd, John Ackerman, and especially George Shulman, as well as to this volume's anonymous readers. Diego Rossello, Nick Dorzweiler, and Lexi Neame provided research assistance and helped prepare the manuscript for publication.

1. "In the fall of 1921, less than a year into his directorship of the *Lehrhaus* and—eerily—months after he wrote his account of philosophical paralysis, Rosenzweig began to notice symptoms" of what would six months later be diagnosed as amyotrophic lateral sclerosis (ALS). By "the spring of 1922, his speech was significantly impaired and he experienced difficulty writing. . . . By the end of 1922, Rosenzweig could no longer write; he remained able to communicate orally to his wife and to a few others close to him—and through these to others as well—until the spring of 1923. At that time the Rosenzweigs purchased a special typewriting machine which allowed Rosenzweig first to type, and then simply to indicate, the letters (and later, the first letters) of the words he wished to communicate, by using a lever to move a disk to the desired letter. As Rosenzweig became further incapacitated, more and more was demanded of his wife, Edith, who would regularly guess the word Rosenzweig wished to convey from Rosenzweig's indication of that word's first letter." Benjamin Pollock, "Franz Rosenzweig," in *Stanford Encyclopedia of Philosophy* (Winter 2009), http://plato.stanford.edu/archives/win2009/entries/rosenzweig/.

2. He took up residence there and eventually became the first professor of Kabbala at the first university in the country, before it was a country. See Cynthia Ozick, "The Heretical Passions of Gershom Scholem," in *The Din in the Head* (New York: Houghton Mifflin, 2006), a book whose title seems to refer to a noise in the head but surely puns as well, in a significant way, on the Hebrew *din*, meaning "law."

3. Jacques Derrida and Gil Anidjar, *Acts of Religion* (New York: Routledge, 2002), 227.

4. Ibid. Is it this fear that leads Scholem, who by then was Gershom in Palestine, to sign his letter to Rosenzweig as Gerhardt?

5. Here is what Derrida calls the monolingualism of the other: the (false) belief that life in a single language is somehow insulated from exposure to or implication in otherness. *Monolingualism of the Other: or, The Prosthesis of Origin* (Stanford, CA: Stanford University Press, 1998).

6. But even revenge happens in language, Derrida points out—"There is always a language of vengeance; vengeance always implicates language" (Derrida and Anidjar, *Acts of Religion*, 207). Without language, what we call revenge is merely killing. Animals do not take revenge, though when humans take revenge, they are often described as animals—insofar as they do not live by law.

7. Ibid., 209.

8. Ibid. For most modern scholars of religion and secularism, too, the problem is not with Hebrew per se but with language or secularization more generally. Secularism demands that theology evacuate certain spheres only to be surprised later that the evacuation was not a true secularization but rather a repression, and a necessarily imperfect

one. For Scholem, however, the situation is unique to Hebrew and a problem that will be uniquely—tragically—Israel's when it occurs.

9. Scholem does not just emplot the shift of Hebrew from sacred to secular as a Fall narrative. He also, thereby, saves biblical, sacred Hebrew from the free play of signification to which language in its fallenness is fated.

10. Michael Walzer, *Exodus and Revolution* (New York: Basic Books, 1985), 3. Further citations will be made parenthetically in text.

11. On the place of *Exodus* in nineteenth-century US racial politics, see Eddie S. Glaude Jr., *Exodus! Religion, Race, and Nation in Early Nineteenth-Century Black America* (Chicago: University of Chicago Press, 2000).

12. Michael Walzer, *What It Means to Be an American* (New York: Marsilio, 1992).

13. Bonnie Honig, *Democracy and the Foreigner* (Princeton, NJ: Princeton University Press, 2001), chap. 5.

14. Walzer refers to his project as an exercise in biblical realism (*Exodus and Revolution* 143). For remarks on Walzer's realism, though referring to other of his works, see Marc Stears, "Making the Nation a Neighborhood," in *Demanding Democracy: American Radicals in Search of a New Politics* (Princeton, NJ: Princeton University Press, 2010). But Walzer finds some solidarity with Scholem (in whose later writings Walzer finds support for his own antiapocalyptic social democratic politics [see *Exodus and Revolution*, 141, citing "Zionism—Dialectic of Continuity and Rebellion," in *Unease in Zion*, ed. Ehud Ben Ezer (New York: Quadrangle / New York Times Book Co., 1974)]). In one way, Walzer's position on Zionism is closer to Rosenzweig's original one: for both, the Promised Land will necessarily be caught up in a this-worldly politics. For Walzer, this is a welcome solicitation out of an otherworldly theological politics and into a more this-worldly alternative. For Rosenzweig, the issue is not politics but Judaism. And the land, whether embroiled in this-worldly politics or the more theological variety, will undermine Judaism's mission.

15. He also finds evidence of a Jewish politics *avant la lettre*, which his later project, *The Jewish Political Tradition*, will attempt to document in detail. Michael Walzer et al., eds., *The Jewish Political Tradition*, vol. 1, *Authority* (New Haven, CT: Yale University Press, 2003), and vol. 2, *Membership* (New Haven, CT: Yale University Press, 2006).

16. Walzer inverts the Argentine liberation theologian Severino Croatto, whom he cites in *Exodus and Revolution*. Croatto, Walzer says, sees Exodus as the story of a "liberation process having all the contours of a political event [that] can very well be interpreted for a Christian conscience—as the will of God" (10).

17. Here Walzer reminds me of Michael Rogin, whose *Ronald Reagan the Movie: And Other Episodes in Political Demonology* (Berkeley: University of California Press, 1988) also argued against apocalyptic politics and focused on the problem of demonization in politics as a problem like absolutism—that is, a form of politics in which opposition as such is barred. Walzer's Exodus book appeared in 1985; Rogin's, in 1988.

18. Resisting the irresistible is, I argue, a mark of an agonistic neo-Arendtian politics. See Bonnie Honig, *Political Theory and the Displacement of Politics* (Ithaca, NY: Cornell University Press, 1993).

19. Citing W. D. Davies, *The Territorial Dimension of Judaism* (Berkeley: University of California Press, 1982), 60.

20. Here it may be of interest to compare Derrida's play on the word *march* at the end of *Monolingualism of the Other*.

21. And, as we shall see, he takes these splittings to license a focus only on the politics of internal enmity and not on those cast as the external enemies of the Israelites.

22. Walzer continues: "Conceived in territorialist terms the promise of milk and honey has a temporal end point: sooner or later, the people will cross the Jordan and enter the land. Conceived in ethical terms the promise is temporally uncertain, for its achievement is not a matter of where we plant our feet but of how we cultivate our spirits" (108).

23. Charles Isbell, "Deuteronomy's Definition of Jewish Learning," *Jewish Bible Quarterly* 31:2 (2003).

24. In this, he is best read, I think, as continuing the line of critique developed by Karl Popper against totalitarianism and since furthered by Fredric Jameson in his critique of utopianism. For bringing Jameson to my attention, I am indebted to Clem Clarke. Fredric Jameson, *Archaeologies of the Future: The Desire Called Utopia and Other Science Fictions* (London: Verso, 2007); Karl R. Popper, *The Open Society and Its Enemies*, 2 vols. (London: Routledge, 1945), and "Utopia and Violence," address to Institut des Arts, Brussels, 1947.

25. Here surely are Spinoza's Jews, so frightened of God that they march not one day as commanded but three days without stopping to leave the scene of their covenant.

26. In a reading of Rosenzweig on language and translation, in which Rosenzweig in effect argues for the ensoulment of language itself, Marc Crepon provides a useful context for these issues and argues that nihilism is the important if unnamed concern in the Scholem letter ("The Inheritance of Languages," trans. Andre Munro; manuscript on file with the author).

27. Derrida and Anidjar, *Acts of Religion*, 226.

28. Ibid., 227.

29. For this reason it is important to study the march and to receive Exodus as a march-centered narrative rather than one focused on the Promised Land and end states.

30. Homer, *The Iliad*, trans. Robert Fagles (New York: Penguin Classics, 1998); Simone Weil, "The *Iliad* or The Poem of Force," in *Simone Weil: An Anthology*, ed. Sian Miles, trans. Mary McCarthy (New York: Grove Press, 1986); Hannah Arendt, *The Human Condition* (Chicago: University of Chicago Press, 1958).

31. Edward W. Said, "Michael Walzer's 'Exodus and Revolution': A Canaanite Reading," *Grand Street* 5:2 (Winter 1986): 86–106.

32. God's wrath is quelled by the disturbingly redemptive passion of Pinchas, after whom the *parsha* is named (Numbers 25:11). This time, as on many other occasions, God might well have wiped out his flock altogether were it not for something that stayed his hand. Other times, in Numbers and Genesis, he is held back from deeper violence by Moses's interventions or Abraham's logic.

33. *Etz Hayim Torah and Commentary*, ed. David L. Lieber (Philadelphia: Jewish Publication Society, 2002), 918.

34. Ibid.

35. Jacques Rancière, "Ten Theses on Politics," *Theory and Event* 5:3 (2001).

36. My own analysis of the intimate connections between xenophobia and xeno-philia is relevant here. See *Democracy and the Foreigner*.

37. This doubleness is embedded in the Israelite temporality as well, by way of Sab-baticals and the Jubilee. When private landowners give the land a rest, the people too get a rest. The sabbatical year exposes everyone to the vagaries of contingency. Rather than master nature, or be mastered by it, all are made vulnerable to it for a year: they may eat only what happens by chance to grow or what has been set aside. The land sabbatical requirement is not merely a rational precursor to crop rotation, which allows the earth to replenish itself, to maintain and recover its fertility. It also replenishes the people, who normally take their livelihood from the land but for one year, every few years, must receive its bounty as an unearned gift (like the manna of the desert gen-eration). The unearned gift is like the result of the lottery by way of which the land is distributed. The years of labor are like the rational distribution of shares, reflecting the needs and contributions of each group.

38. Judith Butler, *Giving an Account of Oneself* (New York: Fordham University Press, 2005), 125.

39. Jacques Rancière, "Literature, Politics, Aesthetics: Approaches to Democratic Disagreement," interviewed by Solange Guénoun and James H. Kavanagh, *SubStance* 92 (2000): 19.

40. This is an idea that Walzer toys with—or something like it—but with which he is also uncomfortable. He admires the aspirational ideal of an entire people equally deserving of equality. But he does not endorse the idea of undeservingness per se. He tracks in Numbers the back and forth between those who believe the chosen people must be led by prophets and lawgivers and those who believe that the people as such are possessed of the gift of prophecy. The universal priesthood and universal prophecy later taken up by Protestantism are featured in the second promise by way of which God constitutes the people at Sinai, the promise that they will be "a kingdom of priests and a holy nation" (108). This "revolutionary aspiration" does not survive "the people's sin with the calf" (109). At that point, the Levitical priesthood is established. The people are not up to the holiness God saw in them as a whole. The promise will be restricted to the Levites. This solves the problem of the people's carnality, or weakness, in a way. But it also creates a problem. For, as Walzer notes, now there is a tension—between the original universality of holinesss and its restrictive application to a particular tribe (110). Out of this tension arises a new kind of opposition to Moses: rival, popular prophecy. When Joshua reports to Moses that Eldad and Medad have been prophesying in the camp—the tabernacle is outside the camp and revelation is delivered only there—Joshua expects Moses to make them stop. But Moses refuses: "Enviest thou for my sake? Would God that all the Lord's people were prophets" (Numbers 11:26–29). Here Walzer says somewhat poignantly, "Moses remembers the promise, though Joshua has already forgotten it." Eldad and Medad are allowed to continue, and independent prophecy "remains a permanent, if often a precarious, feature of Israel's religious life" (110). But the new leadership prevails in the end, and Moses's hope, that of the second promise, is transformed into a messianic promise. One day the people shall be prophets is one of Joel's prophecies. Is everyone holy? Moses would have said that makes holiness too

easy (112). Instead, it is hard. But it is in the Levites' interests to make it harder still (see Walzer's citation of David Brewer, a justice of the US Supreme Court, on voting, 113).

41. Todd May, *The Political Thought of Jacques Rancière: Creating Equality* (University Park: Pennsylvania State University Press, 2008). I did not know Rancière's work in 1992 and 1993 when I published similar critiques of Rawls (in "Rawls on Politics and Punishment," *Political Research Quarterly* 46:1 (1993): 99–125, and in *Political Theory and the Displacement of Politics*, chap. 5). Rancière's distinction between police order and politics helps bring out sharply what is at stake in what I called then the difference between a *virtù* or virtue-based approach and a democratic or liberal approach to justice and inequality, each postulating active or consumer styles of citizenship, respectively.

42. Derrida, *Monolingualism of the Other*, 73.

43. Baldwin, "Exodus," in *God: Stories*, ed. C. Michael Curtis (Boston: Houghton Mifflin, 1998).

44. Derrida, *Monolingualism of the Other*, 72.

CHAPTER 9

THE STATE BETWEEN RACE AND RELIGION

A Conversation

MARTIN LAND AND JONATHAN BOYARIN

After a semester devoted to the critique of essentialist notions of Jewish identity, an undergraduate raises her hand to demand: "I still want to know—is it a race or a religion?" If these somehow remain the default categories in which to place Jewishness as a putative exemplum, what politics of identity have led to such a rigid binary? Moreover, if "culture" has come as a third possible category, does it represent some way out of this binary trap, or is it merely a mask for what it is no longer polite to designate as "race" in educated circles?

THUS BEGAN a proposal-abstract for this essay. The student's question, in one of the last meetings of a 2006 course on "Jewish cultural history," took me, JONATHAN, by surprise. Yet the slightly petulant tone of her question ("I *still* want to know") suggests some prior exchange left unresolved. I cannot quite reconstitute that prior exchange in memory now, but it may be she had actually raised her hand early in the semester and asked, "Is it a race or a religion?" Maybe, to be fair, I'd responded with something like a coy, "I ain't gonna tell you," suggesting that perhaps by the end of the semester, I'd finally provide an answer to the vexing question of the real ground of Jewish identity.[1]

It would have been more enlightening, I suppose, to try to explain that her question wouldn't have made sense until something like the eighteenth or even the nineteenth century; that the attempt to separate out race, religion, and culture was inseparable from questions of governability and identity in the bourgeois state ideal; that the refusal of these categories to respect our attempts to keep them distinct goes far toward explaining the gulf separating that ideal from the violent history of the twentieth century; that the "Jewish question" remains simultaneously anomalous and paradigmatic because Jewishness refuses to sit still as genealogy (a politer term than "race," which, at least in older usages, was not necessarily limited to what we now call biological kinship), religion (certainly if that term is understood to mean, most conveniently for the liberal state, an individual affair primarily consisting of points of "faith" that remain discreetly tucked away in individual brains), or culture (something everyone has, unique but equivalent to everyone else's, like a home address or a Social Security number); that the discourse on Jewishness, friendly and hostile, internal and external, opportunistically draws on all of these categories, especially when it tries to explain where and how continued Jewishness might still be defensible, permissible, feasible, worthwhile, or—dare I say it—even necessary?[2]

How shall we think about the consequences of a history in which liberal democracies, including the Jewish state, have willy-nilly fostered the requirements that Jews be categorized into the imagined unities of race, religion, or both? That liberal democracies do this is not a new insight, especially if we understand "political theology" to indicate not so much (or not merely) the continuity between the authority structures of the church and those of the European monarchy or liberal state, but rather the inevitable and flawed attempt to ground rationales of state exclusion and inclusion in something posited as more abyssal, more unquestionable than state power in itself.[3] Israeli citizenship criteria, for example, rely heavily both on a genealogical conception of Jewish peoplehood and on state-sanctioned clerical authorities for determination of Jewishness in individual cases. Other liberal Western states, as has been argued by scholars such as Jon Stratton,[4] permit assimilation and inclusion of Jews within the dominant collective, but only at the cost of adherence to a covert "whiteness" criterion for membership. These cases suggest that, rather than view our task as the addition of a consideration of "race" to the discursive tradition (following, say, Schmitt and Kantorowicz) on political theology that in any case ultimately

means "Christianity" when it says "religion,"[5] it may be useful to start by
assuming that categories covertly or explicitly deemed racial and/or religious are indispensable to the logic of the state and (for us equally important) by discussing possibilities for generous group identifications that resist
these statist constraints.

I refused my student's invitation to pin Jewishness down as race or religion
not only because the dichotomy hardly applies to the self-understanding of
Jews at most times and places until post-Enlightenment modernity. Rather,
my particular resistance to rhetorics of race and religion turns on how these,
used to ground the governance of identity in liberal nationalisms, have
constituted and continue to constitute naturalized and therefore generally
unrecognized hindrances to contingent, grounded, and reflexive Jewish *identification* on the part of persons who self-identify, to be sure in quite various
fashions, as Jews.

Though this might seem a move in the direction of evacuating the name
"Jew" of any determinate content, I believe our intention is rather to move
notions of Jewishness away from any given set of core criteria, toward consciousness of, and participation in, an almost unimaginably vast range of
repertoires, interpretive debates, and dialogues. This may not only help explain why succeeding generations continue to somehow *want* to be Jewish,
even when the alternative categories of race and religion continue to lose
whatever resonant appeal they once had, but may also, ultimately, help provide new directions for thinking about Jewish and other collective names
beyond the constitutive, and powerfully lingering, aporias of the politics of
identity in modernity.

I know, however, that you wish to insist on something like a moral core
to Jewishness, and I see that you are eager to interrupt.

ASIDE FROM AN EAGERNESS TO INTERRUPT, which has now been attributed
to me, MARTIN, and indeed has been regarded by some commentators as
belonging to an essential core of Jewishness, what specific criteria for classi-
fying Jews as a collectivity could possibly attain sufficiently wide acceptance
as to render the assembled construction useful, analytically or otherwise?
An implicit question underlying much of the foregoing seems to be "useful for whom?" You draw a distinction between two basic approaches to

understanding Jewishness, one that attempts to locate Jews within socio-political categories inherited from historical circumstances of questionable relevance, and another that seeks to infer a classification scheme from patterns of self-identification in the experience of Jewish communities and the testimony of individuals. The former approach, by cataloging Jews as one among several instances of a presupposed classification, be it race, religion, culture, or some other, is clearly useful to the state in its efforts to portray its actions as rational, categorical, and impartial. The latter approach, by reflecting the relatively recent academic disfavor toward classifications of group identity imposed from without (generally from above) and embracing an intersubjective engagement with the people being discussed, is useful to scholars in their search for a discourse that offers a reasonable level of explanatory power (dare I say, a scientific approach).

What is less clear is the usefulness of either approach, as perceived by the Jews under study. If we judge by the contemporary discourse among self-identified Jews, it is a safe guess that no defining conception of Jewishness, perhaps especially a conception offered from within, will be even minimally acceptable to most participants. In the Israeli context certainly, it is far from obvious that the question of what constitutes an overarching Jewishness is as compelling as the struggle among competing prescriptions for living as a Jew, each vision highly parochial but perceived by its partisans as somehow "most authentic." The diversity of contemporary Israeli Jewish life often degenerates into an internal disputation, unfortunately mirroring the externally posed terms of the "Jewish question" based on the categories of race and religion. Having accepted these terms in negotiating with the world powers, whether opportunistically or from a disadvantageous bargaining position, many Jews find themselves trapped within them, unable to even ask whether these categorical assumptions can be adjusted, for fear of consequently undermining their historic position regarding the legitimacy of the State of Israel. Thus, an Israeli undergraduate might very well ask an instructor to characterize the Jews as a religion or a people (a word that in the Middle East performs much of the political work historically associated with the word *race* in America), not to obtain an authoritative answer but, more likely, to locate the teacher, as an individual, on the familiar spectrum of parochial perspectives. The careless instructor might place emphasis on the Jews as a people (probably "secular"), on the Jewish religion ("ultra-orthodox"), on both ("national-religious"), or on neither ("anti-Zionist"), but any attempt to hide behind cageyness would be read as invoking teacher-student hierarchy. The awkward labels in our hypothetical undergraduate's repertoire are the most commonly invoked representations of Jewishness among Israeli Jews, and though they distort a more nuanced understanding through the binaries of race and religion, each of these perspectives has accumulated a sufficiently rich history to provide its advocates with a core of meaning and identity. So, the categories of race and religion, constructed to serve particular political interests in an early European context, applied to the Jews in a much later context, introjected by Jews in the name of achieving political statehood, and reified by that state through its legal structures, ultimately begat new political identities based on partisan relationship to the older categories and a contest among these partisans to legally impose those categories on Israelis, Palestinians, Jews in general, and everyone else.

Where can one begin in trying to unravel this mess? Perhaps the preliminary work of deconstruction, which thankfully prevents ontologizing anything as race, is only half finished, and we must now turn our attention to religion. Despite the relevance of multiple academic perspectives to the study of an individual decision not to steal, how can that decision be uniquely classified as law, philosophy, politics, psychology, sociology, anthropology, biology, or religion? Each discipline can construct analyses of that decision based on its historically successful methods, but while the inseparable signifier and signified make up the workload of the scholar, the referent can remain autonomous and indifferent, until taught to understand itself as inherently belonging to one or another label. Just as the state promotes the reification of categorical distinctions, not only to govern its subjects/citizens but also to negotiate relations with other centers of power, each of these power centers similarly manufactures ontology for the phenomena under its purview. In particular, institutional scholarship establishes spheres of interest and regulates market share among the academic disciplines. For these reasons, controversy over the classification of some issue as religious, medical, legal, or economic often reflects the friction along boundaries between the centers of power involved.

As you hinted, not all "religions" begin with faith or belief, and many do not respect, except as a matter of practical obedience to state power, the division of human activity according to past agreements over realms of authority between competing centers of power. I submit that your proposal for moving away from core criteria toward a more open-ended consciousness and participation is a valuable contribution to understanding religion as such. Within an agreed framework that sees Jewishness as a collection of experiences to be understood phenomenologically, I can feel free to adhere to my particular repertoire and interpretive debates, moral and otherwise.

Now, stop me before I interrupt again.

MARTIN, YOUR RESPONSE seems so lucid that my opening entry now seems full of holes through which I could drive my 2005 Prius, if not a Mack truck. To follow this, I'll have to direct your attention back to that opening entry as well.

The first hole is right there at the beginning. It's hard to imagine beginning an account of Jewishness without at least some postulates, whether or not made explicit, about what Jewish identity is and is not. So it seems unlikely that I really devoted an entire semester to the critique of essentialist notions of Jewish identity without making at least certain key assumptions about shared notions of Jewishness that everyone, the instructor included, brought into the class. I do use one term, "Jewish communities," which, it seems, one could get away with for the length of this essay without deontologizing. The term has its critical attractions, which turn out to be mostly negative, since it avoids some of the problems of racial, religious, or even statist categorization. It also has its sentimental attractions, suggesting a legacy of collective solidarity and autonomy, but we should be wary of being seduced by these, since a host of repressions have also been carried out, by Jews and non-Jews, in the name of Jewish community.

Likewise, suggesting that a distinction something like that between racial and religious differences cannot be traced further back than the Enlightenment is not particularly helpful. One can argue that something like racial discourses can be detected well back into the Middle Ages, and indeed this seems to be the emerging consensus among medievalists.[6] Also, to be sure, the vexed relation of—to vary the terms a bit—communities of genealogy and communities of faith dogged European colonialism from its very beginnings, as witness the decision taken rather early by Spanish missionaries in the New World that natives could not be ordained as priests.[7] More speculatively—because it relies on a counterfactual—I wrote of the importance to the bourgeois state ideal of the separation of race and religion in a way that suggested we might have been better off if that ideal had been fully realized in the twentieth century, as if something like Fukuyama's now-risible "end of history" had arrived rather than the end of the myth of inevitable progress in the wake of World War II. I'm not sure that particular consummation would have been something so devoutly to be wished. And, while we're still looking at my second paragraph, I noticed that although anthropologists and other cultural theorists have been working for decades to dismantle the notion of whole, organic, and functionally equivalent human cultures, within the Jewish world we've been seeing a renewed emphasis on, and funding of efforts to promote, "Jewish culture" (an effort in which I'm certainly complicit) or even something called (oxymoronically to my ears) "cultural Judaism." Speaking of multiple "Jewish cultures" just defers the problem; it doesn't resolve it.

One more point before I begin responding to you rather than to me. I refer to the situated identities of "persons who self-identify . . . as Jews." Am I doing anything beyond paraphrasing Marx here—especially if we compare Marx's "Alp" of the past weighing on past generations to Mount Sinai, which, as the *Midrash* tells us, God was ready to have overturned on our ancestors' heads had they not "chosen" to accept His Law?[8] More pointedly, is this my iteration of a contemporary ideal that in general veers more heavily toward a greater individualism than I would care to defend in theory, and that deprivileges those who take their own Jewishness (whatever its form) to be noncontingent or who refuse to exercise the language of reflexivity that people like you and me find so comforting?

So, then, "useful for whom?" Yes, quite! However, I had already suggested that we were considering categories of race and religion primarily as they are useful to the state. The state—now there's a nice reification for you. In the Israeli context certainly, as you know, it is particularly difficult to separate personal identity from the state (even for those who argue that identities in Israel should not be a matter of state control or intervention, agonistic *engagement* with the state form of social organization is central). And whether or not full citizenship rights "as a Jew" in Israel depend on conformity to a given description of Jewishness, Jewish people who are identified with, contest for, and deploy the power of the Jewish state are manifestly engaged in deciding who is and who is not a Jew; a signal example of this is the attempt by the (Orthodox) Israeli state rabbinate to assert unique jurisdiction, to the exclusion of Orthodox rabbis in the diaspora, over the validity of individual conversions to Judaism and, thus, over those individuals' access to marriage and other rights in Israel. It is not a novel insight but is worth repeating here, that in a "Jewish" state the meaning of Jewishness is inevitably a matter of state politics.

You imagine that an Israeli student asking her instructor whether the Jews are a religion or a people would be trying more to place the teacher politically than to figure out Jewish identity. To be sure, students are students and instructors have power over them everywhere, including not only the power of grading but, of more immediate consequence, the power to make them sit still and listen. So it seems quite likely that in Kansas (as in your Israeli hypothetical), my actual attempt to hide behind cageyness was read as an attempt to withhold knowledge.

Regarding the status of religion as an object of scholarly discourse, especially in relation to the state, while not knowing exactly what is and isn't "religion" doesn't hobble my teaching or research, it is nevertheless somewhat embarrassing at times. As we have moved away from dogma and theology as the subject matter of religious studies, the scope of the field has expanded to encompass so much, at least potentially, that one particular source of embarrassment is precisely that there is so much we do not attend to that, by all rights, we should. Having broken past the barrier of viewing Christianity as the only "religion," we remain with a politics of academic scarcity in which there is only so much attention available to be paid to so many people. As in so many other areas of our lives, the distorted distribution of resources under capitalism exacerbates the politics of identity, making it appear at times that my heritage or identity can be preserved and strengthened only at the cost of yours being marginalized or extinguished. In any case, if part of the reason scholars are supported and tolerated at all is that they help teach the referent "to understand itself as inherently belonging to one or another label," then academic religious studies bears some relation—let's call it "semideterminate" for now—to the politics of the place of religion in any state, liberal, secular or theocratic, Jewish, Christian, Muslim, or officially godless.

When we first contemplated this exchange, you suggested that you'd take issue with any formulation suggesting that Jewishness is whatever anyone calls it. I'd like to invite you now to say more about your particular repertoire regarding the constitution of Jewishness, especially in regard to debates about morality, acknowledging that (as we both know) even though the morality of Jewishness in the Jewish state is fraught in particular ways, the politics of identity are never innocent of the exercise of certain forms of power.

WE SEEM TO AGREE THAT, at least for general scholarly purposes, Jewishness should be understood through patterns of consciousness and participation and cannot be reduced to either race (understood as something associated with genealogy) or religion (understood as faith or adherence to a system of beliefs), despite the heavy reference to these categories made by Jews themselves in attempting to describe their own experience. Having said what Jewishness isn't, can we say anything about what it is? It seems to me that any reasonable approach to that question must address two interrelated difficulties you raise in connection with this empirical/phenomenological understanding of Jewish self-identification: on the one hand, does an accretive catalog of Jewish cultural repertoires deal justly with those who take their particular Jewishness to be noncontingent, and on the other, does the inclusivity of that approach undermine our attempt to distinguish Jewishness from anything else, precisely because it excludes all noncontingent content? How do we discuss the multiplicity of Jewish narratives in a manner that negotiates among diverse repertoires within some recognizable boundary of Jewishness, while neither privileging nor depriviledging any particularistic notions of essential content?

These questions return us precisely to the problem of "freedom of religion" in the liberal state: how can the law grant equal respect to all recognized religions while withholding recognition of any as having special legitimacy? If we follow this analogy, it may be useful, at least for academic work, to recognize a principle of "freedom of Jewishness" that understands the word *Jewishness* as a purely descriptive category, within which every Jewish repertoire, each with its own particularistic notions of essential content, is an equivalent exemplum. Although "freedom of religion" effectively constitutes an equal depriveging of all noncontingent religious experience, the legal intent (if not always the political) is not to challenge the meaning of religion for its adherents but rather to downplay the theological significance of state action toward religion and limit the state's engagement with religion to empirical information available to adherents and nonadherents alike. Perhaps, by limiting the goals of study to a historical accounting of Jewish experience based on empirical information, naturally including personal testimony and text analysis, scholars will be freed to apply their professional skills to the multiplicity of Jewish narratives while accepting neither responsibility nor authority for singling out any one for special endorsement or for inventing some master synthesis that, in any event, most of the Jews under study are likely to reject.

However, "freedom of Jewishness" differs from "freedom of religion" in significant ways. First, unlike the methodological difficulties associated with distinguishing certain human activities as categorically religious, the observation that "Jewishness" generally applies to historically interconnected narratives, including the judgments each narrative makes of the others, provides a basis for operational definition of the boundary. In fact, the importance of the historical perspective in Jewish thought, underpinning the understanding and interpretation of text and found in activities from prayer to "secular" literature and politics, imparts an implicit authority to historicist methodology, or at least makes it less foreign. Second, Zionism notwithstanding, Jews have a long tradition of indifference toward engagement with nonparticipants on the question of whether their particular narrative repertoires are kosher, so it is not clear what fairness a nonparticipant can show toward those who take their Jewishness to be noncontingent beyond respectful recognition that they indeed follow a way of life they regard as possessing transcendent significance. Third, questions about how interpretive debates act to unify the differing repertoires, and how that unity can be represented to nonparticipants, have been a central concern for Jews at least since the ancient Talmudic debates, the interactions with Hellenism, the work of medieval Jewish philosophers, and the disputations.

Proposing an apparently liberal, even laissez-faire, "freedom of Jewishness" may surprise you, in light of my early statement that I do not accept Judaism to be merely the sum total of what Jews do (which I compared to my rejecting the suggestion that mathematics is merely the sum total of whatever mathematicians do). The difference is entirely one of context. Any particular repertoire belongs to the complex web of relationships called Jewishness by virtue of the nature of those relationships, and belonging neither influences nor is influenced by its consistency with other Jewish narratives.

My own Jewish perspective encourages this distinction between the experience of noncontingence from within and the explicit awareness of contingence in representing my perspective to others. I was taught that we are obliged to concern ourselves with what Judaism expects of us, while practicing curiosity and genial open-mindedness toward other repertoires of Jewishness, as long as they do not contradict what we understand Judaism to be capable of accepting. In view of this distinction, "freedom of Jewishness" is not intended as a technical compromise that politely steers away from conflicts over interpretation but as embracing the goal of a psychologically mature relationship between our reflexive experience as subjects and the awareness of relationship and interaction with other different, yet fundamentally equivalent, subjects. Put another way, an intersubjective outlook prohibits the recognition of a public rule based solely on the private experience of one individual or group, and this prohibition is the foundation of an ethical principle. Thus, drawing a line from Hillel to Levinas, by way of Yehuda Halevi, we find ourselves, not having forgotten your original question, discussing morality as the moral core of a particular Jewish repertoire.

In light of Rabbi Hillel's greatest hit, "That which is hateful to you, do not impose on another. That is the whole Torah; the rest is the interpretation; go and learn," it is reasonable to expect that adherents of alternative perspectives will at least acknowledge that the identification of a moral core in Judaism is not too far-fetched. Although no perfect distinction is possible, Jewish law is traditionally divided into ritual law and ethical law, and many followers of Hillel argue that, without second guessing divine intent, the observance of ritual law serves as a practice of mindfulness in regard to the ethical law. According to this line of thinking, in the Sinai covenant our ancestors accepted an obligation to hold ourselves to a high standard of ethical behavior, so our coherence as a collectivity follows from that historical event and is embodied in that commitment (answering for this narrative the question, "Who are the Jews?"). Since the Torah directs us not to look to heaven for instruction—the law as given, debated, interpreted, deconstructed, and reconstructed provides the blueprint for a just society— this ethical structure must include the style of scholarly debate as well as its content. As Jessica Benjamin has said,[9] we may construct the moral thirdness required for ethical relationships through a process of mutual recognition of our subjective interpretations of divine law, but not while insisting on a single absolute statement of divine intent. This understanding is underscored in the remarkable account of Rabbi Eliezer, who successfully obtains divine support for his position in the debate over the oven of Akhni, but is nevertheless overruled by the other rabbis. The Talmud says that this rabbinic independence caused God to smile, reminding Him that the Torah instructs us to settle earthly matters among ourselves without looking to Heaven. Conversely, as pointedly observed by Yeshayahu Leibowitz, this style of debate reminds us not to confuse our emotional needs with divine will.

Of course, the foregoing invites the response that Hillel's canonical formulation logically constrains only the subset of Jewishness informed by Torah, and some may argue that to invoke Hillel in a political context amounts to religious coercion. In a recent essay that appeared in the daily Hebrew newspaper *Haaretz* and was translated for its English edition, A. B. Yehoshua wrote, "Logically, the word Jew belongs much more among terms like French, Chinese or English. The Jewish faith is an optional part of being a Jew, just as Catholicism or Christianity is an optional part of being an Italian or English, or the way Islam is optional for Egyptians. This has been absolutely proven over the last 200 years of Jewish secularism."[10] This narrative, which is not my own but does represent a familiar Jewish repertoire, poses an apparent challenge to the relevance of Hillel to Jewish identity. Logically, this challenge can be further expanded to consider the identities of Chinese or Italians who adopt something they understand to be the Jewish faith without becoming Jews, and Jews who adopt Catholicism or Islam yet remain Jews, but it is interesting to note the inadequate translation as "faith" of the Hebrew *dat*, a word closer in meaning to law, lawfulness, or in the logical sense, known (cf. *data*). Perhaps a more accurate translation of Yehoshua's original would be that "the observance of Jewish law is an optional part of being a Jew," and here again, so long as we bear in mind a proper distinction between what Judaism (or Jewish law) requires and what Jews do, the statement remains logically valid.

Incorporating Jewish law into state law, backed by the state's monopoly on the legitimate use of violence, renders the question of how Jewish law should be determined problematic, and "freedom of Jewishness" is inherently violated. Despite the face Israel presents to the world through the statements and policies of its government, commitment to the ethical law in the general population is probably no better or worse than in other Jewish communities over time. But in this globalized economy, problems of social justice and communal responsibility are posed in the vocabulary of European social democracy and American neoconservatism, with only marginal relevance seen in Jewish ethical law. Thus, even though one assumes that "secular" progressives such as A. B. Yehoshua, who regard ritual law as optional, have a different attitude toward Jewish laws of ethics and social justice, nevertheless (and despite the importance of observant Jews in the concrete daily struggles for justice in Israel), the mainstream view (cf. "The ideas of the ruling class are in every epoch the ruling ideas"[11]) largely relegates Jewish ethics to a fuzzy notion of "compassion" as a chronic Jewish shortcoming and regards observant progressives as largely anomalous.

In this political environment, I am occasionally called upon to explain the peculiar assortment of ritual laws I observe, and consequently about belief in God, divine judgment, and so on, belief being the presumed starting place for observance of Jewish ritual law or concern for the Jewish ethical content of social justice. Exacerbating the general annoyance of these interrogators, I recount my teenage impulse to reconsider Jewish identity while reading *The Autobiography of Malcolm X*, whose emphasis on history and memory as components of identity held a powerful resonance for me as a Jew. Anticipating that resonance, Yehuda Halevi argued in his twelfth-century work *Kuzari* that for its adherents, attachment to Judaism is rooted not in faith in a deity or belief in nature as evidence for a deity but in the existential experience of being raised and educated within a pattern of historical developments, beginning with the events at Sinai, evolving through a vast series of interpretive narratives down to us, and depending on one's teleological viewpoint, continuing beyond the present moment. In this view of Jewish identity, the most significant epistemological assumption for the individual and the community is that our inherited narrative did not originate in a fraud, an assumption essentially comparable to believing that the (now ancient and irreproducible) Apollo moon landings were not actually staged in a Hollywood basement. Although Halevi intended his work as a defense of Judaism, his central insight into the role of historical experience in Jewish identity is essentially up to date, if we understand that experience as a complex network of historically connected narratives, each with a subjective core of interpretive experience, and each recognizing in the other a different and yet fundamentally equivalent subject. This shuffling of Halevi onto the postmodernist escalator then extends to Jewishness, understood in the most inclusive sense, an ethical structure based on intersubjective relationships among the most easily recognized narratives and the less familiar others with which we are more likely to enter into interpretive debate.

A FEW FURTHER THOUGHTS on two questions on which we have, perhaps, already made some progress.

First, what coherent stance can we (defined here as those who take group identity per se as at least primarily contingent, and who in public discourse at least take that stance toward their own identities as well) take toward our fellows who concede the contingency of their identity not at all? I would say that it is useful, among other things, for us to recall that their stance tends to destabilize ours, that which is absolute tending to be more forceful than that which is contingent. In response we tend alternatively to idolize or to demonize our fellows who are "noncontingent." It is wiser, perhaps, to start from a somewhat reductive or quantitative stance and assume, as if identity were a fixed quantum, that more of theirs than of ours is invested in the Jewish name, and to see what the consequences are for their lives and for our mutual relationships—for example, it may be prudent to see noncontingent Jews as bearers of a rich and detailed collective memory of everyday, intimate Jewish life without fashioning them as more "authentically" Jewish than anyone else.

Second, to the extent that we may retain some notion of our own authentic Jewishness, is there a necessary gap in reasoning between that and our assertion that, discursively, nothing that calls itself Jewish, *even if we find it repellent*, is to be declared a priori fraudulent in its claim to that name? Your last communication goes far, I think, toward filling that gap in reasoning. Academic Jewish studies has gone far, even in the few decades since I began to apprentice in that trade, away from the search for (or even assumption of) one normative Jewish tradition and toward recognition of Gershom Scholem's assertion that what's Jewish is what Jews have done and thought. But as a practitioner of that trade, I find that something's lost and something's gained in the embrace of this laissez-faire. A decathexis has been demanded of me. I no longer approach my field of Jewish studies primarily as the study of that which is "my own." The primary question necessarily becomes not "What relation do the people I study have to me?" but rather "What relation do the people I study have to each other?"

I think you are too kind by far to the bizarre and troubling statement by A. B. Yehoshua that you quote. To be sure, I have no wish to dispute the right of anyone to call herself a Jew without adherence to the Jewish faith. Yet the separability of Jewishness from Judaism is not a "logical" but a historical and semantic fact, and his analogy ("just as") proves nothing. Before Emancipation, that is, before "the last 200 years," the possibility of abandoning Judaism but remaining a Jew almost inevitably smacked of a genealogical determinism (what we now call "racism") imposed from outside. This is certainly not the "logic" Yehoshua means to assert, yet that he finds himself back in the same trap points once again to the state's seeming inability to constitute itself without the help of either race, religion, or both. On the other hand, for Jews, but also for "the" French, English, or Italians, the possibility of sharing that nationality without a "religion" presumed its inevitable concomitant is also a matter of the last two hundred years, and by no means fully accomplished: just ask Muslim immigrants to France, England, or Italy. Without that, nationality is a matter of language, territorial-state belonging, and genealogy. How else would he or they know who these putative Jews are? Otherwise, unless Yehoshua is ready to concede that I'm not Jewish (because I don't share his land, language, or citizenship) or that Hebrew-speaking Arab citizens of Israel are (because they do share his land, language, or citizenship), I don't think Hillel has to worry too much.

WELL, THOSE REALLY ARE THE TWO QUESTIONS underlying this entire discussion—in a sense they should be seen as two instances of one big question facing anyone who tempers the authenticity of immediate private perspective with a learned awareness of the contingence of that perspective in public space and time. Private experience being just that, no two people can possibly have identical conceptions of their group identity, so group members must inevitably negotiate practical differences of perspective or fall into endless power struggle and schism. Moreover, unless we accept that group identity can only be a group construction, we are left with an old and somewhat ludicrous conundrum—what literal meaning can be given to the notion of sharing nonidentical group identities? Negotiating difference can be difficult even when all parties share a common identity and an awareness of identity as contingent. Restating your questions, our strategy for understanding identity is ultimately tested by two problematic cases at the boundaries—a party that concedes no awareness of contingence and a party whose demand for recognition strains our ability to find meaningful group identity at all.

The Talmudic process poses Jewish identity as adherence to a central core of law, whose meaning is to be collectively determined, and institutionalizes rule-based interpretive debate as a necessary step in understanding Jewish experience. This insistent awareness of epistemology admits a possibility that is simply not consistent with absolutist noncontingence, the possibility of rethinking a provisional identity, and as I understand Jewish tradition, this point of view is traditional. In this sense, it can be argued that an entirely noncontingent view of Jewish identity should be understood as yet another of the many nontraditional directions Jewishness has taken over the past three hundred years, along with secular assimilationism and Zionism. Again, we adopt a coherent stance toward all Jewish narratives, from absolute noncontingence to antinomian sentimentalism, by defining boundaries for "freedom of Jewishness" that admit as kosher any particular form of Jewishness with a reasonable and recognizable historical connection to Jewish practice. This approach emphasizes the commonality between various claims to a more authentic Jewishness, whether from a thoroughly Westernized Israeli whose assertion rests on his participation in a Hebrew-speaking army or a Haredi appropriating to himself the title Jewish Jew or Torah Jew. Both, with some degree of generosity, can be taken as invitations to similarly draw on our own secure base of identity and similarly exhibit what feels like authentic Jewishness. In considering the problematics of this invitation, I am reminded of a passage you may recall writing, regarding the means by which house slaves, acculturated into the servant class of the white American slaveholders, may have preserved their identification with African culture through attachment to their own memories and contact with field slaves whose connection to African practices was presumably less fully suppressed by the slave system.[12] In countering claims that the assimilation of house slaves into "white culture" rendered their identification artificial, the passage describes the physical and historical circumstances that produced an authentic cultural connection and suggests that emotional factors arising from contact with field slaves—dissonance, guilt, and nostalgia—may have strengthened that identification. Without my suggesting any comparison to the horrors of New World slavery, it occurred to me that your insight into these emotional factors may have been influenced by personal experience as a partially or superficially assimilated American Jew confronting Jews whose detailed Jewishness is unmistakably evident in their presentation of self.

Analogously perhaps, many Israelis perversely regard diaspora Jews as a variety of house slave, privileged to share the master's culture and wealth but deprived of Jewish authenticity and paralyzed by self-hatred (a fault ostensibly evidenced by sensitivity to traditional Jewish ethics). Inevitably, this pattern has been replicated in the view taken by the "frontiersmen" of the Jewish West Bank settlements toward the "degenerate and hedonistic" Jews of Tel Aviv. Speaking for myself, I have become somewhat immune to Jews who regard their Jewishness as less contingent or more authentic than my own.

About twenty years ago, a lesbian reform rabbi was discussing her work on an Israeli TV talk show, until rudely interrupted by another guest, a minor male politician from an "ultra-orthodox party" who dismissively pronounced her views unacceptable. She politely (in American-accented Hebrew) suggested that as religiously committed Jews representing disadvantaged minority groups in Israel, they should recognize their common interest in working together to further pluralism and tolerance. Clearly caught off guard that the *maidele* was not destabilized by his absolutist stance,[13] the politician was further astonished at the suggestion that his authentic community would seek the protection of minority status, as though it were a form of "social deviance" and not the natural ideology for the Land of Israel. Whether drawing on his rich experience as a Jew or as a grubby politician, he exemplified much of what Jean-Luc Nancy had in mind in distinguishing reasoned belief from faith as a form of noncontingent loyalty.[14] The rabbi exemplified the ethical approach advocated by Hillel, drawing on a safe space where she stores her sense of authentic Jewishness. Whether choosing this strategy as a follower of Hillel or as a student of game theory, she admirably confronted potentially destabilizing noncontingence without seeking to destabilize the other.

Since you evidently enjoyed A. B. Yehoshua's statement, I am sure that you will be interested to hear his motivation—to argue against the continued reference to Israel as a Jewish state. In Yehoshua's view, by proclaiming the State of Israel, the founders clearly announced a political entity embodying the People of Israel in organic, divinely inspired, and noncontingent relationship with the Land of Israel, thus rendering any further qualification unnecessary. Applying the term "Jewish state" therefore implies a religious component (and hence, religious coercion) that is not only superfluous (since he views the Jewish religion as optional for Jews) but the primary source of irritation to Palestinian-Arab Israelis. But in viewing the Jews as a people (or race or nation) that incidentally acquired a religious faith, Yehoshua does not abandon his exiled kin, keeping open the possibility of return (a secularized version of traditional notions of repentance).

> There is no need to insist on saying "Jewish state" or "state of the Jewish people" in order to express the validity of the law of return (which grants any Jew who wants to live in Israel automatic citizenship). On the contrary, when we say that Israel is also a Zionist state, we clearly articulate the standing offer to Diaspora Jews to transform from Jews into Israelis, and to return to their original and total Jewishness—in territory, in history and in the experience of living within a community that obligates them.[15]

You have been an articulate exponent of an opposing view—that "the lesson of Diaspora, namely that peoples and lands are not naturally and organically connected" is important for Jews and the world as a whole.[16]

I STAND BY THOSE WORDS. Though I admit I first misread the title of Yehoshua's article—that is, I thought he was explaining the rationale for insisting on a Jewish state rather than questioning that rationale—my reaction to his argument hasn't changed. Genealogy is an inescapable aspect of collective identity through time; it shapes life and is never innocent. When combined with state-territorial dominance, its tendency to facilitate oppression of nonkin is enhanced; when substituted for rhetorics of collective memory (rhetorics that include but are not limited to suffering, that may focus on what is shared through the generations but do not suppress differences among members of the group in time and space), the pressure on exclusive (or dominant) dwelling within a sovereign territory becomes all the greater, since any nonmember of the group present in that territory becomes ipso facto a threat to identity and "security." Though Yehoshua refers to "history" and communal obligation, those are readily available in diasporic communities, so what's left is, again, territory and "nationality," which can only mean biological descent here. On what other possible basis does he assert that those he calls "Diaspora Jews" should come to Israel "to return to their original and total Jewishness"?[17]

In any case, I'm a hopeless candidate as far as he's concerned. I *like* the fact that my Jewishness depends on interaction—some good, some not so good—with other peoples. My Jewishness is not original. I don't want it to be. It's derived, with some twists I've come up with on my own at the cost of considerable personal effort, and again, that's just how I like it. I can't begin to imagine what he thinks "total Jewishness" means. It sounds like some creepy marketing campaign. I don't especially want to have the last word, but I really don't even want to argue about this, even with a great writer. And I know that other smart and moral and worldly people agree with him. I'm outta here. Good-bye.

WHETHER CONSTRUED NARROWLY, as the applicability of particular religious constructs to sociopolitical organization, or broadly, as the influence of religious identity on political behavior, political theology takes off from the claim that religion is a distinct and identifiable category whose relationship to politics admits universal conclusions. Although the foregoing discussion focuses on Jewish experience, it points to the difficulties in clearly distinguishing race and religion as formal categories with regard to one historically significant case and is thus relevant to the claim of universality. A different traditional approach to Jewish identity grounded in ethical relations—referencing notions of kinship and theology but not requiring a clear distinction—may provide a useful model in political theology.

A democratic state can be understood as dealing in matters of public record, respectfully accommodating but remaining agnostic toward expressions of subjective experience. Moreover, since theology is only sharply distinguished from history, philosophy, law, and literature insofar as it deals with issues not intersubjectively available for controlled study, its relevance to democracy seems naturally limited to its overlap with these other ways of thinking. One need not assert an inevitable connection between Carl Schmitt and the particular state, whose legal philosophy he worked to formalize, to suspect that positioning the state in analogy to God is not a secure base for democracy. Put another way, to the extent that what is conventionally denominated as "religious thought" cannot be unambiguously distinguished from the shared habits of mind among a particular kinship group, it remains unlikely that religion can provide a basis for democratic constitutional principle without similarly sacralizing race.

Notes

1. If Henry Goldschmidt's *Race and Religion among the Chosen Peoples of Crown Heights* (New Brunswick, NJ: Rutgers University Press, 2006) had already been published then, I could have cited it as a textbook analysis of the way the state, in order to manage the politics of group difference, forces neighboring group identities into these respective and limited categories, and how they are swallowed, resisted, and manipulated by the people(s) themselves. Goldschmidt also points out, among other insights, that what's culture to some (e.g., foodways for African Americans and Afro-Caribbeans) is law for others (their Lubavitch Hasidic neighbors)—making the neighborhood barbecue a less-than-ideal candidate for fostering state-sponsored unity.

2. Marc Ellis has insisted, plausibly enough, on the claim that continued Jewish identity is unthinkable without the continued viability of Palestinian identity. I suppose I could imagine a variety of post-Jewishness that, God forbid, would focus on mourn-

ing Jewishness as a result of the final abandonment of Palestinian dreams for redemption, but what a dreary prospect for all of us that is.

3. As Claude Lefort has reminded us, Hegel already recognized how ultimately untenable it was to assert religion as a "private" sphere that could be merely additive to an originary state identity. "The Permanence of the Theologico-Political?," in *Political Theologies: Public Religions in a Post-secular World*, ed. Hent de Vries (New York: Fordham University Press, 2006), 149.

4. Jon Stratton, *Coming Out Jewish: Constructing Ambivalent Identities* (London: Routledge, 2000).

5. Lefort, "The Permanence of the Theologico-Political?," 159.

6. See, for example, David Nirenberg, "Race and the Middle Ages: The Case of Spain and Its Jews," in *Rereading the Black Legend: The Discourses of Religious and Racial Difference in the Renaissance Empires*, ed. Margaret R. Greer, Walter D. Mignolo, and Maureen Quilligan (Chicago: University of Chicago Press, 2007), 71–88; Geraldine Heng, "The Romance of England: *Richard Coeur de Lyon*, Saracens, Jews, and the Politics of Race and Nation," in *The Postcolonial Middle Ages*, ed. Jeffrey Jerome Cohen (New York: St. Martin's Press, 2000), 135–171.

7. See Jonathan Boyarin, *The Unconverted Self: Jews, Indians, and the Identity of Christian Europe* (Chicago: University of Chicago Press, 2009).

8. "Men make their own history, but they do not make it as they please; they do not make it under self-selected circumstances, but under circumstances existing already, given and transmitted from the past. The tradition of all dead generations weighs like a nightmare on the brains of the living." Karl Marx, *The Eighteenth Brumaire of Louis Napoleon* (Moscow: Progress Publishers, 1937).

9. Jessica Benjamin, personal communication.

10. A. B. Yehoshua, "Why Do We Insist on a 'Jewish' State?," *Haaretz*, October 6, 2009.

11. Karl Marx and Friedrich Engels, *Die deutsche Ideologie* (Moscow: Marx-Engels Institute, 1932).

12. Daniel Boyarin and Jonathan Boyarin, "Diaspora: Generation and the Ground of Jewish Identity," *Critical Inquiry* 19 (1993): 693–725.

13. The word *maidele* is Yiddish for "little girl," used in Israel as a pejorative address to an adult woman.

14. Jean-Luc Nancy, personal communication.

15. Yehoshua, "Why Do We Insist?"

16. Boyarin and Boyarin, "Diaspora," 723.

17. The question has significant, although of course still hypothetical, practical consequences, since Yehoshua clearly wants to retain "the law of return" to Israel *for Jews* (however that identity is to be determined) and to Palestine for Palestinians *who are not Jews*.

CHAPTER 10

FROM POLITICAL THEOLOGY TO VERNACULAR PROPHECY

Rethinking Redemption

GEORGE SHULMAN

Historians often note that great critics of white supremacy in the United States—from Frederick Douglass, William Lloyd Garrison, and Henry Thoreau to Martin Luther King and James Baldwin—are drawn to specifically *prophetic* language to address dimensions of politics precluded by liberal discourse. But how shall we theorize prophecy as a *genre* of political language (and of political theory) in relation to liberalism and race? In ways that historians rarely appreciate, critics of white supremacy in the United States are also drawn to prophetic language because politics involves persuasion, persuasion requires starting with your audience, and prophecy—not only liberal individualism—remains a passionate frame of reference in American politics. For these critics, prophecy is not a dead ("biblical") genre but vernacular "political theology," the ordinary language even of those who believe they are secular. Critics of white supremacy are drawn to prophecy less in a strategic or voluntarist sense, as if they stand outside of and choose to use a language their audience is inside, and more in an embodied sense; they are gripped by and bespeak a vernacular legacy, even as they rework it as a language in and for politics.

To assess prophetic language in theoretical and political terms, then, we should start with the question of definition. What is prophecy? Prophecy

names a social practice appearing in many cultures, which commentators
link to shamanism, ecstatic vision, founder myths, charisma, political demagoguery, and social criticism. It is a social role that mediates between human
beings and powerful realities they neither understand nor control to address their fateful choices as a community. But prophecy also is a changeable, contested *social practice*. After all, there was profound conflict between
those (call them "house prophets") who worked for Israel's royal house
and voiced God's unconditional support for it, and those now canonized
as "the" prophets, who condemned the idolatry of state power by voicing
a God that holds monarchy and nation to account. People thus revise the
practice of prophecy and argue about who counts as a prophet and which
words to endow with (or recognize as having) authority. Simon and Gar-
funkel sing "the words of the prophets are written on the subway walls and
tenement halls," to signal how "prophecy" surrounds us still, as we count
some voices and ignore others—at our peril.

Prophecy is an *office*—a public practice—open to revision, but in cultures
bearing biblical traces prophecy also is a genre of speech, with characteristic
narrative forms and tropes, cadences of speech, registers of voice. Figures
such as William Blake or Friedrich Nietzsche, and American literary artists
and social critics, assume the office as they take up and revise the language.
But what marks the genre, and how shall we assess its political bearing?

Biblical prophets condemn idolatry, social injustice, and monarchical power by telling a story about a chosen people who strayed from the
founding covenant, first principles, and God that once redeemed them from
Egyptian bondage. Prophets seek what they call a "turn," which is translated into English as "repentance," a turn by which Hebrews can reconstitute themselves as a community. Martin Buber thus argues that biblical
prophets neither decree a fate nor predict the future but rather seek a "decision" about the constitutive commitments and practices of the people they
address.[1] But the biblical genre bears a vexed relation to politics because it
lacks an Aristotelian dimension. For prophets denounce idolatry in the name
of a God whose higher authority is beyond question; they denounce social
injustice but do not conceive a valid pluralism among compelling truths and
worthy goods. After all, they defend monotheism, and so a unitary idea of
community, against a cosmopolitan multiculturalism! They also invent the

idea of redemption, which seems to promise deliverance not only from oppression but from the conflict, contingency, and history that are constitutive conditions of a specifically political life.

It matters greatly, therefore, that in the United States a self-declared democracy forges national identity by prophetic language. Surely, elites repeatedly use the idea of a redeemer nation to justify imperial power, and they link the redemption of a special American promise to a politics that purifies the social body of impulses, practices, and alien peoples signifying corruption. From Puritanism to Jerry Falwell, uses of prophetic language seem to *inherently* support social control, the centering of cultural authority, and violence in the name of redemption. In response to such rhetoric in the last twenty years, many political theorists have reaffirmed private rights and liberal constitutionalism, a language of pluralism, or norms of civil deliberation. Yet the political meaning of prophecy remains contingent, I would argue, if we note the cohort of thinkers and actors who have used prophetic language to criticize white supremacy. Indeed, in doing so they pose questions silenced by liberalism and on behalf of democratic projects.

Indeed, it even seems impossible to think about race in the United States without being impelled toward prophecy as a form of political theory and practice. But what is it that American critics of white supremacy seek in or draw from the genre of prophecy, and have they revised it to make democratic claims in a political way? Answers to these two questions appear by attending to the biblical idea of prophecy as an office involving certain kinds of speech: critics of white supremacy draw on the depiction of prophets as *messengers* who *announce*, as *witnesses* who *testify*, as *watchmen* who *warn* of danger, and as *singers* who *lament* and thus endow history and suffering with meaning.

First, prophecy is the office of "messengers" who announce. For Blake, prophets are poets who bring forth seminal poetic fictions. In words so powerful as to become a truth—Wallace Stevens says "supreme fiction"—that subsequent generations live by, their announcements remake the passionate frame of reference through which audiences orient self-reflection and agency.[2] But the prophetic office is specifically to announce *unspeakable* truths, which people deny at great cost to others and themselves. Amos declares that God does not unconditionally support the Hebrews but holds them accountable for their injustice and may declare war on them because of it. And Nietzsche, likewise, assumes the office of prophecy to announce the death of God. To announce conditions we must acknowledge if we are to flourish—whether a just God or a universe beyond good and evil—is a prophet's office. Prophets speak unequivocally and imperatively not because of theism but because of the kind of claim they make; whether Jeremiah or Baldwin, such messengers seek not obedient submission to dogma but what Stanley Cavell calls acknowledgment—of conditions of finitude we must accept, and of idolatrous fictions we must relinquish, if we are not to live in bad faith and sterility.[3]

Second, critics of white supremacy draw on prophecy as the office of those who bear witness. They not only say what they see, like a legal witness; they name and condemn the disavowals by which a regime or community constitutes itself; "testifying" about disavowal and its destructive consequences, prophetic witnesses must say what they see *and stand against it*. They bear the voice not only of God but of those Toni Morrison calls the "disremembered and unaccounted for."[4] To bear witness is to make present what has been made absent, to count what has not been counted as real. By testifying, prophetic witnesses re-member or re-found a body divided and haunted by what and who are forgotten.

Accordingly, critics of white supremacy bear witness against both the unjust exclusion by which a republic at once constitutes and betrays itself and ongoing disavowal that this is the case. Again, militant judgment signals not theism or moral absolutism but a grasp of the difference between knowledge and acknowledgment. For they address not a lack of knowledge to remedy by information, or a cognitive error to remedy by reason, but a motivated blindness about the reality of others, our conduct toward them, and so about who we think we are.

At issue for them is not the inescapable partiality of human vision, or our inevitable imbrication in discourse, but a willful innocence about domination that is culpable because it can be overcome. As Baldwin testifies: "One must strive to be tough and philosophical concerning destruction and death, but it is not permissible that the authors of devastation also be innocent. It is the innocence that constitutes the crime."[5] He names no mere "gap" between what people say about their ideals and their actual conduct but a denial of reality so profound that their professed values seem hollow, and they seem not hypocritical but deranged. He does not attack dogmatism to pluralize valuable optics but rather addresses a willful blindness about domination to reconstitute a regime.

As prophets from Jeremiah to Baldwin warn, those who deny reality pay the penalty of self-destruction. Third, therefore, prophecy is the office of watchmen who would *forestall* danger. It is for this reason that we typically associate prophecy with "prediction," as if prophets were making a causal claim. By warning of "the fire next time," however, Baldwin does not decree a fate or make a prediction but states the consequence of our conduct as a contingent future we can avoid if we "amend our ways," as Jeremiah says. The office of prophecy is thus to emphasize choice and agency but warn of the point when it is too late to avert the relentlessly unfolding consequences of conduct.

What then is the prophetic answer to disavowal and its penalties? Biblical prophecy claims that what God requires of us is not esoteric but accessible, not a transcendent Archimedean point to reach by abstraction but a "turn" toward what is nearby, to become present to it. As turn is translated as a repentance that means acknowledging (and trying to overcome) past conduct, so Baldwin provokes whites to what he calls "acceptance" of the reality of their history.[6] To register the costs of our conduct, and to count those we have disavowed, is to shift our judgments of pervasive practices we have long deemed legitimate and to recast (how we understand) our first principles and ideas of membership, which reconstitutes community. This insistence on capacities to act otherwise makes prophecy a language of freedom.

Jeremiah and Baldwin both seek a decision about practices they depict as constitutive and fateful. Likewise, they exercise authority by narrating a certain perspective on the past and its meaning: Jeremiah makes idolatry and Baldwin makes white supremacy the defining fact in their stories. Each knows his perspective is "contestable," but for each, we who contest it are denying the meaning of our history and conduct. Depicting amnesia, disavowal, and self-destruction, these "titans of the holy curse," as Weber calls them, offer fateful judgments on which our lives depend rather than opinions or stories whose comparable validity we must grant to achieve civility. Accordingly, they do not use deliberative reason to validate or mediate conflicting claims but rather use poetry, and what Frederick Douglass calls scorching irony, to recast at visceral levels what and whom we count as real.[7]

What is dangerous—and needful—in prophecy is this demand for decisive choices between commitments, practices, and narratives depicted as antithetical. Danger arises in the Schmittian register that seems to deny plurality as an axial principle of democratic politics. Yet for Jeremiah and Baldwin, this register is needful because the issue is domination and its disavowal. The constitutively political value of their speech is suggested by Jacques Rancière. In *Dis-agreement* he argues that all regimes enfranchise some by subordinating others: a "whole" is always constituted partially, by exclusion, by way of a "part that has no part." The subordinated exist demographically so to speak, but they become properly political subjects only as they translate their injury into claims about "wrong." By speech and action that engage the enfranchised across lines of difference, they also provoke the reconstitution of the whole. In Rancière's terms, then, as critics of white supremacy use prophetic speech to stand with "the part that has no part," they make claims about wrong to restructure the whole. Speech relating a part to the whole may fail to persuade, and violence may be an aspect of dis-agreement, but the *political* office of prophecy is to provoke this reconstitution.[8]

Implicit in Rancière is the idea that reconstitution occurs by shifting how people judge the meaning of their practices, but inescapably, that means recasting people's relationship to the past, their understanding of its meaning. If Rancière theorizes constitutive exclusion, it is but a step to say that amnesia is its symptom, and prophecy, by remembering what people too readily forget, returns them to origins to reconstitute community. But remembering can appear in two different narrative modalities.

The jeremiads of Frederick Douglass or Martin Luther King return whites to origins in a Machiavellian sense, by reinterpreting and renewing first principles long practiced in viciously exclusive ways, corrupted by forgetting, or idolized in reified forms. In contrast, Baldwin rejects jeremiadic narrative: like Nietzsche, he depicts a coming-to-terms with a past that is haunting and imprisoning because it is horrific and because it has been denied. The problem is an unredeemed past, and the question is not how to get free from it but how to redeem it in the sense of changing our relationship to it, both how we imagine it and how we bear and use it.

But critics of white supremacy do not turn to prophecy only because its modes of address are a language of and for politics. They also turn to prophecy because politics involves persuasion, persuasion means starting with audiences, and in America prophecy is vernacular theology in the idiom of redemption. Critics of white supremacy turn to prophecy to link race and politics to redemption, the vernacular language in America for speaking about agency and temporality.

What I mean by vernacular political theology is illustrated by a revealingly unexceptional episode: Trent Lott, Republican senator from Mississippi, was once forced to resign as majority leader because at a birthday dinner for Strom Thurmond he expressed regret that Thurmond's white supremacy agenda had not been made national policy; when Lott was reinstated by the Republican caucus in November 2006 after they lost control of the Senate, John McCain commented, "We all believe in redemption. Thank God."[9] This "we" thanks a God of atonement who stands for mercy if we repent, but also, "thank God" we believe in redemption because otherwise, as Hannah Arendt argues, we are trapped by our history, by acts whose wayward and injurious consequences are boundless and binding.[10] But in a way that Arendt does not argue, which Thurmond and Lott exemplify, practices of domination generate, for master and slave, rhetorics of redemption.

That McCain says "we" unreflectively, and that he seems not to doubt either the promise of redemption or its theistic author, is my initial point: "religion" is itself the surface of what Tocqueville calls an "involuntary agreement" or "grammar" beneath argument, indeed, beneath every aspect of American life.[11] Surely "redemption" is a commodity to acquire, as celebrities and politicians perform obviously hypocritical rituals to "apologize for" and "put behind" them racist outbursts and other kinds of injurious or self-exposing conduct. But the idiom of redemption can work as a commodity and is available for debasement because it remains alive in the culture; not so long ago both New Right rage at and black support for Bill Clinton were voiced in terms of redemption, and the Bush era surely demonstrated that the concept relates adversaries across other profound differences.

McCain's statement illustrates, therefore, that prophecy is not articulated doctrinally as theology but lived as common sense and narrative, condensed in a word, *redemption*. The context of that statement also signifies how the idiom of redemption is inseparably tied to the history and politics of a republic constituted by racial exclusion. The racial "we" and the redemption in which we believe are the two sides of the American ordinary. For Lott's unthinking endorsement of Thurmond's white supremacy, and his all-too-easy redemption illustrate how racial domination remains both constitutive and intractable. And when McCain—himself baited in 2000 for having adopted a black baby—defends redemption, he knows that Lott stands in for a white nation, whose redemption from racial sins McCain and Lott also accredit too readily. But the "we" who believe in it are not only those invested in sustaining supremacy and innocence, for adversaries who are invested in freedom also invoke redemption. Just as Arendt links forgiveness to freedom and both to redemption, so most great critics of white supremacy have spoken in redemptive terms, to grapple with the intractability of origins in the name of human capacities for self-overcoming, natality, and the miraculous. By starting with this incident, therefore, I am framing political theology less as philosophy and more as a rhetorical practice, and I am embedding that practice in an American ordinary constituted by relations of racial domination and by redemption as a vernacular language that is used both to sustain and to contest that domination.

Still, what is this redemption in which we believe, "thank God"? I have concluded that there are two different but related idioms of redemption, each originating in relation to domination. One idiom depicts redemption *from* captivity in Egypt or exile and oppression in Babylon, then from sin and from history. Redemption then seems like a noun denoting final freedom "from" a condition and sure achievement of another, but "redeeming from" is also a verb, an ongoing practice of making-free by action.

The other idiom depicts redemption *of* history: to "redeem" suffering or crime means to endow it with meaning, to atone for it or heal it, to make it justified, worthwhile, of value. In this idiom, masters and slaves, from reverse perspectives, seek to redeem domination—the crime or the injury. By this idiom we identify as guilty agents to redeem shameful acts and restore our worthiness; as subalterns subject to power, we also redeem a history of suffering or a wounding experience of oppression, sometimes by drawing value from it and making it meaningful, sometimes by seeking vengeance, reparation, or vindication.

Lincoln invokes this second cluster of meanings when he narrates a story in which the sin of slavery is redeemed by Civil War deaths, which in turn "we the living" must redeem by our own dedication to the principle for which they died—or death and suffering are in vain.[12] Martin Luther King invokes Moses to depict redemption *from* white supremacy, but when he calls on whites to "redeem" the American promise, he means make good on it; and by making amends for conduct that violates the promise of equality, they "redeem" themselves and "make whole" a union rent by injustice.[13] In this sense Baldwin and Morrison call us to redeem the past in a Nietzschean sense, because we cannot escape it or change it.

The idioms of redemption *from* (oppression) and redemption *of* (past suffering or crime) form a grammar; in individual and collective senses, redeeming involves making-free and making-meaningful. Arendt deems politics redemptive, and Nietzsche calls *amor fati* (love of fate) "my redemption" because they grasp this double sense. But we can see why redemption readily goes awry, as Nietzsche most acutely analyzes. For if we seek deliverance from conditions that are in fact fundamental to life, our practice of redemption bespeaks resentment and enacts violence. And if we imagine "unconditional truth," as if to solve once and for all the *problem* of the meaning of our suffering, we erase the gap between art and life and create a "true world by which to devalue the actual one."[14]

The damage wrought by redemptive language is indeed staggering, and by no means only in American history. Clearly, overt violence is authorized by promises of redemption as deliverance: as redemption from Egypt dispossesses Canaanites, so the saved are produced by marking the preterits—those not elect, the pagans and racialized others who embody unredeemed life. Violence thus bridges the avowedly redemptive practices of Christianity and liberalism as emancipatory projects. In a parallel way Weber sees the Christian quest for redemption generating the iron cage of worldly asceticism.[15] Likewise, for heirs of Nietzsche, redemptive rhetoric in religious and then secular forms justifies resentment, generates herd morality, and entails nihilism.

In one idiom, rhetorics of redemption as deliverance always seem to identify the saved by marking the damned, and always seem to purify conditions seen to stain life rather than wrestle with conditions that constitute it. In the second idiom, if we lodge the redemption of our suffering or the meaning of our lives in our children, our possessions or our work, in community, in art, or in politics, we seem to impose an unfeasible burden and enact an imprisoning investment. Reckoning with redemption thus impels the question: what must people do to themselves and others to gain redemption as they construe it? As Baldwin always asks, what is the price of the ticket?[16]

For Talal Asad, the discourses of late modern power are authorized by this aspiration to forge a "we" and "redeem" it.[17] The danger was intensified after 9/11, as ruling American elites revitalized the myth of America as a redeemer nation. It seems credible to conclude, therefore, that the survival of democratic life depends on disenchanting redemptive myths layer by layer, from liberal internationalism and human rights to teleological narratives in providential or progressive forms. If so, then the vocation or "office" of the theorist must be to drain communities and political action of redemptive meaning, to chasten dogmatism, unmask power, and foster reverence for endangered human diversity. Our task is not to justify resistance but to reveal the practices by which every justification is a form of power. Deidealization of language, especially of redemptive and democratic rhetoric, is the only way to expose how ideals, taken up in the logics and ruses of power, are practiced at human expense.

Disillusioning practices need not be gloomy, however. Just think of the nonredemptive Marxism, Groucho's, the voice of irreverent play, endlessly fertile and disruptive, standing against every form of order and authority, every piety and virtue. Such iconoclastic yet inventive negativity sees meaning-making itself as a coercive imposition of order and propriety, and any specific form of meaning as a vanity to ridicule. If we arrogantly devalue life in the effort to bestow meaning, and if we are imprisoned by the forms of meaning we make for ourselves and impose on others, the only way to escape self-defeat is shameless irreverence. By extension, a kind of liberatory antipolitics is performed by those who unmask the promises and mock the arts that elicit our investment in schemes of redemption. Against

those he calls "teachers of the purpose of existence," Nietzsche above all
defends the laughter of a "gay science" that subverts all convictions and
motivational frameworks, while embracing the unredeemed matter we
are.[18] No wonder that jesters from Groucho to Philip Roth find in sex acts
and pleasure what Roth calls a "redeeming corruption," a blessed release
from the tyranny of meaning.[19]

Such a tension between the Apollonian and Dionysian suggests a tragic
(Cornel West says tragi-comic) rather than redemptive vision.[20] Indeed, some
theorists do invoke a tragic ethos to both highlight and counter the dangers
of redemptive rhetoric. They seek a vocabulary to oppose: teleological narrative in the form of theodicy or providential design; dreams of communi-
tarian fullness; longings to purify "the human stain." In these ways a "tragic"
orientation toward life does seem more congenial to an agonistic politics. In
response to the political question—what kind of language is needful now?—
it is credible to argue that neoliberalism and its evangelical alter ego can be
countered best by a tragic (rather than theistic) ethos of finitude.

But perhaps another genre is not necessary; perhaps a tragic perspective
on redemption already has been fashioned in American culture, as a minority yet still vernacular voice: there is the African American tradition of the
blues, and other poets, songsters, literary artists, and critics retell—as tragedy—the stories of redemption driving the culture. They criticize the motives and worldly consequences of practices their audiences call redemptive,
showing that what their audiences call redemption entails brutally violent
as well as bewilderingly self-defeating forms of action. Yet those who address race typically redefine rather than renounce redemption.

Some prophetic voices—Jeremiah, Douglass, John Brown, and King—do
not narrate redemption as tragedy. Some—like Thoreau—remain ensnared
by the redemptive logic whose costs they partly see. In contrast, Baldwin
and Morrison (like Nietzsche) present more complex visions. Unlike other
prophetic voices, they question rather than expound the idea of deliverance
from captivity, trouble rather than avow the idea of a redemptive promise
in politics, dramatize what is problematic and not just needful in efforts to
redeem the past, and mark the limits and not only the power of language
to redeem suffering. They stage redemption as a problem, but they make it
impossible "to pass on," as they try to redeem the history whose haunting

crimes and horrors they unblinkingly narrate. In sum, they forge a tragic perspective on redemption by the way they confront both American language and history.

Why is this ambivalent engagement preferable to directly unmasking justificatory schemes? Why *retell* rather than simply renounce stories of redemption? Baldwin and Morrison, like Nietzsche and Arendt, retell prevailing redemptive stories to dramatize both their grip and their dangers. But they also rework redemption because human beings require a sense of purpose or meaning: redemption is a problem, but human beings cannot flourish unless, by creating ways to make life (seem) worthwhile, they resist the wisdom of Silenus—better not to have been born. Likewise, human beings must "redeem" the past because they cannot escape or change it: they must fashion a fruitful relationship to the past, or they live by amnesia, resentment, and repetition. As Arendt's engagement with Silenus at the end of *On Revolution* shows so beautifully, meaning-making is the other side of the freedom that makes politics redemptive.

They retell rather than renounce stories of redemption, because redemption is so intimately tied to freedom and to meaning. What, then, makes life worthwhile? For Nietzsche, making riddle, chance, and accident "cohere" by the art of *narrative*, so that we become not only subjects but authors and actors. For Arendt it is *action*, a capacity for initiative and generativity she associates with miracles and attributes to faith. That she turns to biblical exemplars to depict this "natality" is no more coincidental than Morrison quoting Paul (citing Hosea) for the epigraph to *Beloved*. But Morrison, like Baldwin before her, is thereby emphasizing *love*, which is devalued by Arendt and Nietzsche, but central to prophecy's view of redemption as a collective (that is, political) aspiration and practice.

Like Arendt and Nietzsche, however, Baldwin and Morrison rework redemption while insisting that we acknowledge the darkness surrounding us, which art, love, or action can momentarily illuminate but never banish. As Baldwin asserts at the end of *The Fire Next Time*: "Everything now, we must assume, is in *our* hands"—not in God's—and "we have no right to assume otherwise."[21] If he thus echoes Nietzsche's sense of *amor fati* as the greatest weight, necessary to take on yet impossible to bear, however, he here politicizes what Nietzsche calls "my redemption." To assume there is a providential design is bad faith, but to assume it is in *my* hands alone (as Nietzsche often suggests) is to avoid the politics Baldwin signals by "our," a community not pregiven but conjured into being, if at all, by redemptive language.

It has been the office of prophecy to *conjure*—to represent and summon—capacities for redemption by love, art, and action in the face of desperate suffering or domination. After two failed reconstructions, though, it seems that no speech or action in concert, trumpets blasting and pitchers smashing, can shake the walls of race. Yet no guarantee secures these walls or precludes contest. The appearance of intractability does not justify relinquishing the truth—or should I say faith?—that significant change remains a possibility we cannot preclude. Baldwin thus says, "I know that what I am asking is impossible. But in our time, as in every time, the impossible is the least one can demand—and one is, after all, emboldened by the spectacle of human history in general, and American history in particular," which testifies "to nothing less that the perpetual achievement of the impossible."[22] Redemption—necessary to dream and (im)possible to realize—names the bent bow of democratic desire.

Notes

An earlier version of portions of this chapter appeared in George Shulman, *American Prophecy: Race and Redemption in American Political Culture* (Minneapolis: University of Minnesota Press, 2008).

1. Martin Buber, *The Prophetic Faith* (New York: Harper & Row, 1949).

2. Wallace Stevens, *The Necessary Angel: Essays on Reality and Imagination* (New York: Vintage, 1951).

3. Stanley Cavell, *Must We Mean What We Say?* (Cambridge: Cambridge University Press, 1976).

4. Toni Morrison, *Beloved* (New York: New American Library, 1987), 274.

5. James Baldwin, *The Fire Next Time*, in *The Price of the Ticket: Collected Nonfiction 1948–1985* (New York: St. Martin's Press, 1985), 334.

6. Ibid., 373.

7. Max Weber, *Ancient Judaism* (New York: Free Press, 1952), 293; Frederick Douglass, "The Meaning of July Fourth for the Negro," in *The Life and Writings of Frederick Douglass*, ed. Phillip S. Foner (New York: International Publishers, 1952), 2:181–204.

8. Jacques Rancière, *Dis-agreement: Politics and Philosophy*, trans. Julie Rose (Minneapolis: University of Minnesota Press, 1999).

9. "In Senate Shift, Big Comeback for Trent Lott," *New York Times*, November 15, 2006, http://www.nytimes.com/2006/11/16/us/politics/16lott.html.

10. Hannah Arendt, *The Human Condition* (Chicago: University of Chicago Press, 1998).

11. Alexis de Tocqueville, *Democracy in America*, 2 vols. (New York: Vintage, 1990).

12. Abraham Lincoln, "Second Inaugural Address," in *Abraham Lincoln, Great Speeches* (New York: Dover, 1991).

13. Martin Luther King Jr., "Letter from Birmingham Jail," in *Testament of Hope: The Essential Writings and Speeches of Martin Luther King Jr.* (New York: HarperCollins, 1986).

14. Hannah Arendt, *On Revolution* (New York: Viking, 1971); Friedrich Nietzsche, *Thus Spake Zarathustra*, trans. Walter Kaufmann (London: Penguin, 1996), 137–41.

15. Max Weber, *The Protestant Ethic and the Spirit of Capitalism* (New York: W. W. Norton, 2007).

16. Baldwin, *The Price of the Ticket*.

17. Talal Asad, *Formations of the Secular: Christianity, Islam, Modernity* (Stanford: Stanford University Press, 2003).

18. Friedrich Nietzsche, *The Gay Science*, trans. Walter Kaufmann (New York: Vintage, 1974).

19. Philip Roth, *The Human Stain* (New York: Houghton Mifflin, 2000), 37.

20. Cornel West, "Black Strivings in a Twilight Civilization," in *Cornel West Reader* (New York: Basic Books, 1999), 106.

21. Baldwin, *The Fire Next Time*, 379.

22. Ibid.

Index

Agamben, Giorgio, 15, 49, 57
agape: Barth on, 108; Stapel on, 63, 65–70
al-Qaeda, 46, 48
Améry, Jean, 25
Amos, 236–37
Anderson, Benedict, 85
Anidjar, Gil, 17, 174, 180–81, 187n19
An-Na'im, Abdullahi Ahmed, 46–47
Annales School, 27
Antichrist, 13
anti-Semitism: Brunner's, 38, 42;
    distinguished from Islamophobia,
    168; Du Bois's, 123–28; Fichte's, 80n5;
    Schmitt's, 9, 12, 15
Antrim, Zayde, 45
Arendt, Hannah, 114, 199, 240–42, 245
Asad, Talal, 116, 243
Ataturk, Kemal, 46

Baldwin, James, 127, 192–93, 207, 234,
    237–39, 242–46
Balibar, Étienne, 85–88
baptism, 57, 105, 177, 182–83
Barth, Karl, 81n15, 84–85, 90–101, 108
Bauman, Zygmunt, 106
Bedouins, 45
Benjamin, Jessica, 224
Benjamin, Walter, 49, 145
bestiality, 177–79
Bidault, Georges, 1
bin Laden, Osama, 46
Bismark, Otto von, 28, 89

black theology, 6
Body of Christ, 1, 11
Blake, William, 235–36
Bloom, Allan, 158, 160, 162, 164, 165
Blum, Edward, 120, 125
Blut und Boden, 23–26, 50
Boose, Lynda E., 175–76, 184
Boyarin, Jonathan, 181–82, 186n15
Braudel, Fernand, 27
Brown, John, 244
Brunner, Otto, 22–23, 26–50
Buber, Martin, 235
Butler, Judith, 203

Cain, mark of, 183
Canaanites, 199–200, 242
Canne, John, 193
Carter, J. Kameron, 7–8, 114
Cavanaugh, William T., 19n8
Cavell, Stanley, 129, 158, 164, 187n30, 237
census, 14, 201–3
Certeau, Michel de, 143
Césaire, Aimé, 1–4, 7, 17, 108
Chakrabarty, Dipesh, 16
chance, 203–4, 211n37. *See also*
    contingency
Chow, Rey, 87
Christianity: Barth's criticism of, 91–92,
    108; Césaire on, 1–3, 7, 17; contrasted
    with Judaism, 60; interchangeable
    with religion, 214–15, 220; political
    theology associated with, 214–15;

Christianity (*continued*): secularism
and, 17; secularization and, 28;
Shakespeare's use of, 180, 183–84
Christmas, 2–3
Christology: Barth's, 101; Du Bois's, 101;
Lessing's, 72; Stapel's, 68–70
circumcision, 176, 179–82
Clinton, Bill, 240
Cohen, Tom, 158
Collins, George "Shorty," 138–39
colonialism, 219; Césaire on, 1–2, 7–8;
German, 24, 87–89
communion, 1–4
Conrad, Joseph, 25
contingency, 94, 95, 121, 129, 130, 135,
149, 203–6, 236, 238; of identity, 215,
223, 226, 228, 229
Crepon, Marc, 210n26
Croatto, Severino, 209n16
Cross, George, 141, 151
Crummell, Alexander, 121

Danson, Laurence, 158
Darré, Walther, 24
Dawson, Michael, 117–18
death: Baldwin on, 237; Barth on, 96; Du
Bois on, 104–7; Foucault on, 14–15;
Thurman on, 143, 145–52
Declaration of Independence, 87
democracy: democratic desire, 205, 246;
Derrida on, 14; prophecy in, 236; role
of contingency in, 204; secularism
and, 115; theology and, 232
Derrida, Jacques, 13–14, 191–92, 198, 207
Douglass, Frederick, 116, 127, 234, 239,
244
Du Bois, W. E. B., 84–85, 97–107, 112–14,
117–30, 149

Eckhart, Meister, 143
Egypt: ancient, 192–200, 235, 241, 242;
contemporary, 16, 44–47, 224
Eliezer, Rabbi, 224
Ellis, Marc, 232n2

Ellison, Ralph, 129
enemy: Schmitt on, 9, 162; Shakespeare's
depiction of, 162–64, 166–68, 178,
185; Stapel on, 55, 56, 58, 62–64, 68,
71–76; Walzer on, 194, 199
Engels, Friedrich, 34, 35, 36, 52n21
equality, 35, 47, 116, 120, 204–6, 242
eros: Barth on, 108; found in Exodus,
202; Stapel on, 65–70
eschaton, 12–14; the West as, 85, 88, 93–94,
108
Europe, 1, 3, 7; Christian, 175, 184;
modernity's origins in, 16
exception, state of, 15, 90
exceptionalism: American, 114, 118, 121,
122, 125, 128, 192; Exodus story and,
192, 194
Exodus, 129, 192–200, 206–7

Falwell, Jerry, 236
Fanon, Frantz, 108
Fellowship of Reconciliation, 139
feud, 29–32, 37, 39, 44; terrorism as, 46,
48
Feuerbach, Ludwig, 63
Fichte, Johann Gottlieb, 41, 57, 80n5
Fiedler, Leslie, 165
Foucault, Michel, 14–15, 95, 203
Franklin, Benjamin, 193
freedom: Arendt on, 241; Exodus and,
198; as goal of political theology,
136–38; prophecy as language of,
238; redemption and, 241; religious,
221–23; Thurman on, 146, 150, 152
Fukuyama, Francis, 219

Garden of Eden, 74–75
Gierke, Otto, 36
Glaude, Eddie, 121, 195
Gogarten, Friedrich, 55, 57
Goldberg, David Theo, 153n2
Goldschmidt, Henry, 232n1
Gourgouris, Stathis, 131n11
Gramsci, Antonio, 134

Greenblatt, Stephen, 158
Griese, Friedrich, 25
Gypsies, 33, 38, 47

Haekel, Ernst Heinrich, 24
Hagen, Louis, 82n23
Haggard, H. Rider, 25
Halevi, Yehuda, 223, 225–26
Hall, Stuart, 134–36, 152–53
Hamsun, Knut, 25, 38
Harris, Sam, 117
Haushofer, Karl, 24
Haxthausen, Baron August von, 33–36,
    42
Hebrew, 79, 189–91, 193, 198, 227–29
Hegel, G. W. F., 27–28, 89, 94, 196, 233n3
Heidegger, Martin, 50, 146–47, 150
Herzl, Theodor, 57, 189
Hickman, Jared, 16
Hillel, 223–24, 228, 230
Hirsch, Emanuel, 55, 57
Hitchens, Christopher, 117
Hitler, Adolf, 7, 22, 24, 42, 78; rise to
    power, 88; Stapel on, 69
Hobbes, Thomas, 39, 159
Holocaust, 12, 44
Homer, 199
homo sacer, 15
Honig, Bonnie, 19n6, 129
hope, 107, 122
Horgan, John, 48

idolatry, 235, 238
idols, 40, 97, 108, 196
immigration, 88; immigrants and Jews,
    128, 130
Indochina War, 1
innocence, 237, 241
Irish Republican Army, 48
Iroquois, 34–35
Islamophobia, 168
Israel, 44, 124, 216, 219–20, 225, 230–31;
    America as, 114; Israeli citizenship,
    214, 220; Palestinian-Arab Israelis,

230; prophets in, 235. *See also*
    Israelites; Palestine
Israelites, 194–97, 199–201, 206, 235–37

JanMohamed, Abdul, 107–8
Jeremiah, 237–39, 244
Jesus: Du Bois on, 103–4; liberal Jesus,
    73–74; Stapel on, 55–56, 60, 62, 66,
    72–74, 79–80
Jew, the: Brunner on, 38–39; Césaire
    on, 2, 7; Derrida on, 14; Du Bois
    on, 114, 123–28; Foucault on, 15;
    origins of race and, 8; Schmitt on, 9;
    Shakespeare on, 157, 163–64, 166–68,
    180; Stapel on, 58, 73–76
Jewishness, 213–32
Jones, Rufus, 143–44, 147
Joseph of Nazareth, 73, 103
jouissance, 191–92, 204–6
Jubilee, 211n37
Judy, Ronald A. T., 101

Kant, Immanuel, 59, 60, 71–72, 80n5, 89,
    140, 143
Kantorowicz, Ernst, 39–40, 156–57,
    160–62, 214
katechon, 13
Kazin, Michael, 49
King, Martin Luther, Jr., 116, 118, 234,
    239, 242, 244
Koonz, Claudia, 88
Korach, 195, 197, 198, 206
Kozbi, 201–2
Kramer, Michael, 125–27

Lacan, Jacques, 107, 205
LaFarge, John, 155n25
laïcité, 43
Land, 29–33, 36–47
Lasch, Christopher, 119
law: Jewish, 224–25, 228; law of life,
    65–67, 70, 71, 75, 76, 78; natural and
    positive, 28–31
Lefort, Claude, 233n3

Leibowitz, Yeshayahu, 224

Leiner, Mordechai Yosef (The Isbitzer), 201–2, 207

Lenin, Vladimir, 80n15, 195; Leninists, 193–96, 199

Lessing, Gotthold Ephraim, 59, 60, 71–72

Levinas, Emmanuel, 223

Levites, 196, 206

Lewis, Bernard, 45

Lewis, David Levering, 112, 125, 128

liberalism: Du Bois's, 120; Martin Luther King's, 118; prophecy and, 236; redemption and, 242; religion and, 114–15; Schmitt's criticism of, 10

Lilla, Mark, 93, 116

Lincoln, Abraham, 242

Lindbeck, George, 20n16

Long, Charles, 137, 148, 149, 153

Loomba, Ania, 163

Lott, Trent, 240–41

lottery, 203–4

love: *amor fati*, 242; analogy with body public, 159–60; Barth on, 108; Césaire on, 3; Du Bois on, 103–6; freedom to, 119; God's, 202; improper, 178; law related to, 157, 161–62; political theological approaches to, 6; prophecy and, 245–46; Stapel on, 58, 59, 61–64, 66, 71–72, 74. *See also* agape; eros

luck, 203

Lupton, Julia, 163, 165, 170n21, 175, 176, 180, 186n10

Luther, Martin, 54, 57, 61–63, 65, 68–70

lynching, 100, 105–7

Mahmood, Saba, 16

Maine, H. S., 33–37

Maistre, Joseph de, 22, 27

Malagasy Uprising, 1

Malcolm X, 225

manna, 191–92, 204–6, 211n37

Marcuse, Herbert, 141

Marx, Groucho, 243

Marx, Karl, 34, 35, 36, 52n21, 141, 219

May, Todd, 205

McCain, John, 240–41

Melville, Herman, 114

messianism: imperialism and, 74, 89, 94; Jewish, 72, 73, 206–7; messianic politics, 193; political, 56–58, 193; secular, 55, 64, 71, 72, 73, 76, 77

Metz, Johann Baptist, 12

Milbank, John, 49

miscegenation, 176–78

modernity, 16, 50, 83–85, 92, 94, 109; antimodernity, 64; death and, 107, 145, 148; Jews in, 215; modernity's underside, 97, 136; race and, 137; Stapel on, 55, 61, 75, 76

Moltmann, Jürgen, 12

Morgan, Lewis Henry, 34–36, 42

Morrison, Toni, 107, 237, 242, 244–45

Moses, 195–96, 242

mulatto, Jesus as, 102–4

Muslims, 45–47, 166, 175–80, 183–85

Nancy, Jean-Luc, 230

Nasser, Gamal, 46

natality, 241, 245

National Socialism, 23–24; Barth and, 93; Brunner and, 49; Foucault on, 15; haunting political theology, 7; Kantorowicz and, 39–40; Schmitt and, 7, 9; Stapel and, 58–59, 77–80

nationalism, 36, 45, 85–88, 95, 125, 136, 215

Nazis. *See* National Socialism

negritude, 1, 110n30

new atheists, 117

Niebuhr, Barthold Georg, 33, 42

Nietzsche, Friedrich, 28, 42–43, 56, 237, 242, 244–46

O'Donovan, Oliver, 116

ordinary, the, 3, 148; American ordinary, 241

original sin, 55, 60, 61, 64, 65, 68, 74, 75

pagans, 1–3, 242; in Shakespeare, 163,
    177, 180, 183–85; Stapel on, 61–62, 65,
    68, 79
Palestine, 44, 75, 124, 188–91, 198, 200.
    See also Israel; Palestinians
Palestinians, 44, 46, 180, 217, 230. *See also*
    Palestine
Palin, Sarah, 48
Patterson, Orlando, 106
Paul, 13, 56–57, 60–68, 70, 159, 180,
    187n23, 245
Peterson, Erik, 12, 56–57
Pilate, 63
Pinchas, 201–2
plague, 195, 197, 201–2
Political Theology (journal), 8
populism, 23, 48–49
Prometheus, 100
prophecy, 234–46; Césaire on, 3, 4;
    Shulman on, 116, 123
Protestant, approach to religion, 4, 7, 15,
    16

Rabin, Yitzkhak, 44
Rancière, Jacques, 204–6, 239
Rashi, 201–2
Ratzel, Friedrich, 24
Rawls, John, 114, 204–6
Red Tory, 49
redemption, 84, 113, 207, 236, 240–46
Reimarus, Hermann Samuel, 72
Riehl, W. H., 22
Ritter, Karl, 24
Rogin, Michael, 126, 209n17
Rolls, Albert, 159
Rorty, Richard, 114
Rosenzweig, Franz, 188–92, 198, 200,
    207
Roth, Philip, 244

Sabbath, 195, 197
Said, Edward, 16–17, 199–200
Schleiermacher, Friedrich Daniel, 59, 77,
    89, 141

Schmitt, Carl, 9–14, 22, 23, 26, 214, 232;
    approach to political theology, 5,
    6; Brunner's use of, 29–30, 33, 37;
    compared with Kantorowicz, 161–62;
    embrace of, 49
Scholem, Gerhardt (Gershom), 188–93,
    198–201, 227
Schreiner, Olive, 138–41
Scott, Nathan, 141, 146
secularism, 17, 208n8; Jewish, 224
secularization, 4–5, 50; Brunner's
    refusal of, 28; of Exodus, 200, 207; of
    Hebrew, 189–90, 198; Kantorowicz's
    account of, 40, 161; mistranslation of,
    50; Stapel on, 55–60, 63–64, 68, 70,
    71, 73–76
Sermon on the Mount, 62
Shakespeare, William: *Hamlet*, 156, 166;
    Merchant of Venice, 157–59, 163–68,
    181, 183; *Othello*, 157–60, 163–68,
    174–185; *Richard II*, 156–57, 159, 162
Shapiro, James, 163, 166
Shulman, George, 113, 116, 118, 123,
    129
Silenus, 245
Singh, Nikhil Pal, 118
slavery, 146, 149, 151; Du Bois on,
    99, 102, 119; Exodus and, 194,
    198; mastery and slavery, 95, 97;
    redemption of, 241–42
Sölle, Dorothee, 12
sovereignty, 3, 6, 11–12, 14; Brunner
    on, 29, 32, 37–39; Foucault on, 14;
    household, 31, 34–35; linked with sin,
    96; sovereign body, 157, 159; Stapel
    on, 59, 61, 63, 68–70, 76
Spencer, Herbert, 34
spirituals, 121, 142–53
Stapel, Wilhelm, 54–80
Stevens, Wallace, 236
Stout, Jeffrey, 115
Stratton, Jon, 214
subjectivity, formation of, 83–88, 97, 104
supersessionism, 13, 98

Taliban, 46–47

Taubes, Jacob, 13, 57, 170n26

Taylor, Charles, 4–5

Tea Party, 48

terrorists, 46, 48

Thurman, Howard, 137–53

Thurmond, Strom, 240–41

tikkun olam, 202, 204, 207

Tocqueville, Alexis de, 115, 240

translation, 16, 145

Trinity, 12; Stapel on, 57, 63

tzitzit, 195, 197

umma, 45–47

United Nations, 44

Vattimo, Gianni, 50

violence: Brunner on, 30–31; Christ
    as model of, 65; divine, 198; of
    Exodus, 195–99, 201–2; imperialism
    and, 108; of the past, 207; political
    biology as, 71; prophecy and, 236;

redemption and, 242, 244; religious,
    4, 49; terrorism and, 48; Walzer's
    domestication of, 195–97

Wallace, Michelle, 135

Walzer, Michael, 129, 192–203, 206–7

Weber, Max, 51n18, 238, 242

Weil, Simone, 199

Weinbaum, Alys, 87–88

West, Cornel, 244

whiteness, 87–89, 92; Baldwin on, 127;
    Césaire on, 2, 7; Du Bois on, 100, 103,
    121; Jews and, 214; white supremacy,
    236–37, 240, 242

Wright, Richard, 105, 107

Yaffe, Martin, 164

Yehoshua, A. B., 224–25, 227, 230–31

Zimri, 201–2

Zionism, 58–59, 75, 222, 228; Scholem-
    Rosenzweig debate, 188–93, 198, 201

Žižek, Slavoj, 49